BAGH O BAHAR

BAGH O BAHAR

AMIR KHUSROW,
MIR AMMAN,
DUNCAN FORBES

ISBN: 978-93-90215-39-3

Published: 1874

LECTOR HOUSE LLP
E-MAIL: lectorpublishing@gmail.com

BAGH O BAHAR

OR

TALES OF THE FOUR DARWESHES.

TRANSLATED FROM THE HINDUSTANI OF

MIR AMMAN OF DIHLI

BY

DUNCAN FORBES, LL.D.,

Professor of Oriental Languages in King's College, London; Member of the Royal Asiatic Society of Great Britain and Ireland, author of several works on the Hindustani and Persian Languages.

(TRANSLATION OF MIR AMMAN DIHLAVI'S URDU ADAPTATION OF THE PERSIAN TALE, QISSAH-I CHAHAR DARVISH, ATTRIBUTED TO AMIR KḤUSROW)

1874.

PREFACE.

The *Bagh O Bahar*, or "Garden and Spring," has, for the last half century, been held as a classical work throughout our Indian empire. It highly deserves this distinguished fate, as it contains various modes of expression in correct language; and displays a great variety of Eastern manners and modes of thinking. It is an excellent introduction not only to the colloquial style of the *Hindustani* language, but also to a knowledge of its various idioms and popular phrases.

The tale itself is interesting, if we bear in mind the fact, that no Asiatic writer of romance or history has ever been consistent, or free from fabulous credulity. The cautious march of undeviating truth, and a careful regard to *vraisemblance*, have never entered into their plan. Wildness of imagination, fabulous machinery, and unnatural scenes ever pervade the compositions of Oriental authors,—even in most serious works on history and ethics. Be it remembered, that *jinns*, demons, fairies, and angels, form a part of the *Muhammadan* creed. The people to this day believe in the existence of such beings on the faith of the *Kur,an*; and as they are fully as much attached to their own religion as we are to ours, we ought not to be surprised at their credulity.

I have rendered the translation as literal as possible, consistent with the comprehension of the author's meaning. This may be considered by some a slavish and dull compliance; but in my humble opinion we ought, in this case, to display the author's own thoughts and ideas; all we are permitted to do, is to change their garb. This course has one superior advantage which may compensate for its seeming dulness; we acquire an insight into the modes of thinking and action of the people, whose works we peruse through the medium of a literal translation, and thence many instructive and interesting conclusions may be drawn.

To the present edition numerous notes are appended; some, with a view to illustrate certain peculiarities of the author's style, and such grammatical forms of the language as might appear difficult to a beginner; others, which mainly relate to the manners and customs of the people of the East, may appear superfluous to the Oriental scholar who has been in India; but in this case, I think it better to be redundant, than risk the chance of being deficient. Moreover, as the book may be perused by the curious in Europe, many of of whom know nothing of India, except that it occupies a certain space in the map of the world, these notes were absolutely necessary to understand the work. Finally, as I am no poet, and have a most thorough contempt for the maker of mere doggerel rhymes, I have translated the pieces of poetry, which are interspersed in the original, into plain and humble prose.

D. FORBES

58, BURTON CRESCENT,
July, 1857.

CONTENTS

THE PETITION OF MIR AMMAN, OF DILLI.

Which was Presented to the Gentlemen Managers of the College [of Fort William].

May God preserve the gentlemen of great dignity, and the appreciators of respectable men. This exile from his country, on hearing the command [issued by] proclamation,[1] hath composed, with a thousand labours and efforts, the "Tale of the Four Darweshes," [entitled] the *Bagh O Bahar*[2] [i.e. Garden and Spring,] in the *Urdu, e Mu'alla*[3] tongue. By the grace of God it has become refreshed from the perusal of all the gentlemen[4] [of the college]. I now hope I may reap some fruit from it; then the bud of my heart will expand like a flower, according to the word of *Hakim Firdausi,*[5] who has said [of himself] in the *Shahnama,*

"Many sorrows I have borne for these thirty years;
But I have revived Persia by this Persian [History.][6]
I having in like manner polished the *Urdu* tongue,
Have metamorphosed *Bengal* into *Hindustan.*"[7]

---

[1] The proclamation of the Marquis Wellesley, after the formation of the college of Fort William; encouraging the pursuit of Oriental literature among the natives by original compositions and translations from the Persian, &c, into *Hindustani.*

[2] "The *Bagh O Bahar,*" i.e. "The Garden and Spring;" which may be better called, "The Garden of Spring," or the "Garden of Beauty." The less appropriate title of "*Bagh O Bahar*" was chosen merely in order that the Persian letters composing these words, might, by their numerical powers, amount to 1217, the year of the Hijra in which the book was finished.—Vide Hind. Gram., page 20.

[3] *Mir Amman* himself explains the origin and derivation of these words in his preface, and we cannot appeal to a better authority.

[4] Literally, "in consequence of its being traversed or walked over."

[5] *Hakim Firdausi,* the Homer of Persia, who wrote the history of that country, in his celebrated epic entitled the "*Shah-nama,*" or Book of Kings.

[6] I have translated into plain prose all the verses occurring in the original. I have not the vanity to think myself a poet; and I have a horror of seeing mere doggrel rhymes—such as the following—

"Mighty toil I've borne for years thirty,
I have revived Persia by this *Pursi.*"

These elegant effusions are of the "Non hominies, non Dî, &c." description.

[7] That is to say, he has introduced the elegance and correctness of the *Urdu* language, or that of the Upper Provinces, into *Bengal.* In fact, the *Bengalis* who speak a wretched jargon of what they are pleased to call *Hindustani,* (in addition to their native tongue,) would scarcely be understood at *Agra* or *Dilli;* and those two cities are the best sites to acquire the real *Urdu* in perfection; there the inhabitants speak it not only correctly but elegantly.

You gentlemen are yourselves appreciators of merit. There is no need of representation [on my part]. O God! may the star of your prosperity ever shine!

MIR AMMAN'S PREFACE.

"The Name of God, Most Merciful and Gracious."

The pure God! what an [excellent] Artificer he is! He who, out of a handful of dust, hath created such a variety of faces and figures of earth. Notwithstanding the two colours [of men], one white and one black, yet the same nose and ears, the same hands and feet, He has given to all. But such variety of features has He formed, that the form and shape of one [individual] does not agree with the personal appearance of another. Among millions of created beings, you may recognise whomsoever you wish. The sky is a bubble in the ocean of his [eternal] unity; and the earth is as a drop of water in it; but this is wonderful, that the sea beats its thousands of billows against it, and yet cannot do it any injury. The tongue of man is impotent to sound the praise and eulogy of Him who has such power and might! If it utter any thing, what can it say? It is best to be silent on a subject concerning which nothing can be said.

VERSE.

"From earth to heaven, He whose work this is,
If I wish to write his praise, then what power have I;
When the prophet himself has said, 'I do not comprehend Him.'
After this, if any one pretends to it, he is a great fool.
Day and night the sun and moon wander through their course, and behold his works—
Yea, the form of every individual being is a sight of surprise:
He, whose second or equal is not, and never will be;
No such a unique Being, Godhead is every way fit.
But so much I know, that He is the Creator and Nourisher.
In every way his favour and beneficence are upon me."

And blessings on his friend, for whose sake He created the earth and heavens, and on whom He bestowed the dignity of prophet.

VERSE.

"The pure body of *Mustafa* is an emanation of Divine light,
For which reason, it is well known that his body threw no shadow.[8]
Where is my capacity, that I should sufficiently speak his praise;
Only with men of eloquence this is an established rule."[9]

[8] The Muhammadans believe that the body of their prophet cast no shadow. *Mustafa* means "The Chosen," "The Elected," one of Muhammad's titles.

[9] As a general rule, all Muhammadan books begin with a few sentences devoted to the praise of God and the eulogy of the prophet Muhammad; to which some add a blessing

And blessings and salvation be on his posterity, who are the twelve *Imams*.[10]

VERSE.

"The praise of God and the eulogy of the prophet having here ended;
Now I begin that which is requisite to be done.
O God! for the sake of the posterity of thy prophet,[11]
Render this my story acceptable to the hearts of high and low."

The reasons for compiling this work are these, that in the year of the *Hijra*, 1215, A.D. 1801, corresponding to the[12] *Fasli* year 1207, in the time of his Excellency the noble of nobles, Marquis Wellesley, Lord Mornington, Governor-general, (in whose praise the judgment is at a loss, and the understanding perplexed, and in whom God has centred all the excellent qualities that great men ought to possess. In short, it was the good fortune of this country that such a chief came here, from whose happy presence multitudes enjoy ease and happiness. No one can now dare to injure or wrong another; and the tiger and the goat drink at the same *ghat*;[13] and all the poor bless him and live,)[14] the pursuit of learning came into vogue, and the gentlemen of dignity perceived that by acquiring the *Urdu* tongue, they might hold converse with the people of India, and transact with perfect accuracy the affairs of the country; for this reason many books were compiled during

---

on the twelve *Imams*.

[10] The twelve *Imams* are the descendants of the prophet, by his daughter *Fatima*, who was married to her cousin-german *'Ali*, who is considered as the first *Imam*; the other eleven were the following, viz., *Hasan*, the son of *'Ali; Husain*, the son of *'Ali*; *'Ali*, surnamed *Zainu-l-'Abidin*, son of *Husain; Muhammad*, son of the last mentioned; *Ja'far Sadik*, son of *Muhammad; Musa-l-Kazim*, son of *Ja'far; 'Al-i Raza*, son of *Musa; Muhammad*, son of *'Ali Raza; 'Ali 'Askari*, son of *Muhammad; Hasan 'Askari*: and lastly *Muhammad Mahdi*. With regard to this last and twelfth *Imam*, some say, very erroneously, that he is yet to appear. Now the fact is, the twelfth *Imam* has appeared. He lived and died like the rest of the sainthood; otherwise what would be the use of praying for him? The Muhammadans offer up prayers for the dead, but I never heard of their praying for the unborn.

[11] Much nonsense has been written about this *Fasli* aera. We are told that "it dates from the Christian year 592¾"! but the fact is that it was established no further back than the reign of Akbar. It was engrafted on the Hijri aera in the first year of that monarch's reign, with this proviso, that the *Fasli* years should thenceforth go on increasing by *solar* calculation, and not by lunar; hence, every century the Hijri aera gains three years on the *Fasli*, and in Mir Amman's time the difference had amounted to nearly eight years.

[12] Much nonsense has been written about this *Fasli* aera. We are told that "it dates from the Christian year 592¾"! but the fact is that it was established no further back than the reign of Akbar. It was engrafted on the Hijri aera in the first year of that monarch's reign, with this proviso, that the *Fasli* years should thenceforth go on increasing by *solar* calculation, and not by lunar; hence, every century the Hijri aera gains three years on the *Fasli*, and in Mir Amman's time the difference had amounted to nearly eight years.

[13] A *ghat* is a long flight of steps, of stone or brick, leading to a river for the purpose of bathing, drawing water, embarking or disembarking. It is a high object of ambition in India, among the wealthier classes of natives, to construct these *ghats*, and this species of useful ostentation has produced some magnificent structures of the kind on the rivers *Ganges*, and *Jumna*, which are of great public utility.

[14] The reader will do well in the first place to pass over this very clumsy parenthesis in the original; and return to it after he has finished the rest of the paragraph.

this same year, according to orders.

To those gentlemen who are learned, and speak the language of *Hindustan*,[15] I address myself, and say, that this "Tale of the Four Darwesh" was originally composed by *Amir Khusru*,[16] of *Dihli*[17] on the following occasion; the holy *Nizamu-d-Din Auliya*, surnamed *Zari-Zar-bakhsh*,[18] who was his spiritual preceptor, (and whose holy residence was near *Dilli*, three *Kos*[19] from the fort, beyond the red gate, and outside the *Matiya* gate, near the red house), fell ill; and to amuse his preceptor's mind, *Amir Khusru* used to repeat this tale to him, and attend him during his sickness. God, in the course of time, removed his illness; then he pronounced this benediction on the day he performed the ablution of cure:[20] "That whoever will hear this tale, will, with the blessing of God, remain in health:" since which time this tale, composed in Persian, has been extensively read.

Now, the excellent and liberal gentleman, the judge of respectable men, Mr. John Gilchrist, (may his good fortune ever increase as long as the *Jamuna* and *Ganges* flow!) with kindness said to me, "Translate this tale into the pure *Hindustani* tongue, which the *Urdu* people, both *Hindus* and *Musalmans*, high and low, men, women and children, use to each other." In accordance with his honour's desire, I commenced translating it into this same dialect, just such as any one uses in common conversation.

But first this guilty being, *Mir Amman*, of *Dilli*, begs to relate his own story: "That my forefathers, from the time of King *Humayun*, served every king, in regular descent, with zeal and fidelity; and they[21] also (i.e. the kings), with the eye of protection, ever justly appreciated and rewarded our services. *Jagirs*, titles and rewards, were plentifully bestowed on us; and we were called hereditary[22] vas-

---

[15] The Honourable Company's European servants, civil, military, and medical.

[16] A celebrated Persian poet of *Dilli*; his odes are very elegant, and have great poetical genius; he was, as a Persian poet, inferior to none: he is the original author of this "Tale of the Four Darwesh."

[17] The author seems to use *Dilli* or *Dihli* indifferently for the northern metropolis of India, vulgarly called *Delhi*.

[18] *Zari Zar-bakhsh* means the bestower of gold; *Nizamu-d-Din Auliya* was a famous holy personage of Upper India, and holds the first rank in the list of the saints of *Hindustan*. His shrine is at *Dilli*, and resorted to by thousands of devotees, and many tales are told of his inspired wisdom, his superior beneficence, his contempt of the good things of this world, and his uncommon philanthropy.

[19] The *Kos* is a measure of distance nearly equal to two English miles, but varying in different provinces.

[20] The *Muhammadans*, after being cured of sickness or wounds, also their women, after recovery from child-bed, always bathe in luke-warm water; which is called the ablution of cure.

[21] A mere novice in the language would say that *Mir Amman* writes "bad grammar" here! He uses the singular pronoun "*wuh*" instead of "*we*." Now *Mir Amman* distinctly tells us that he gives us the language *as it is*. He did not make it—and, furthermore, nothing is more common among *Hindustani* writers than to use the singular for the plural, and "vice versâ."—Vide Grammar, page 114.

[22] Mr. Ferdinand Smith adds the following note: "How proud the slave seems of his chains!—but such is the nature of Asiatic minds, under the baneful influence of Asiatic

sals, and old servants; so that these epithets were enrolled in the royal archives.[23] When such a family (owing to which all other families were prosperous) dwindled to such a point! which is too well[24] known to require mention, then *Suraj Mal*, the *Jat*,[25] confiscated our *Jagir*, and *Ahmad Shah* the *Durrani*,[26] pillaged our home. Having sustained such various misfortunes, I abandoned that city, which was my native land, and the place of my birth. Such a vessel, whose pilot was such a king, was wrecked; and I began to sink in the sea of destitution! a drowning person catches at a straw, and I sustained life for some years in the city of *'Azim-abad*,[27] experiencing both good and bad fortune there. At length I left it also—the times were not propitious; leaving my family there, I embarked alone in a boat, and came in quest of a livelihood[28] to Calcutta, the chief of cities. I remained unemployed for some time, when it happened that *Nawwab Dilawar Jang* sent for me, and appointed me tutor to his younger brother, *Mir Muhammad Kazim Khan*. I stayed with him nearly two years; but saw not my advantage [in remaining there any longer.] Then, through the assistance of *Mir Bahadur 'Ali Munshi*, I was introduced to Mr. John Gilchrist (may his dignity be lasting.) At last, by the aid of good fortune, I have acquired the protection of so liberal a person, that I hope better days; if not, even, this is so much gain, that I have bread to eat, and having stretched my feet, I repose in quiet; and that ten persons in my family, old and young, are fed; and bless that patron. May God accept [their prayers!]

"The account of the *Urdu* tongue I have thus heard from my ancestors;—that the city of *Dilli*, according to the opinion of the *Hindus*, was founded in the earliest times,[29] and that their *Rajas* and subjects lived there from the remotest antiquity, and spoke their own peculiar *Bhakha*.[30] For a thousand years past, the *Musalmans*

---

despotism." Now, this criticism is absurd enough. Have not we in England the titles of "Ladies in waiting," "Grooms," &c., innumerable, which honours are borne by our nobility and gentry?

[23] The family of *Taimur*, or Tamerlane; a pageant of which royal race still sits on the throne of *Dilli*, under the protection of the British government. He is happier, and has more comforts of life, than his family have had for the last century.

[24] Literally, "why explain that which is self evident" a Persian saying.

[25] The founder of the *Jut* principality; they were once very powerful in *Upper-Hindustan*. *Ranjit Sing, Raja* of *Bhartpur* at the commencement of the present century, who so gallantly defended that place against our arms, was a son of *Suraj Mal*, who was killed while reconnoitring the *Mughal* army. The *Jats* are the best agriculturists in India, and good soldiers in self defence; for since the spirit which *Suraj Mal* infused, evaporated, they have always preferred peace to war. They built some of the strongest places in India.

[26] *Ahmad Khan*, the *Durrani* or *Afghan*, became king of *Kabul* after the death of *Nadir Shah*. He was the father of *Taimur Shah*, who kept *Upper Hindustan* in alarm for many years with threats of invasion. *Shuja'u-l-Mulk*, whom we seated on the throne of *Kabul* some fifteen years ago, was descended from him.

[27] *'Azim-abid* is the *Muhammadan* name of *Patna*. On the *Muhammadan* conquest, many of the *Hindu* names of cities were changed for *Muhammadan* names, such as *Jahangir-abad* or *Jahangir-nagar* for *Dacca, Akbar-abad* for *Agra, Shahjahan-abad* for *Dilli*, &c.

[28] Literally, "water and grain."

[29] Literally, "has existed during the four *jugas*," or fabulous ages of the *Hindus*, i.e., since the creation of the world.

[30] The *Bhakha*, or *Bhasha*, par excellence, is the *Hindu* dialect spoken in the neighbour-

have been masters there. *Mahmud* of *Ghazni*[31] came [there first]; then the *Ghori* and *Lodi*[32] became kings; owing to this intercourse, the languages of the *Hindus* and *Musalmans* were partially blended together. At last *Amir Taimur*[33] (in whose family the name and empire remain to this day), conquered *Hindustan*. From his coming and stay, the *bazar* of his camp was settled in the city; for which reason the *bazar* of the city was called *Urdu*.[34] Then King *Humayun*, annoyed by the *Pathans*, went abroad [to Persia]; and at last, returning from thence, he punished the surviving [*Pathans*], and no rebel remained to raise strife or disturbance.

When King *Akbar* ascended the throne, then all tribes of people, from all the surrounding countries, hearing of the goodness and liberality of this unequalled family, flocked to his court, but the speech and dialect of each was different. Yet, by being assembled together, they used to traffic and do business, and converse with each other, whence resulted the common *Urdu* language. When his majesty *Shahjahan Sahib Kiran*[35] built the auspicious fort, and the great mosque,[36] and caused the walls of the city to be built; and inlaid the peacock throne[37] with precious stones, and erected his tent, made of gold and silver brocade; and *Nawwab' Ali Mardan Khan* cut the canal[38] [to *Dilli*]; then the king, being pleased, made great rejoicings, and constituted the city his capital. Since that time it has been called *Shajahan-abad*, (although the city of *Dilli* is distinct from it, the latter being called

hood of *Agra, Mathura,* &c. in the *Braj* district; it is a very soft language, and much admired in *Upper Hindustan,* and is well adapted for light poetry. Dr. Gilchrist has given some examples of it in his grammar of the *Hindustani* language, and numerous specimens of it are to be found in the *Prem Sagar,* and other works published more recently.

[31] *Mahmud,* the first monarch of the dynasty of *Ghazni,* was the son of the famous *Sabaktagin*. Ha invaded *Hindustan* in A.H. 392, or A.D. 1002. The dynasty was called *Ghaznawi,* from its capital *Ghazna,* or as now commonly written *Ghazni.*

[32] Two dynasties of kings who reigned in *Upper Hindustan* before the race of *Taimur.*

[33] *Timur,* (or *Taimur* as it is pronounced in India) invaded *Hindustan* A.D. 1398.

[34] The *bazar,* that part of a city where there are most shops; but the word is applied to various parts of a city, where various articles are sold, as the cloth *bazar,* the jewel *bazar,* &c.

[35] *Shahjahan* was the most magnificent king of *Dilli,* of the race of *Taimur, Sahib Kiran* was one of his titles, and means, Prince of the Happy Conjunction; i.e. the conjunction of two or more auspicious planets in one of the signs of the Zodiac at the hour of birth. Such was the case at the birth of *Taimur,* who was the first we read of as *Sahib-Kiran.* As a contradistinction, *Shahjahan* is generally called *Sahib Kirani Sani,* or the second *Sahib Kiran.* It never waw applied, as Ferdinand Smith states, to *all* the emperors of *Dilli.* It may be mentioned, that a very extraordinary conjunction of the planets in the sign Libra took place in A.D. 1185, just about the period of *Jangis Khan's* appearance as a conqueror; but I am not aware that he was thence called a *Sahib Kiran,* as he did not happen to be *born* under the said conjunction.

[36] The fort, or rather fortified place, of *Dilli,* and the great mosque, called the *Juma' Masjid.*

[37] The famous *Takhti Ta,us,* or peacock throne, made by the magnificent *Shahjahan,* the richest throne in the world; it was valued at seven millions sterling. Tavernier, the French jeweller and traveller, saw it and describes it in his work. It was carried away by *Nadir Shah* when he plundered *Dilli* in 1739.

[38] The expensive and useless canal which brought fresh water to *Dilli,* whilst the limpid and salutary stream of the *Jumna* flowed under its walls. The advantages of irrigation to the country, through which it passed, were nothing compared to the expense of its construction.

the old city, and the former the new,) and to the bazar of it was given the title of *Urdu-e Mu'alla.*[39]

From the time of *Amir Taimur* until the reign of *Muhammad Shah,* and even to the time of *Ahmad Shah,* and *Alamgir* the Second, the throne descended lineally from generation to generation. In the end, the *Urdu* language, receiving repeated polish, was so refined, that the language of no city is to be compared to it; but an impartial judge is necessary to examine it. Such a one God has at last, after a long period, created in the learned, acute and profound Mr. John Gilchrist, who from his own judgment, genius, labour and research, has composed books of rules [for the acquisition of it]. From this cause, the language of *Hindustan* has become general throughout the provinces, and has been polished anew; otherwise no one conceives his own turban, language and behaviour, to be improper. If you ask a countryman, he censures the citizen's idiom, and considers his own the best; "well, the learned only know [what is correct]."[40]

When *Ahmad Shah Abdali,* came from *Kabul* and pillaged the city of *Dilli, Shah 'Alam* was in the east.[41] No master or protector of the country remained, and[42] the city became without a head. True it is, that the city only flourished from the prosperity of the throne. All at once it was overwhelmed with calamity: its principal inhabitants were scattered, and fled wherever they could. To whatever country they went, their own tongue was adulterated by mixing with the people there; and there were many who, after an absence of ten to five years, from some cause or other, returned to *Dilli,* and stayed there. How can they speak the pure language of *Dilli*? somewhere or other they will slip; but the person who bore all misfortunes, and remained fixed at *Dilli* and whose five or ten anterior generations lived in that city, and who mixed in the company of the great, and the assemblies and processions of the people, who strolled in its streets for a length of time, and even after quitting it, kept his language pure from corruption, his style of speaking will certainly be correct. This humble being [viz. *Mir Amman*], wandering through many cities, and viewing their sights, has at last arrived at this place.

[39] Literally, "the supreme camp or market."

[40] A Persian expression.

[41] *Shah 'Alam* the emperor of *Dilli,* was then towards *Patna* a tool in the hands of *Shuja'u-d-Daula, the Nawwab* of *Lakhnau, and Kasim 'Ala Khan, the Nawwab* of *Murshid-abad.*

[42] Alluding to the confusion which reigned in *Upper Hindustan* after the assassination of *'Alamgir* the Second, and the flight of *Shah 'Alam. Upper Hindustan* was then in a sad plight, ravaged alternately by the *Abdalis,* the *Marhattas,* and the *Jats*—the king a pageant, the nobles rebellious, the subjects plundered and oppressed, and the country open to every invader—though this was near 100 years ago, and although they had some government, justice, and security from 1782 to 1802, yet the country had not even then recovered from the severe shock.

INTRODUCTION.

I now commence my tale; pay attention to it, and be just to its merits. In the "Adventures of the Four Darwesh,[43]" it is thus written, and the narrator has related, that formerly in the Empire of *Rum*[44] there reigned a great king, in whom were innate justice equal to that of *Naushirwan*,[45] and generosity like that of *Hatim*.[46] His name was *Azad-Bakht*, and his imperial residence was at Constantinople,[47] (which they call Istambol.) In his reign the peasant was happy, the treasury full, the army satisied, and the poor at ease. They lived in such peace and plenty, that in their homes the day was a festival, and the night was a *shabi barat*[48]. Thieves, robbers, pickpockets, swindlers, and all such as were vicious and dishonest, he utterly exterminated, and no vestige of them allowed he to remain in his kingdom.[49] The doors of the houses were unshut all night, and the shops of the *bazar* remained open. The travellers and wayfarers chinked gold as they went along, over plains and through woods; and no one asked them, "How many teeth have you in your mouth,"[50] or "Where are you going?"

There were thousands of cities in that king's dominions, and many princes

---

[43] The word is used in the singular, both by *Mir Amman* and the original author, *Amir Khusru* according to a well-known rule in Persian syntax, viz., "a substantive accompanied by a numerical adjective dispenses with the plural termination," as "*haft roz*," "seven days," not "*haft rozha*. The Persian term *darwesh*, in a general sense, denotes a person who has adopted what by extreme courtesy is called a religious life, closely akin to the "mendicant friar" of the middle ages; i.e., a lazy, dirty, hypocrital vagabond, living upon the credulous public. The corresponding term in Arabic is *Fakir*; and in *Hindi, Jogi*.

[44] The word *Rum* means that empire of which Constantinople is the capital, and sometimes called, in modern times, Romania. It was originally applied to the Eastern Roman Empire, and, at present, it denotes Turkey in Europe and Asia.

[45] *Naushirwan* was a king of Persia, who died in A.D. 578. He is celebrated in oriental history for his wisdom and justice. During his reign *Muhammad* the prophet was born. The Persian writings are full of anecdotes of *Naushirwan's* justice and wisdom.

[46] *Hatim* or rather *Hatim Tai*, is the name of an Arab chief, who is celebrated for his generosity and his mad adventures, in an elegant Persian work called *Kissae Hatim Tai*. This work was translated into English for the Asiatic Translation Fund in 1830.

[47] Called also *Kustuntuniya* by the Persians, and *Istambol*, also *Islambol*, by the Turks.

[48] The *shabi barat* is a Mahometan festival which happens on the full moon of the month of *Sha'ban*; illuminations are made at night, and fire-works displayed; prayers are said for the repose of the dead, and offerings of sweetmeats and viands made to their manes. A luminous night-scene is therefore compared to the *shabi barat*.

[49] I warrant you there were no "tickets of leave" granted in those blessed days.

[50] This means an impertinent, or rather a *chaffing*, question, like our own classic interrogation, "Does your mother know you'ra out?"

paid him tribute. Though he was so great a king, he never for a moment neglected his duties or his prayers to God. He possessed all the necessary comforts of this world; but male issue, which is the fruit of life, was not in the garden of his destiny, for which reason he was often pensive and sorrowful, and after the five[51] regulated periods of prayer, he used to address himself to his Creator and say, "O God! thou hast, through thy infinite goodness blest thy weak creature with every comfort, but thou hast given no light to this dark abode.[52] This desire alone is unaccomplished, that I have no one to transmit my name and support my old age.[53] Thou hast everything in thy hidden treasury; give me a living and thriving son, that my name and the vestiges of this kingdom may remain."

In this hope the king reached his fortieth year; when one day he had finished his prayers in the Mirror Saloon,[54] and while telling his beads, he happened to cast his eyes towards one of the mirrors, and perceived a white hair in his whiskers, which glittered like a silver wire; on seeing it, the king's eyes filled with tears, and he heaved a deep sigh, and then said to himself, "Alas! thou hast wasted thy years to no purpose, and for earthly advantages thou hast overturned the world. And all the countries thou hast conquered, what advantage are they to thee? Some other race will in the end squander these riches.

Death hath already sent thee a messenger;[55] and even if thou livest a few years, the strength of thy body will be less. Hence, it appears clearly from this circumstance, that it is not my destiny to have an heir to my canopy and throne. I must one day die, and leave everything behind me; so it is better for me to quit them now, and dedicate the rest of my days to the adoration of my Maker."

Having in his heart made this resolve, he descended to his lower garden.[56] Having dismissed his courtiers, he ordered that no one should approach him in

---

[51] It is incumbent on every good *Musalman* to pray five times in the twenty-four hours. The stated periods are rather capriciously settled:—1st. The morning prayer is to be repeated between daybreak and sunrise; 2nd. The prayer of noon, when the sun shows a sensible declination from the meridian; 3rd. The afternoon prayer, when the sun is near the horizon that the shadow of a perpendicular object is twice it's length; 4th. The evening prayer, between sunset and close of twilight; 5th. The prayer of night, any time during the darkness. The inhabitants of Iceland and Greenland would find themselves sadly embarrassed in complying with these pious precepts, bequeathed by *Muhammad* to the *true believers,* as they call themselves.

[52] The Asiatics consider *male* children as the light or splendour of their house. In the original there is a play upon the word "*diya*" which, as a substantive signifies "a lamp;" and as a verbal participle it denotes "given," or "bestowed."

[53] The literal meaning is—"There is no one as the bearer of his name, and the giver of water."

[54] The Mirror Saloon, called by the Persians, and from them by the *Hindustanis, Shish Mahall,* is a grand apartment in all oriental palaces, the walls of which are generally inlaid with small mirrors, and their borders richly gilded. Those of *Dilli* and *Agra* are the finest in *Hinduistan.*

[55] "The messenger was the white hair in his majesty's whiskers.

[56] Called in the original, *Pain Bagh.* Most royal Asiatic gardens have a *Pain Bagh* or lower terrace adorned with flowers, to which princes descend when they wish to relax with their courtiers.

future, but that all should attend the Public Hall of Audience,[57] and continue occupied in their respective duties. After this speech the king retired to a private apartment, spread the carpet of prayer,[58] and began to occupy himself in devotion: he did nothing but weep and sigh. Thus the king, *Azud Bakhht* passed many days; in the evening he broke his fast with a date and three mouthfuls of water, and lay all day and night on the carpet of prayer. Those circumstances became public, and by degrees the intelligence spread over the whole empire, that the king having withdrawn his hand from public affairs, had become a recluse. In every quarter enemies and rebels raised their heads, and stepped beyond the bounds [of obedience]; whoever wished it, encroached on the kingdom, and rebelled; wherever there were governors, in their jurisdictions great disturbance took place; and complaints of mal-administration arrived at court from every province. All the courtiers and nobles assembled, and began to confer and consult.

At last it was agreed, "that as his Highness the *Wazir* is wise and intelligent, and in the king's intimacy and confidence, and is first in dignity, we ought to go before him, and hear what he thinks proper to say on the occasion," All the nobles went to his Highness the *Wazir*, and said: "Such is the state of the king and such the condition of the kingdom, that if more delay takes place, this empire, which has been acquired with such trouble, will be lost for nothing, and will not be easily regained." The *Wazir* was an old, faithful servant, and wise; his name was *Khiradmand,* a name self-significant.[59] He replied, "Though the king has forbidden us to come into his presence, yet go you: I will also go—may it please God that the king be inclined to call me to his presence." After saying this, the *Wazir* brought them all along with him as far as the Public Hall of Audience, and leaving them there, he went into the Private Hall of Audience,[60] and sent word by the eunuch[61] to the royal presence, saying, "this old slave is in waiting, and for many days has not beheld the royal countenance; he is in hopes that, after one look, he may kiss the royal feet, then his mind will be at ease." The king heard this request of his *Wazir*, and inasmuch as his majesty knew his length of services, his zeal, his talents, and his devotedness, and had often followed his advice, after some consideration, he said, "call in *Khiradmand.*" As soon as permission was obtained, the *Wazir* ap-

---

[57] The *Diwani' Amm,* or Public Hall of Audience in eastern palaces, is a grand saloon where Asiatic princes hold a more promiscuous court than in the *Diwani Khass,* or the Private Hall of Audience.

[58] The *Musalla,* is generally in Persia a small carpet, but frequently a fine mat in *Hindustan,* which is spread for the performance of prayer. The devotee kneels and prostrates himself upon it in his act of devotion. It is superfluous to remark that the *Muhammadans* pray with their face turned towards *Mecca,* as far as they can guess its direction. Jerusalem was the original point, but the prophet, (it is said,) in a fit of anger, changed it to *Mecca.*

[59] *Khiradmand* means wise; as a man's name it corresponds to our "Mr. Wiseman," or as the French have it "Monsieur le Sage." It does not necessarily follow, however, that every Mr. Wiseman is a sage.

[60] The *Diwani Khass,* or Private Hall of Audience, is a grand saloon, where only the king's privy councillors or select officers of state are admitted to an audience.

[61] As Asiatic princes in general pass the most part of their time in the *haram* or in seclusion, eunuchs are the usual carriers of messages, &c.

peared in the royal presence, made his obeisance, and stood with crossed arms.[62] He saw the king's strange and altered appearance, that from extreme weeping and emaciation his eyes were sunk in their sockets,[63] and his visage was pale.

Khiradmand could no longer restrain himself, but without choice, ran and threw himself at [the king's] feet. His majesty lifted up the *Wazir's* head with his hands, and said, "There, thou hast at last seen me; art thou satisfied? Now go away, and do not disturb me more—do thou govern the empire." *Khiradmand,* on hearing this, gnashing his teeth, wept said, "This slave, by your favour and welfare, can always possess a kingdom; but ruin is spread over the empire from your majesty's such sudden seclusion, and the end of it will not be prosperous. What strange fancy has possessed the royal mind! If to this hereditary vassal your majesty will condescend to explain yourself, it will be for the best—that I may unfold whatever occurs to my imperfect judgment on the occasion. If you have bestowed honours on your slaves, it is for this exigency, that your majesty may enjoy yourself at your ease, and your slaves regulate the affairs of the state; for if your imperial highness is to bear this trouble, which God forbid! of what utility are the servants of the state?" The king replied, "Thou sayest true; but the sorrow which preys on my mind is beyond cure.

"Hear, O *Khiradmand!* my whole age has been passed in this vexatious career of conquest, and I am now arrived at these years; there is only death before me; I have even received a message from him, for my hairs are turned white. There is a saying; 'We have slept all night, and shall we not awake in the morning?' Until now I have not had a son, that I might be easy in mind; for which reason my heart is very sorrowful, and I have utterly abandoned everything. Whoever wishes, may take the country and my riches. I have no use for them. Moreover, I intend some day or other, to quit everything, retire to the woods and mountains, and not show my face to any one. In this manner I will pass this life of [at best but] a few days' duration. If some spot pleases me, I shall sit down on it; and by devoting my time in prayers to God, perhaps my future state will be happy; this world I have seen well, and have found no felicity in it." After pronouncing these words, the king heaved a deep sigh, and became silent.

Khiradmand had been the *Wazir* of his majesty's father, and when the king was heir-apparent he had loved him; moreover, he was wise and zealous. He said (to *Azad Bakht,*) "It is ever wrong to despair of God's grace; He who has created the eighteen thousand species of living beings[64] by one fiat, can give you children without any difficulty. Mighty sire, banish these fanciful notions from your mind, or else all your subjects will be thrown into confusion, and this empire,—with what trouble and pains your royal forefathers and yourself have erected it!—will

[62] The posture of respect, as to stand motionless like a statue, the eyes fixed on the ground, and the arms crossed over the waist.

[63] Literally, "rings or circles had formed round his eyes, and his visage had turned yellow." The term "yellow" is used among the dark-complexioned people of the East in the same sense as our word "pale," or the Latin "pallidus," to indicate fear, grief, &c.

[64] The Asiatics reckon the animal species at 18,000; a number which even the fertile genius of Buffon has not attained. Yet the probability is, that the orientals arc nearer the true mark; and the wonder is, how they acquired such correct ideas on the subject.

be lost in a moment, and, from want of care, the whole country will be ruined; God forbid that you should incur evil fame! Moreover, you will have to answer to God, in the day of judgment, when he will say, 'Having made thee a king, I placed my creatures under thy care; but thou hadst no faith in my beneficence, and thou hast afflicted thy subjects [by abandoning thy charge.'] What answer will you make to this accusation? Then even your devotion and prayers will not avail you, for the heart of man is the abode of God, and kings will have to answer only for the justice[65] of their conduct. Pardon your slave's want of respect, but to leave their homes, and wander from forest to forest, is the occupation of hermits,[66] but not that of kings. You ought to act according to your allotted station: the remembering of God, and devotion to him, are not limited to woods or mountains: your majesty has undoubtedly heard this verse, 'God is near him, and he seeks him in the wilderness; the child is in his arms, and there is a proclamation [of its being lost] throughout the city.'

"If you will be pleased to act impartially, and follow this slave's advice, in that case the best thing is, that your Majesty should keep God in mind every moment, and offer up to him your prayers. No one has yet returned hopeless from his threshold. In the day, arrange the affairs of state, and administer justice to the poor and injured; then the creatures of God will repose in peace and comfort under the skirt of your prosperity. Pray at night; and after beseeching blessings for the pure spirit of the Prophet, solicit assistance from recluse *Darweshes* and holy men, [who are abstracted from worldly objects and cares;] bestow daily food on orphans, prisoners, poor parents of numerous children, and helpless widows. From the blessings of these good works and benevolent intentions, if God please, it is to be fervently hoped that the objects and desires of your heart will all be fulfilled, and the circumstances for which the royal mind is afflicted, will likewise be accomplished, and your noble heart will rejoice! Look towards the favour of God, for he can in a moment do what he wishes." At length, from such various representations on the part of *Khiradmand* the *Wazir, Azad Bakht's* heart took courage, and he said, "Well, what you say is true; let us see to this also; and hereafter, the will of God be done."

When the king's mind was comforted, he asked the *Wazir* what the other nobles and ministers were doing, and how they were. He replied, that "all the pillars of state are praying for the life and prosperity of your majesty; and from grief for your situation, they are all in confusion and dejected. Show the royal countenance to them, that they may be easy in their minds. Accordingly, they are now waiting in the *Diwani Amm*." On hearing this, the king said, "If God please, I will hold a court to-morrow: tell them all to attend." *Khiradmand* was quite rejoiced on hearing this promise, and lifting up his hands, blessed the king, saying, "As long as this earth and heaven exist, may your majesty's crown and throne remain. Then taking leave [of the king,] he retired with infinite joy, and communicated these pleasing

[65] There is a well-known Eastern saying, that, "On the part of a king, one hour's administration of justice will be of more avail to him on the day of judgment than twenty years of prayer."

[66] Literally, "*Fakirs* and *Jogis*;" either term denotes "hermit" the former being applied to a *Musalman*, the latter to a *Hindu*.

tidings to the nobles. All the nobles returned to their homes with smiles and gladness of heart. The whole city rejoiced, and the subjects became boundless [in their transports at the idea] that the king would hold a general court the next day. In the morning, all the servants of state, noble and menial, and the pillars of state, small and great, came to the court, and stood each according to his respective place and degree, and waited with anxiety to behold the royal splendour.

When one *pahar*[67] of the day had elapsed, all at once the curtain drew up, and the king, having ascended, seated himself on the auspicious throne. The sounds of joy struck up in the *Naubat-Khana*,[68] and all the assembly offered the *nazars*[69] of congratulation, and made their obeisance in the hall of audience. Each was rewarded according to his respective degree and rank, and the hearts of all became joyful and easy. At midday[70] his majesty arose and retired to the interior of the palace; and after enjoying the royal repast, retired to rest. From that day the king made this an established rule, viz., to hold his court every morning, and pass the afternoons in reading and in the offices of devotion; and after expressing penitence, and beseeching forgiveness from God, to pray for the accomplishment of his desires.

One day, the king saw it written in a book, that if any one is so oppressed with grief and care as not to be relieved by [any human] contrivance, he ought to commit [his sorrows] to Providence, visit the tombs of the dead, and pray for the blessing of God on them,[71] through the mediation of the Prophet; and conceiving himself nothing, keep his heart free from the thoughtlessness of mankind; weep as a warning to others, and behold [with awe] the power of God, saying, "Anterior to me, what mighty possessors of kingdoms and wealth have been born on earth! but the sky, involving them all in its revolving circle, has mixed them with the dust." It is a bye-word, that, "on beholding the moving handmill, *Kabira*,[72] weeping, exclaimed, 'Alas! nothing has yet survived the pressure of the two millstones.'"

"Now, if you look [for those heroes], not one vestige of them remains, except a heap of dust. All of them, leaving their riches and possessions, their homes

[67] In India, the day was formerly divided into four equal portions, called *pahars* or watches, of which the second terminated at noon; hence, *do-pahar-din*, mid-day. In like manner was the night divided; hence, *do-pahar-rat*, midnight. The first *pahar* of the day began at sunrise, and of the night at sunset; and since the time from sunrise to noon made exactly two *pahars*, it follows that in the north of India the *pahar* must have varied from three and a-half hours about the summer solstice, to two and a-half in winter, the *pahars* of the night varying inversely. A shallow commentator has said that "the *pahar* or watch is three hours, and that the day commences at six a.m.," which is altogether incorrect.

[68] The *Naubat-khana*, or the royal orchestra, is, in general, a large room over the outer gate of the palace for the martial music.

[69] *Nazars*, presents made to kings, governors, and masters, &c., on joyful occasions, and on public festivals, generally in silver and gold.

[70] Literally, "when two *pahars* had elapsed." —V. note on *pahar*, supra.

[71] "On them," i.e., for the souls of the dead.

[72] A celebrated *Hindu* poet of Upper *Hindustan*; his poetry is of a sombre hue, but natural and sympathetic; the simile here is, that no creature has yet survived the pressure of the heavens and the earth; the heavens, being in motion, representing the upper millstone, and the earth (supposed to be at rest), the lower millstone.

and offsprings, their friends and dependants, their horses and elephants, are lying alone! All these [worldly advantages] have been of no use to them; moreover, no one by this time, knows even their names, or who they were; and their state within the grave cannot be discovered; (for worms, insects, ants, and snakes have eaten them up;) or [who knows] what has happened to them, or how they have settled their accounts with God? After meditating on these words in his mind, he should look on the whole of this world as a perfect farce; then the flower of his heart will ever bloom, and it will not wither in any circumstance." When the king read this admonition in the book, he recollected the advice of *Khiradmand* the *Wazir*, and found that they coincided. He became anxious in his mind to put this in execution; "but to mount on horseback, [said his majesty to himself,] and take a retinue with me, and go like a king, is not becoming; it is better to change my dress, and go at night and alone to visit the graves of the dead, or some godly recluse, and keep awake all night; perhaps by the mediation of these holy men, the desires of this world and salvation in the next, may be obtained."

Having formed this resolution, the king one night put on coarse and soiled clothes, and taking some money with him, he stole silently out of the fort, and bent his way over the plain; proceeding onwards, he arrived at a cemetery, and was repeating his prayers with a sincere heart. At that time, a fierce wind continued blowing, and might be called a storm. Suddenly the king saw a flame at a distance which shone like the morning star; he said to himself, "In this storm and darkness this light cannot shine without art, or it may be a talisman; for if nitre and sulphur be sprinkled in the lamp, around the wick, then let the wind be ever so strong, the flame will not be extinguished—or may it not be the lamp of some holy man which burns? Let it be what it may, I ought to go and examine it; perhaps by the light of this lamp, the lamp of my house also may be lighted,[73] and the wish of my heart fulfilled." Having formed this resolution, the king advanced in that direction; when he drew near, he saw four erratic *fakirs*,[74] with *kafnis*[75] on their bodies, and their head reclined on their knees; sitting in profound silence, and senselessly abstracted. Their state was such as that of a traveller, who, separated from his country and his sect, friendless and alone, and overwhelmed with grief, is desponding and at a loss. In the same manner sat these four *Fakirs*, like statues,[76] and a lamp placed on a stone burnt brightly; the wind touched it not, as if the sky itself had been its shade,[77] so that it burnt without danger [of being extinguished.]

On seeing this sight, *Azad Bakht* was convinced [and said to himself] that "as-

[73] A figurative expression, denoting, "I may yet have a son and heir."

[74] *Fakirs* are holy mendicants, who devote themselves to the expected joys of the next world, and abstract themselves from those of this silly transitory scene; they are generally fanatics and enthusiasts—sometimes mad, and often hypocrites. They are much venerated by the superstitious Asiatics, and are allowed uncommon privileges, which they naturally often abuse.

[75] The *kafni* is a kind of short shirt without sleeves, of the colour of brick dust, which *Fakirs* wear.

[76] Literally, "paintings on a wall."

[77] The *fanus* is a large glass shade open at the top, placed over a lamp or candle as a protection from wind, or bats, &c., when the windows are all open, as is generally the case in hot weather.

suredly thy desires will be fulfilled, by the blessing [resulting from] the footsteps of these men of God; and the withered tree of thy hopes shall revive by their looks, and yield fruit. Go into their company, and tell thy story, and join their society; perhaps they may feel pity for thee, and offer up for thee such a prayer as may be accepted by the Almighty." Having formed this determination, he was about to step forward, when his judgment told him, O fool, do not be hasty! Look a little [before thee.] What dost thou know as to who they are, from whence they have come, and where they are going? How can we know but they may be *Devs*[78] or *Ghuls*[79] of the wilderness, who, assuming the appearance of men, are sitting together? In every way, to be in haste, and go amongst them and disturb them, is improper. At present, hide thyself in some corner, and learn the story of these *Darweshes*." At last the king did so, and hid himself in a corner with such silence, that no one heard the sound of his approach; he directed his attention towards them to hear what they were saying amongst themselves. By chance one of the *Fakirs* sneezed, and said, "God be praised."[80] The other three *Kalandars*,[81] awakened by the noise he made, trimmed the lamp; the flame was burning bright, and each of them sitting on his mattrass, lighted their *hukkas*,[82] and began to smoke. One of these *Azads*[83] said, "O friends in mutual pain, and faithful wanderers over the world! we four persons, by the revolution of the heavens, and changes of day and night, with dust on our heads, have wandered for some time, from door to door. God be praised, that by the aid of our good fortune, and the decree of fate, we have to-day met each other on this spot. The events of to-morrow are not in the least known, nor what will happen; whether we remain together, or become totally separated; the night is a heavy load,[84] and to retire to sleep so early is not salutary. It is far better that we relate, each on his own part, the events which have passed over our heads in this world, without admitting a particle of untruth [in our narrations;] then the night will pass away in words, and when little of it remains, let us retire to rest." They all replied, "O leader, we agree to whatever you command. First you begin your own history, and relate what you have seen; then shall we be edified."

---

[78] The *Dev* is a malignant spirit, one of the class called *jinn* by the Arabs, vide Lane's "Arabian Nights," vol. i. p. 30. The *jinn* or genii, however, occasionally behave very handsomely towards the human race, more especially towards those of the *Muhammadan* faith.

[79] The *Ghul* is a foul and intensely wicked spirit, of an order inferior to the *jinn*. It is said to appear in the form of any living animal it chooses, as well as in any other monstrous and terrific shape. It haunts desert places, especially burying grounds, and is said to feed on dead human bodies.

[80] This is a general exclamation when Asiatics sneeze, and with them, as with the ancients, it is an ominous sign.

[81] *Kalandars* are a more fanatic set of *Fakirs*. Their vow is to desert wife, children, and all worldly connexions and human sympathies, and to wander about with shaven heads.

[82] The introduction of the *hukka* is an improvement of *Mir Amman's*; as that luxury was unknown in Europe and Asia at the time of *Amir Khusru*.

[83] The term *Azad*, "free, or independent," is applied to a class of Darweshes who shave the beard, eyelashes and eyebrows. They vow chastity and a holy life, but consider themselves exempt from all ceremonial observances of the *Muhammadan* religion.

[84] Literally, "is an immense mountain."

ADVENTURES OF THE FIRST DARWESH.

The first *Darwesh*, sitting at his ease,[85] began thus to relate the events of his travels:

> "Beloved of God, turn towards me, and hear this helpless one's narrative.
> Hear what has passed over my head with attentive ears,
> Hear how Providence has raised and depressed me.
> I am going to relate whatever misfortunes I have suffered; hear the whole narrative."

O my friends, the place of my birth, and the country of my forefathers, is the land of Yaman;[86] the father of this wretch was *Maliku-t-Tujjar*,[87] a great merchant, named *Khwaja Ahmad*. At that time no merchant or banker was equal to him. In most cities he had established factories and agents, for the purchase and sale (of goods); and in his warehouses were *lakhs* of *rupis* in cash, and merchandise of different countries. He had two children born to him; one was this pilgrim, who, clad in the *kafni*[88] and *saili*,[89] is now in your presence, and addressing you, holy guides; the other was a sister, whom my father, during his life time, had married to a merchant's son of another city; she lived in the family of her father-in-law. In short, what bounds could be set to the fondness of a father, who had an only son, and was so exceedingly rich! This wanderer received his education with great tenderness under the shadow of his father and mother; and began to learn reading and writing, and the science and practice of the military profession; and likewise the art of commerce, and the keeping of accounts. Up to [the age of] fourteen years, my life passed away in extreme delight and freedom from anxiety; no care of the world entered my heart. All at once, even in one year, both my father and

---

[85] The phrase *do zanu ho baithna* denotes a mode of sitting peculiar, more especially, to the Persians. It consists in kneeling down and sitting back on one's heels, a posture the very reverse of *easy*, at least, so it appears to us good Christians, accustomed to the use of chairs &c.

[86] Arabia Felix, the south-west province of the peninsula.

[87] *Maliku-t-Tujjar* means the chief of merchants; it is a Persian or Arab title. The first title the East India Company received from the court of *Dilli* was *'Umdatu-t-Tujjar*, or the noble merchants. *Haji Khalil*, the ambassador from Persia to the Bengal government, who was killed at Bombay, was *Maliku-t-Tujjar*; and after him *Muhammad Nabi Khan*, who likewise was ambassador from the Persian court, and came to Bengal; he has since experienced the sad uncertainty of Asiatic despotism; being despoiled of his property, blinded, and turned into the streets of *Shiraz* to beg.

[88] The peculiar dress worn by *fakirs*. V. *"Qanooni Islam"*

[89] The *seli*, or *saili*, is a necklace of thread worn as a badge of distinction by a certain class of *fakirs*.

mother died by the decree of God.

I was overwhelmed with such extreme grief, that I cannot express [its anguish.] At once I became an orphan! No elder [of the family] remained to watch over me. From this unexpected misfortune I wept night and day; food and drink were utterly disregarded. In this sad state I passed forty days: on the fortieth day,[90] [after the death of my parents,] my relations and strangers of every degree assembled [to perform the rites of mourning.] When the *Fatiha*[91] for the dead was finished, they tied on this pilgrim's head the turban of his father;[92] they made me understand, that, "In this world the parents of all have died, and you yourself must one day follow the same path. Therefore, have patience, and look after your establishment; you are now become its master in the room of your father; be vigilant in your affairs and transactions." After consoling me [in this friendly manner,] they took their leave. All the agents, factors and employés [of my late father] came and waited on me; they presented their *nazars*, and said, "Be pleased to behold with your own auspicious eye the cash in the coffers, and the merchandise in the warehouses." When all at once my sight fell on this boundless wealth, my eyes expanded. I gave orders for the fitting up of a *diwan-khana*;[93] the *farrashes*[94] spread the carpets, and hung up the *pardas*[95] and magnificent *chicks*.[96] I took handsome servants into my service; and caused them to be clothed in rich dresses out of my treasury. This mendicant had no sooner reposed himself in [the vacant] seat [of his father] than he was surrounded by fops, coxcombs, "thiggars[97] and sornars," liars and flatterers, who became his favourites and friends. I began to have them constantly in my company. They amused me with the gossip of every place, and every idle, lying tittle tattle; they continued urging me thus. "In this season of youth, you ought to

[90] The fortieth day is an important period in *Muhammadan* rites; it is the great day of rejoicing after birth, and of mourning after death. To dignify this number still more, sick and wounded persons are supposed, by oriental novelists, to recover and perform the ablution of cure on the fortieth day. The number "forty" figures much in the Sacred Scriptures, for example, "The flood was forty days upon the earth." The Israelites forty years in the wilderness, &c., &c.

[91] The *Fatiha* is the opening chapter of the *Kur,an*, which, being much read and repeated, denotes a short prayer or benediction in general.

[92] This is the general mode of investiture in *Hindustan* to offices, places, &c.; to which a *khil'at*, or honorary dress, is added.

[93] That part of a dwelling where male company are received.

[94] *Farrashes* are servants whose duty it is to spread carpets, sweep them and the walls; place the *masnads*, and hang up the *pardas* and *chicks*, pitch tents, &c.

[95] *Pardas* are quilted curtains, which hang before doors, &c.

[96] *Chicks* are curtains, or hanging screens, made of fine slips of *bamboos*, and painted and hung up before doors and windows, to prevent the persons inside from being seen, and to keep out insects; but they do not exclude the air, or the light from without. If there is no light in a room, a person may sit close to the *chick*, and not be seen by one who is without.—However, no description can convey an adequate idea of *pardas* and *chicks* to the mere European.

[97] I hope the reader will pardon me for the use of this old-fashioned Scottish expression which conveys the exact meaning of the original, viz., "*muft par khane-pine-wale*", i.e, "gentlemen who eat and drink at another's cost." The English terms, "parasites," or "diners out," do not fully express the meaning, though very near it.

drink[98] of the choicest wines, and send for beautiful mistresses to participate in the pleasures thereof, and enjoy yourself in their company."

In short, the evil genius of man is man: my disposition changed from listening constantly [to their pernicious advice.] Wine, dancing, and gaming occupied my time. At last matters came to such a pitch, that, forgetting my commercial concerns, a mania for debauchery and gambling came over me. My servants and companions, when they perceived my careless habits, secreted all they could lay hand on; one might say a systematic plunder took place. No account was kept of the money which was squandered; from whence it came, or where it went:

"When the wealth comes gratuitously, the heart has no mercy on it."[99]

Had I possessed even the treasures of *Karun,*[100] they would not have been sufficient to supply this vast expenditure. In the course of a few years such became all at once my condition, that, a bare skull cap for my head, and a rag about my loins, were all that remained. Those friends who used to share my board, and [who so often swore][101] to shed their blood by the spoonful for my advantage, disappeared; yea, even if I met them by chance on the highway, they used to withdraw their looks and turn aside their faces from me; moreover, my servants, of every description, left me, and went away; no one remained to enquire after me, and say, "what state is this you are reduced to?" I had no companion left but my grief and regret.

I now had not a half-farthing's worth of parched grain [to grind between my jaws,] and give a relish to the water I drank: I endured two or three severe fasts, but could no longer bear [the cravings of] hunger. From necessity, covering my face with the mask of shamelessness, I formed the resolution of going to my sister; but this shame continued to come into my mind, that, since the death of my father, I had kept up no friendly intercourse with her, or even written her a single line; nay, further, she had written me two or three letters of condolence and affection, to which I had not deigned to make any reply in my inebriated moments of prosperity. From this sense of shame my heart felt no inclination [to go to my sister,] but except her house, I had no other [to which I could resort.] In the best way I could, on foot, empty-handed, with much fatigue and a thousand toils, having traversed the few [intervening] stages, I arrived at the city where my sister lived, and reached her house. My sister, seeing my wretched state, invoked a blessing upon me, embraced me with affection, and wept bitterly; she distributed [the customary offerings to the poor] on the occasion of my safe arrival, such as oil, vegetables, and small coins,[102] and said to me, "Though my heart is greatly rejoiced at this

[98] Literally, "quaff the wine of the *Ketaki,* and pluck the flower of the rose." The *Ketaki,* a highly odoriferous flower, was used in giving fragrance to the wine.

[99] A Persian proverb, like our own "Lightly come, lightly go."

[100] A personage famed for his wealth, like the Croesus of the Greeks.

[101] The reader will observe, in the original, that the terms *rah-bat,* a "highway," and *bhent-mulakat,* "a meeting," consist each of two nouns denoting precisely the same thing, only one of them is of *Musalman* usage, and the other *Hindu.* Such expressions are very common in the language.

[102] Literally, "black *takas,*" or copper coins, in opposition to "white" or silver; an expression similar to what we, in the vernacular call "browns."

meeting, yet, brother, in what sad plight do I see you?" I could make her no reply, but shedding tears, I remained silent. My sister sent me quickly to the bath, after having ordered a splendid dress to be sewn for me. I having bathed and washed, put on these clothes. She fixed on an elegant apartment, near her own, for my residence. I had in the morning *sharbat,*[103] and various kinds of sweetmeats for my breakfast; in the afternoon, fresh and dried fruits for my luncheon; and at dinner and supper she having procured for me *pulaos,*[104] *kababs,*[105] and bread of the most exquisite flavour and delicious cookery; she saw me eat them in her own presence; and in every manner she took care of me. I offered thousands upon thousands of thanksgivings to God for enjoying such comfort, after such affliction [as I had suffered.] Several months passed in this tranquillity, during which I never put my foot out of my apartment.

One day, my sister, who treated me like a mother, said to me, "O brother, you are the delight of my eyes, and the living emblem of the dead dust of our parents; by your arrival the longing of my heart is satisfied; whenever I see you, I am infinitely rejoiced; you have made me completely happy; but God has created men to work for their living, and they ought not to sit idle at home. If a man becomes idle and stays at home, the people of the world cast unfavourable reflections on him; more especially the people of this city, both great and little, though it concerns them not, will say, on your remaining [with me and doing nothing,] 'That having lavished and spent his father's worldly wealth, he is now living on the scraps from his brother-in-law's board.' This is an excessive want of proper pride, and will be our ridicule, and the subject of shame to the memory of our parents; otherwise I would keep you near my heart, and make you shoes of my own skin, and have you wear them. Now, my advice is that you should make an effort at travelling; please God the times will change, and in place of your present embarrassment and destitution, gladness and prosperity may be the result." On hearing this speech my pride was roused; I approved of her advice, and replied, very well, you are now in the place of my mother, and I will do whatever you say. Having thus received my consent, she went into the interior of her house, and brought out, by the assistance of her female slaves and servants, fifty *toras*[106] of gold and laid them before me, saying, "A caravan of merchants is on the point of setting out

---

[103] *Sharbat* is a well-known oriental beverage, made in general with vegetable acids, sugar and water; sometimes of sugar and rose water only; to which ingredients some good *Musalmans*, on the sly, add a *leettle* rum or brandy.

[104] *Pulao*, (properly "*pilav*," as pronounced by the Persians and Turks,) is a common dish in the East. It consists of boiled rice well dried and mixed with eggs, cloves and other spices, heaped up on a plate, and inside of this savoury heap is buried a well-roasted fowl, or pieces of tender meat, such as mutton, &c.; in short, any good meat that may be procurable.

[105] *Kabab* is meat roasted or fried with spices; sometimes in small pieces, sometimes minced, sometimes on skewers, but never in joints as with us, though they make *kababs* of a whole lamb or kid.

[106] The *tora* is a bag containing a thousand pieces (gold or silver). It is used in a collective sense, like the term *kisa*, or "purse," among the Persians and Turks; only the *kisa* consists of five hundred dollars, a sum very nearly equal to 1000 *rupis*.

for Damascus.[107] Do you purchase with this money some articles of merchandise. Having put them under the care of a merchant of probity, take from him a proper receipt for them: and do you also proceed to Damascus. When you arrive there in safety, receive the amount sales of your goods, and the profit which may accrue [from your merchant,] or sell them yourself [as may be most convenient or advantageous."] I took the money and went to the *bazar*;[108] and having bought articles of merchandise, I delivered them over in charge to an eminent merchant, and set my mind at ease on receiving a satisfactory receipt from him. The merchant embarked with the goods on board a vessel, and set off by sea,[109] and I prepared to go by land. When I took leave of my excellent sister, she gave me a rich dress and a superb horse with jewelled harness; she put some sweetmeats in a leather bag and hung it to the pummel of my saddle, and she suspended a flask of water from the crupper; she tied a sacred rupee on my arm,[110] and having marked my forehead with *tika*,[111] "Proceed," said she, suppressing her tears, "I have put thee under the protection of God; thou showest thy back in going, in the same happy state show me soon your face." I also said, after repeating the prayer of welfare, "God be your protector also. I obey your commands." Coming out from thence, I mounted my horse, and having placed my reliance on the protection of the Almighty, I set forward, and throwing two stages into one, I soon reached the neighbourhood of Damascus.

In short, when I arrived at the city gate, the night was far advanced, and the door-keepers and guards had shut them. I made much entreaty, and added, "I am a traveller, who has come a long journey, at a great rate; if you would kindly open the gates, I could get into the city and procure some refreshment for myself and my horse." They rudely replied from within, "There is no order to open the gates at this hour; why have you come so late in the night?" When I heard this plain answer of theirs, I alighted from my horse under the walls of the city, and spreading my housing, I sat down; but to keep awake, I often rose up and walked about. When it was exactly midnight,[112] there was a dead silence. What do I see but a chest descending slowly from the walls of the fortress! When I beheld this [strange sight], I was filled with surprise, thinking what talisman is this! perhaps God, taking pity on my perplexity and my misfortunes, has sent me here some bounty from his hidden treasure. When the chest rested on the ground, I approached it

[107] The word in the original is *Damishk*, an Indian corruption of the Arabic *Dimashk*, which latter mode of pronunciation I have followed in my printed edition.

[108] The grand street where all the large shops are. In oriental towns of considerable size, there is generally a distinct *bazar* for each species of goods, such as "the cloth *bazar*," "the jewellery *bazar*," &c.

[109] The merchant would have rather a puzzling voyage of it, if he went by sea from Yaman to Damascus.

[110] The sacred rupee, or piece of silver, is a coin which is dedicated to the *Imam Zamin*, or "the guardian *Imam*, (a personage nearly allied to the guardian saint of a good Catholic), to avert evils from those who wear them tied on the arm, or suspended from the neck.

[111] To mark the forehead with *tika*, or curdled milk, is a superstitious ceremony in *Hindustan*, as a propitious omen, on beginning a voyage or journey. It is probable that the *Musulmans* of India borrowed this ceremony, among several others, from the *Hindus*.

[112] Literally, "when half the night was on this side, and half on that."

with much fear, and perceived it was of wood. Instigated by curiosity, I opened it; I beheld in it a beautiful lovely woman (at the sight of whom the senses would vanish), wounded and weltering in her blood, with her eyes closed, and in extreme agonies. By degrees her lips moved, and these sounds issued slowly from her mouth, "O faithless wretch! O barbarous tyrant! Is this deed which thou hast done, the return I merited for all my affection and kindness! Well, well! give me another blow [and complete thy cruelty]: I entrust to God the executing of justice between myself and thee." After pronouncing these words, even in that insensible state, she drew the end of her *dopatta*[113] over her face; she did not look towards me.

Gazing on her, and hearing her exclamations, I became torpid. It occurred to me, what savage tyrant could wound so beautiful a lady! what [demon] possessed his heart, and how could he lift his hand against her! she still loves him,[114] and even in this agony of death, she recollects him! I was muttering this to myself; the sound reached her ear; drawing at once her veil from her face, she looked at me. The moment her looks met mine, I nearly fainted, and my heart throbbed with difficulty; I supported myself by a strong effort, and taking courage, I asked her, "tell me true, who art you, and what sad occurrence is this I see; if you will explain it, then it will give ease to my heart." On hearing these words, though she had scarce strength to speak, yet she slowly uttered, "I thank you! how can I speak? my condition, owing to my wounds, is what you see; I am your guest for a few moments only; when my spirit shall depart, then, for God's sake, act like a man, and bury unfortunate me in some place, in this chest; then I shall be freed from the tongue of the good and bad, and you will earn for yourself a future reward." After pronouncing these words, she became silent.

In the night I could apply no remedy; I brought the chest near me, and began to count the *gharis*[115] of the remaining night. I determined, when the morning came, to go into the city and do all in my power for the cure [of this beautiful woman]. The short, remaining night became so heavy[116] a load, that my heart was quite restless. At last, after suffering much uneasiness, the morning approached—the cock crowed, and the voices of men were heard. After performing the morning prayer, I inclosed the chest in a coarse canvas sack, and just as the gates opened, I entered the city. I began to inquire of every man and shop-keeper where I could find a mansion for hire; and after much search, I found a convenient, handsome house, which I rented. The first thing I did, was to take that beautiful woman out of the chest, and lay her on a soft bed made up of flocks of cotton, which I had

[113] The *dopatta* is a large piece of cloth worn by women, which covers the head and goes round the body; the act of drawing her *dopatta* over her face is mentioned as a proof of her modesty. Men likewise wear the *dopatta* flung over the shoulders, or wrapped round the waist. It is often of gauze and muslin.

[114] This is *Mir Amman's* plain expression. Ferdinand Smith's translation savours somewhat of the Hibernian, viz., "She still loves him who has murdered her."

[115] "The *ghari* is the 60th part of 24 hours, or 24 of our minutes. It may be observed that the *ghari* was a fixed quantity, not subject to variation, like the *pahar*, which last, in the north of India, was made to vary from seven to nine *gharies*, according to the season of the year, or as it referred to the day or night in the same season. Since the introduction of European watches and clocks, the term *ghari* is applied to the Christian hour of sixty minutes.

[116] Literally, "became such a mountain."

removed to a corner. I then placed a trusty person near her, and went in search of a surgeon. I wandered about, asking of every one I met who was the cleverest surgeon in the city, and where he lived. One person said, "There is a certain barber who is unique in the practice of surgery, and the science of physic; and in these arts is quite perfect. If you carry a dead person to him, by the help of God, he will apply such remedies as will bring him to life. He dwells in this quarter [of the city,] and his name is *'Isa*."[117]

On hearing this agreeable intelligence, I went in search of him, and after several inquiries, I found out his abode from the directions I had received. I saw a man with a white beard sitting under the portico of his door, and several men were grinding materials for plasters beside him. For the sake of complimenting him, I made him a respectful *salam*,[118] and said,—"having heard of your name and excellent qualities, I am come [to solicit your assistance.] The case is this: I set out from my country for the purpose of trade, and took my wife with me, from the great affection I had for her; when I arrived near this city, I halted at a little distance, as the evening had set in. I did not think it safe to travel at night in an unseen country; I therefore rested under a tree on the plains. At the last quarter of the night, I was attacked by robbers; they plundered me of all the money and the property they could find, and wounded my wife, from avidity for her jewels. I could make no resistance, and passed the remainder of the night as well as I could. Early in the morning I came into this city, and rented a house; leaving her there, I am come to you with all speed. God has given you this perfection in your profession; favour this [unfortunate] traveller, and come to his humble dwelling; see my wife, and if her life should be saved, then you will acquire great fame, and I will be your slave as long as I live." *'Isa*, the surgeon, was very humane and devout; he took pity on my misfortune, and accompanied me to my house. On examining the wounds, he gave me hopes, and said, "By the blessing of God, this lady's wounds will be cured in forty days; and I will then cause to be administered to her the ablution of cure."

In short, the good man having thoroughly washed all the wounds with the decoction of *nim*,[119] he cleansed them; those that he found fit for stitching, he sewed up; and on the others he laid lint and plasters, which he took out of his box, and tied them up with bandages, and said with much kindness, "I will continue to call morning and evening; be thou careful that she remain perfectly quiet, so that the stitches may not give way; let her food be chicken broth administered in small quantities at a time, and give her often the spirit of *Bed-Mushk*,[120] with rose water,

---

[117] *'Isa* is the name of Jesus among the *Muhammadans*; who all believe, (from the New Testament, transfused into the *Kuran*,) in the resurrection of Lazarus, and the numerous cures wrought by our Saviour. This, perhaps, induced *Mir Amman* to call the wonder-performing barber and surgeon *'Isa*.

[118] The Arabic expression is *salam 'alaikum* or *'alaika*, i.e. "Peace be on you" or "on thee." This mode of greeting is used only towards *Musulmans*; and when it has passed between them, it is understood to be a pledge of friendly confidence and sincere good will.

[119] The *nim* is a large and common tree in India, the leaves of which are very bitter, and used as a decoction to reduce contusions and inflammations; also to cleanse wounds.

[120] The spirit drawn from the leaves of an aromatic tree which grows in *Kashmir*, called *Bed-Mushk*; it is a tonic and exhilarating.

so that her strength may be supported." After giving these directions, he took his leave. I thanked him much with joined hands,[121] and added, "From the consolation you have bestowed, my life also has been restored; otherwise, I saw nothing but death before me; God keep you safe." And after giving him *'Itr*[122] and *betel*, I took leave of him. Night and day I attended on that beautiful lady with the utmost solicitude; rest to myself I renounced as impious, and in the threshold of God I daily prayed for her cure.

It came to pass that the merchant [who had charge of my merchandise,] arrived, and delivered over to me the goods I had entrusted to his care. I sold them as occasion required, and began to spend the amount in medicines and remedies. The good surgeon was regular in his attendance, and in a short time all the wounds filled up, and began to heal; a few days after she performed the ablution of cure. Joy of a wonderful nature arose [in my heart]! A rich *khil'at*,[123] and [a purse of] gold pieces I laid before *'Isa*, the surgeon. I ordered elegant carpets to be spread for that fair one[124], and caused her to sit upon the *masnad*.[125] I distributed large sums to the poor [on the joyous occasion,] and that day I was as happy as if I had gained possession of the sovereignty of the seven climes.[126] On that beautiful lady's cure, such rosy, pure colour appeared in her complexion, that her face shone like the sun, and sparkled with the lustre of the purest gold. I could not gaze on her without being dazzled with her beauty.[127] I devoted myself entirely to her services, and zealously performed whatever she commanded. In the full pride of beauty and consciousness of high rank, if ever she condescended to cast a look on me, she used to say, "Take care, if my good opinion is desirable to you, then never breathe a syllable in my affairs; whatever I order, perform without objection; never

[121] A humble deportment when addressing superiors in India; and through complaisance, used sometimes to equals.

[122] An act of ceremony ever observed amongst the well-bred in India, when a visitor takes leave. *'Itr* is the essence of any flower, more especially of the rose (by us corruptly called "otto of roses"); and *betel* is a preparation of the aromatic leaf so generally used in the East, more especially in India. The moment they are introduced, it is a hint to the visitor to take leave.

[123] The *khil'at* is a dress of honour, in general a rich one, presented by superiors to inferiors. In the zenith of the *Mughal* empire these *khil'ats* were expensive honours, as the receivers were obliged to make rich presents to the emperor for the *khil'ats* they received. The *khil'at* is not necessarily restricted to a rich dress; sometimes, a fine horse, or splendid armour, &c., may form an item of it.

[124] The word *pari*, "a fairy," is frequently used figuratively to denote a beautiful woman.

[125] *Masnad* means literally a sort of counterpane, made of silk, cloth, or brocade, which is spread on the carpet, where the master of the house sits and receives company; it has a large pillow behind to lean the back against, and generally two small ones on each side. It also, metaphorically, implies the seat on which kings, *nawwabs*, and governors sit the day they are invested with their royalty, &c. So that to say that *Shah-'Alam* sat on the *masnad* on such a day, means that he was on that day invested with royalty.

[126] Asiatics divide the world into seven climes; so to reign over the seven climes means, metaphorically, to reign over the whole world; king of the seven climes was one of the titles of the Mogul emperors.

[127] Literally, "it was not in the power of eyesight to dwell upon her splendour."

utter a breath in my concerns, otherwise you will repent." It appeared, however, from her manners, that the return due to me for my services and obedience, was fully impressed on her mind. I also did nothing without her consent, and executed her commands with implicit obedience.

A certain space of time passed away in this mystery and submission—I instantly procured for her whatever she desired. I spent all the money I had from the sale of my goods, both principal and interest. In a foreign country [where I was unknown], who would trust me? that by borrowing, affairs might go on. At last, I was distressed for money, even for our daily expenses, and thence my heart became much embarrassed. With this anxious solicitude I pined daily, and the colour fled from my face; but to whom could I speak [for aid]? What my heart suffered, that it must suffer. "The grief of the poor man [preys] on his own soul."[128] One day the beautiful lady, from her own penetration, perceived [my distressed state] and said, "O youth! my obligations [to you] for the services [you have rendered] me are engraven on my heart as indelible as on stone; but their return I am unable to make at present. If there be any thing required for necessary expenses, do not be distressed on that account, but bring me a slip of paper, pen, and ink." I was then convinced that this fair lady must be a princess of some country, or else she would not have addressed me with such boldness and haughtiness. I instantly brought her the writing materials,[129] and placed them before her—she having written a note in a fair hand, delivered it to me, and said, "There is a *Tirpauliya*[130] near the fort; in the adjoining street is a large mansion, and the master of that house is called *Sidi Bahar*;[131] go and deliver this note to him."

I went according to her commands, and by the name and address she had given me, I soon found out the house; by the porter I sent word of the circumstance [of my having brought] a letter. The moment he heard [my message,] a handsome young negro, with a flashy turban on his head, came out to me; though his colour was dark, his countenance was full of animation. He took the note from my hand, but said nothing, asked no questions, and at the same pace [without a pause] entered the house. In a short time he came out, accompanied by slaves, who carried on their heads eleven sealed trays covered with brocade. He told the slaves, "Go with this young man, and deliver these trays." I, having made my salutation, took my leave of him, and brought [the slaves with their burdens] to our house. I dismissed the men from the door, and carried in the trays entrusted to me to the presence of the fair lady. On seeing them she said, "Take these eleven bags of gold pieces and appropriate the money to necessary expenses; God is most bountiful." I

[128] A Persian proverb, somewhat illustrative of a story told of a West India "nigger," whom his master used to over-flog. "Ah, massa," said Sambo, "poor man dare not vex—him damned sorry though."

[129] The *Kalam-dan*, literally "the pen-holder," means here the small tray containing pens, inkstand, a knife, &c.

[130] *Tirpauliya* means three arched gates; there are many such which divide grand streets in Indian cities, and may be compared to our Temple Bar in London, only much more splendid.

[131] Ethiopian, or Abyssinian slaves, are commonly called *Sidis*. They are held in great repute for honesty and attachment.

took the gold, and began to lay it out in immediate necessaries. Although I became more easy in my mind, yet this perplexity continued in my heart. "O God, [said I to myself,] what a strange circumstance is this! that a stranger, whose person is unknown to me, should, on the mere sight of a bit of paper, have delivered over to me so much money without question or inquiry. I cannot ask the fair lady to explain the mystery, as she has beforehand forbidden me." Through fear, I was unable to breathe a syllable.

Eight days after this occurrence, the beloved fair one thus addressed me:—"God has bestowed on man the robe of humanity which may not be torn or soiled; and although tattered clothes are no disparagement to his manhood, yet in public, in the eyes of the world he has no respect paid to him [if shabbily clothed]. So take two bags of gold with thee, and go to the *chauk*,[132] to the shop of *Yusuf* the merchant, and buy there some sets of jewels of high value, and two rich suits of clothes, and bring them with thee." I instantly mounted my horse, and went to the shop described. I saw there a handsome young man, clothed in a saffron-coloured dress, seated on a cushion; his beauty[133] was such, that a whole multitude stopped in the street from his shop as far as the *bazar* to gaze at him. I approached him with perfect pleasure, having made my "*salam 'alaika.*" I sat down, and mentioned the articles required. My pronunciation was not like that of the inhabitants of that city. The young merchant replied with great kindness, "Whatever you require is ready, but tell me, sir, from what country are you come, and what are the motives of your stay in this foreign city? If you will condescend to inform me on these points, it will not be remote from kindness." It was not agreeable to me to divulge my circumstances, so I made up some story, took the jewels and the clothes, paid their price, and begged to take my leave. The young man seemed displeased and said, "O sir, if you wished to be so reserved, it was not necessary to show such warmth of friendly greeting in your first approach. Amongst well-bred people these[134] amicable greetings are of much consideration." He pronounced this speech with such elegance and propriety, that it quite delighted my heart, and I did not think it courteous to be unkind and leave[135] him so hastily; therefore, to please him, I sat down again and said, I agree to your request with all my heart,[136] and am ready [to obey your commands.]

He was greatly pleased with my compliance, and smiling he said, "If you will honour my poor mansion [with your company] to-day, then having a party of pleasure, we shall regale our hearts for some hours [in good cheer and hilarity."] I

---

[132] The *chauk* is in general a large square in Asiatic cities, where are situated the richest shops; it is sometimes a large wide street.

[133] In the original there is a play on the word *'alam* which signifies "beauty," "the world," also "a multitude of people," or what the French call "tout le monde."

[134] Literally, "the observance of the [form of greeting] "*sahib salamat*," or "*salam 'alaika*," by which he had been at first accosted by his customer.—Vide note 118 on this subject, page 23.

[135] The verb *uthna* like the Persian *bar-khastan* is used idiomatically in the sense of "to go away," to "vanish."

[136] Literally, "your command is on my head and eyes," a phrase imitated from the Persian "*ba sar o chashm.*"

had never left the fair lady alone [since we first met,] and recollecting her solitary situation, I made many excuses, but that young man would not accept any; at last, having extorted from me a promise to return as soon as I had carried home the articles I had purchased, and having made me swear [to that effect,] he gave me leave to depart. I, having left the shop, carried the jewels and the clothes to the presence of the fair lady. She asked the price of the different articles, and what passed at the merchant's. I related all the particulars of the purchase, and the teasing invitation I had received from him. She replied, "It is incumbent on man to fulfil whatever promise he may make; leave me under the protection of God, and fulfil your engagement; the law of the prophet requires we should accept the offers of hospitality." I said, "My heart does not wish to go and leave you alone, but such are your orders, and I am forced to go; until I return, my heart will be attached to this very spot." Saying this, I went to the merchant's: he, seated on a chair, was waiting for me. On seeing me, he said, "Come, good sir, you have made me wait long."[137]

He instantly arose, seized my hand, and moved on; proceeding along, he conducted me to a garden; it was a garden of great beauty; in the basons and canals fountains were playing; fruits of various kinds were in full bloom, and the branches of the trees were bent down with their weight;[138] birds of various species were perched on the boughs, and sung their merry notes, and elegant carpets were spread in every apartment [of the grand pavilion which stood in the centre of the garden]. There on the border of the canal, we sat down in an elegant saloon; he got up a moment after and went out, and then returned richly dressed. On seeing him, I exclaimed, "Praised be the Lord, may the evil eye be averted!"[139] On hearing this, exclamation, he smiled, and said, "It is fit you, too, should change your dress." To please him, I also put on other clothes. The young merchant, with much sumptuousness, prepared an elegant entertainment, and provided every article of pleasure that could be desired; he was warm in his expressions of attachment to me, and his conversation was quite enchanting. At this moment a cupbearer appeared with a flask [of wine] and a crystal cup, and delicious meats of various kinds were served up. The salt-cellars were set in order, and the sparkling cup began to circulate. When it had performed three or four revolutions, four young dancing boys, very beautiful, with loose, flowing tresses, entered the assembly, and began to

[137] The phrase *"rah dekhna,"* literally to look at the road," (by which a person is expected to come;) hence, very naturally and idiomatically it signifies "to be anxiously waiting for one." Again, *rah dikhana* is the causal form, signifying "to make one wait," of "keep one waiting."

[138] The word *janwar* means "an animal," in general; but it is frequently used in the more restricted sense of "a bird".

[139] The "evil eye" is a supersitious motion entertained by the ignorant in *all* countries even until this day. The Asiatics suppose that uncommon qualities of beauty, fortune or health, raise an ominous admiration admiration, which injures the possessor. To tell parents that their children are stout and healthy, is a *mal-à-propos* compliment; also to congratulate women on their healthy appearance is often unwelcome; the same ridiculous and supersitious accompany all admiration of beauty, fortune, &c. For this reason the visitor, in this case, do not compliment his host on the beauty of his person or the splendour of his dress; but instead make use of the above exclamation.

sing and play. Such was the scene, and such the melody, that had *Tan-Sen*[140] been present at that hour, he would have forgot his strains; and *Baiju-Ba,ora*[141] would have gone mad. In the midst of this festivity, the young merchant's eyes filled suddenly with tears, and involuntarily two or three drops trickled down [his cheeks]; he turned round and said to me, "Now between us a friendship for life is formed; to hide the secrets of our hearts is approved by no religion. I am going to impart a secret to you, in the confidence of friendship and without reserve. If you will give me leave I will send for my mistress into our company, and exhilarate my heart [with her presence]; for in her absence, I cannot enjoy any pleasure."

He pronounced these words with such eager desire, that though I had not seen her, yet my heart longed for her. I replied, your happiness is essential to me, what can be better [than what you propose]; send for her without delay; nothing, it is true, is agreeable without the presence of the beloved one. The young merchant made a sign towards the *chick* and shortly a black woman, as ugly as an ogress, on seeing whom one would die without [the intervention of] fate, approached the young man and sat down. I was frightened at her sight, and said within myself, is it possible this she-demon can be beloved by so beautiful a young man, and is this the creature he praised[142] so highly, and spoke of with such affection! I muttered the form of exorcism,[143] and became silent. In this same condition, the festive scene of wine and music continued for three days and nights; on the fourth night, intoxication and sleep gained the victory; I, in the sleep of forgetfulness, involuntarily slumbered; next morning the young merchant wakened me, and made me drink some cups of a cooling and sedative nature. He said to his mistress, "To trouble our guest any longer would be improper."

He then took hold of both my hands, and we stood up. I begged leave to depart; well pleased [with my complaisance], he gave me permission [to return home]. I then quickly put on my former clothes, and bent my way homewards, waited on the angelic lady. But it had never before occurred in my case, to leave her by herself and remain out all night. I was quite ashamed of myself for being absent three days [and nights], and I made her many apologies, and related the whole circumstances of the entertainment, and his not permitting me [to come home sooner]. She was well acquainted with the manners of the world, and smiling said, "What does it signify, if you had to remain to oblige your friend; I cheerfully pardon you, where is the blame on your part; when a man goes on occasions of this sort to any person's house, he returns when the other pleases to let him. But you having eaten

[140] A celebrated musical performer in upper *Hindustan*, and considered as the first in his art. He lived in the reign of *Akbar*, somo 300 years ago.

[141] A celebrated singer in upper *Hindustan*, who lived about 600 years ago. *Tan-Sen* and *Ba,ora* are still held in the highest reverence by singers and musical performers. In the original, there is a play on the words to *tan* and *ba,ora* which scarcely needs to be pointed out.

[142] The original is, *"jis Ki itni ta'rif aur ishtiyak zahir kiya,"* where the word *kiya* agrees with *ishtiyak* only, being the noun nearest. A shallow critic would be apt to say that this is bad grammar.

[143] *"La haul parhna,"* to repeat or recite the *"La haul,"* or more fully, *"La haul wa la kuwwat illa b-Illahi;"* meaning, "there is no power nor strength but in God." An exclamation used by *Musalmans* in cases of sudden surprise, misfortune, &c.

and drunk at his entertainments for nothing, will you remain silent, or give him a feast in return? Now I think it proper you should go to the young merchant, and bring him with you, and feast him two-fold greater than he did you. Give yourself no concern about the materials [for such an entertainment]; by the favour of God, all the requisites will soon be ready, and in an excellent style, the hospitable party will obtain splendour." According to her desire, I went to the jeweller, and said to him, "I have complied with your request most cheerfully, now do you also in the way of friendship, grant my request." He said, "I will obey you with heart and soul."

Then I said, "If you will honour your humble servant's house with a visit, it will be the essence of condescension. That young man made many excuses and evasions, but I would not give up the point. When [at length] he consented, I brought him with me to my house; but on the way I could not avoid making the reflection, that "if I had had the means, I could receive my guest in a style which would be highly gratifying to him. Now I am taking him with me, let us see what will be the result." Absorbed in these apprehensions, I drew near my house. Then how was I surprised to see a great crowd and bustle at the door; the street had been swept and watered; silver mace and club bearers[144] were in waiting. I wondered greatly [at what I saw], but knowing it to be mine own house, I entered, and perceived that elegant carpets befitting every apartment, were spread in all directions, and rich *masnads* were laid out. *Betel* boxes, *gulab-pashes, 'itr-dans, pik-duns*[145] flower pots, narcissus-pots, were all arranged in order. In the recesses of the walls, various kinds of oranges and confectionery of various colours were placed. On one side variegated screens of *talk*, with lights behind them were displayed, and on the other side tall branches of lamps in the shape of cypresses and lotuses, were lighted up. In the hall and alcove camphorated candles were placed in golden candlesticks, and rich glass shades were placed over thorn; every attendant waited at his respective post. In the kitchen the pots continued jingling; and in the *ab-dar-khana*[146] there was a corresponding preparation; jars of water, quite new, stood on silver stands, with percolators attached, and covered with lids. Further on, on a platform, were placed spoons and cups, with salvers and covers; *kulfis*[147] of ice were arranged, and the goglets[148] were being agitated in saltpetre.

In short, every requisite becoming a prince was displayed. Dancing girls and boys, singers, musicians and buffoons, in rich apparel, were in waiting, and singing in concert. I led the young merchant in, and seated him on the *masnad*;[149] I

[144] The insignia of state among the grandees of India.

[145] The *gulab-pash* is a silver or gold utensil, like a French bottle, to sprinkle rose water on the company; the *'itr-dan* one to hold essences, and *pik-duns* are of brass or silver to spit in, called by the French *crachoirs*.

[146] The *abdar-khana* a room appropriated to the cooling of water in ice or saltpetre, by the servant called the *abdar*.

[147] Small leaden mugs with covers for the congelation of ice.

[148] To cool the water which they contain; they are made of pewter.

[149] The *masnad* and its large back pillow are criterions of Asiatic etiquette. To an inferior or dependant, the master of the house gives the corner of the *masnad* to sit on; to an equal or intimate friend, he gives part of the large pillow to lean on; to a superior, he abandons the whole pillow, and betakes himself to the corner of the *masnad*.

was all amazement [and said to myself] "O God, in so short a time how have such preparations been made?" I was staring around and walking about in every direction, but I could nowhere perceive a trace of the beautiful lady; searching for her, I went into the kitchen, and I saw her there, with an upper garment on her neck, slippers on her feet, and a white handkerchief thrown over her head, plain and simply dressed, and without any jewels.

> "She on whom God hath bestowed beauty has no need of ornaments;
> Behold how beautiful appears the moon, without decorations."

She was busily employed in the superintendence of the feast, and was giving directions for the eatables, saying, "have a care that [this dish] may be savoury, and that its moisture, its seasoning and its fragrance, may be quite correct." In this toil that rose-like person was all over perspiration.

I approached her with reverence, and having expressed my admiration of her good sense, and the propriety of her conduct, I invoked blessings upon her. On hearing my compliments, she was displeased, and said, "various deeds are done on the part of human beings which it is not the power of angels [to perform]: what have I done that thou art so much astonished? Enough, I dislike much talk; but say, what manners is this to leave your guest alone, and amuse yourself by staring about; what will he think of your behaviour? return quickly to the company, and attend to your guest, and send for his mistress, and make her sit by him." I instantly returned to the young merchant, and shewed him every friendly attention. Soon after, two handsome slaves entered with bottles of delicious wine, and cups set with precious stones, and served us the liquor. In the meantime, I then observed to the young merchant, I am in every way your friend and servant; it were well that your handsome mistress, to whom your heart is attached, should honour us with her presence; it will be perfectly agreeable to me, and if you please, I will send a person to call her. On hearing this, he was extremely pleased, and said, "Very well, my dear friend, yon have [by your kind offer] spoken the wish of my heart." I sent a eunuch [to bring her]. When half the night was past, that foul hag, mounted on an elegant *chaudol,*[150] arrived like an unexpected evil.

To please my guest I was compelled to advance, and receive her with the utmost kindness, and place her near the young man. On seeing her, he became as rejoiced as if he had received all the delights of the world. That hag also clung round the neck of that angelic youth. The [ludicrous] sight appeared, in plain truth, such as when over the moon of the fourteenth night, an eclipse comes. As many people as were in the assembly began to put their fore-fingers between their teeth,[151] saying [to themselves] "How could such a hag subdue the affections of this young man!" The eyes of all were turned in that direction. Disregarding the amusements of the entertainment, they began to attend only to this strange spectacle. Some apart observed, "O friends, there is an antagonism between love and reason! what judgment cannot conceive, this cursed love will show. You must behold *Laili* with

[150] A kind of *palki* or sedan, for the conveyance of the women of people of rank in India.

[151] A sign of afflicting surprise.

the eyes of *Majnun*.[152] All present exclaimed, "Very true, that is the fact."

According to the directions of the lady, I devoted myself to attending on my guests; and although the young merchant pressed me to eat and drink equally with himself, yet I refrained from fear of the fair [one's displeasure], and did not give myself up to eating and drinking, or the pleasures of the entertainment. I pleaded the duties of hospitality as my excuse for not joining him [in the good cheer]. In this scene of festivity three nights and days passed away. On the fourth night,[153] the young merchant said to me with extreme fondness, "I now beg to take my leave; for your good sake I have utterly neglected my affairs these three days, and have attended you. Pray do you also sit near me for a moment, and rejoice my heart," I in my own heart imagined that "if I do not comply with his request at this moment, then he will be grieved; and it is necessary I should please my new friend and guest;" on which account I replied, "it is a pleasure to me to obey the command of your honour;" for "a command is paramount to ceremony"[154]. On hearing this, the young merchant presented me a cup of wine, and I drank it off; then the cup moved in such quick successive rounds, that in a short time all the guests in the assembly became inebriated and stupefied; I also became senseless.

When the morning came, and the sun had risen the height of two spears,[155] my eyes opened, but I saw nothing of the preparations, the assembly, or the beautiful lady—only the empty house remained—but in a corner [of the hall] something lay folded up in a blanket; I unfolded it, and saw the corpses of the young merchant and of his [black] woman, with their heads severed from their bodies. On seeing this sight, my senses forsook me, and my judgment was of no avail [in explaining to me] what this was and what had happened. I was staring about me, in every direction with amazement, when I perceived a eunuch (whom I had seen in the preparations of the entertainment). I was somewhat comforted on seeing him, and asked him an explanation of these strange events. He replied briefly, "What good will it do thee to hear an explanation of what has happened, that thou askest it?"

I also reflected in my mind, that what he said was true; however, after a short pause, I said to the eunuch, well, do not tell it to me; but inform me in what apartment is the beloved lady. He answered, "Certainly; whatever I know I will relate to thee; but [I am surprised] that a man like thee, possessed of understanding, should, without her ladyship's permission, and without fear or ceremony, have indulged in a wine-drinking party after an intimacy of only a few days.[156] What does all this mean?"

I became much ashamed of my folly [and felt the justice] of the eunuch's rep-

[152] *Majnun*, a lover famed in eastern romance, who long pined in unprofitable love for *Laili*, an ugly hard-hearted mistress. The loves of *Yusuf* and *Zulaikh@a, Khusru* and *Shirin*, also of *Laili* and *Majnun*, are the fertile themes of Persian romance.

[153] The *Muhammadans* reckon their day from sunset.

[154] By sitting and drinking with the young merchant, when he ought to wait on his guests, and attend to their entertainment.

[155] A figurative and highly poetic expression as old as Homer. In this instance it is said to signify that the sun had been two *gharis* above the horizon.

[156] Literally, "a friendship of two days," where the number two is employed indefinitely to denote "few."

robation. I could make no other reply than to say, "indeed I have been guilty, pardon me." At last the eunuch, becoming gracious, pointed out the beloved lady's abode, and took his leave; he himself went to bury the two beheaded bodies. I was free from any participation in that crime, and was anxious to meet the beautiful lady. After a painful and difficult search, I arrived at eventide in that street, [where she then was] according to (the eunuch's) direction; and in a corner near the door I passed the whole night in a state of agitation. I did not hear the sound of any person's footsteps, nor did any bne ask me about my affairs. In this forlorn state the morning came; when the sun rose, the lovely fair one looked at me from a window in the balcony of the house. My heart only knows the state of joy I felt at that moment. I praised the goodness of God.

In the meanwhile, an eunuch came up to me, and said, "Go and stay in this [adjoining] mosque; perhaps your wishes may, in that place, be accomplished, and you may yet gain the desires of your heart." According to his advice I got up from the place [where I had passed the night], and went to the mosque; but my eyes remained fixed in the direction of the door of the house, to see what might appear from behind the curtain of futurity. 1 waited for the arrival of evening with the anxiety of a person who keeps the fast [of *Ramazan*].[157] At last the evening came, and the heavy day was removed from my heart. All at once the same eunuch who had given me the directions to find out the lady's house, came to the mosque. After finishing the evening prayer, having come up to me, that obliging person, who was in all my secrets, gave me much comfort, and taking me by the hand, led me along with him, proceeding onwards at last having made me sit down in a small garden, he said: "Stay here until your desire [of seeing your mistress] be accomplished." Then he himself having taken his leave, went, perhaps, to impart my wishes to the beautiful lady. I amused myself with admiring the beauty of the flowers of the garden, and the brightness of the full moon, and the play of the fountains in the canals and rivulets, a display like that of the mouths of *Sawan* and *Bhadon*; but when I beheld the roses, I thought of the beautiful rose-like angel, and when I gazed on the bright moon, I recollected her moon-like face. All these delightful scenes without her were so many thorns in my eyes.

At last God made her heart favourable to me. After a little while that lovely

[157] The month of *Ramazan* consisting of thirty days, is the Lent of the *Muhammadans*. During tgat whole period, a good *Musalman* or "true believer," is not allowed either to eat, or drink, or smoke from sunrise to sunset. This naturally explains the anxiety they must feel for the arrival of evening; more especially in high latitudes, should the *Ramazan* happen in the middle of summer. As a mere religions observance this same fast, enjoined by *Muhammad*, is the most absurd, the most demoralizing, and the most hurtful to health that ever was invented by priestcraft. The people are forced to starve themselves during the whole day, and consequently they overeat themselves during the whole night, when they ought to be asleep in their beds, as nature intended. Hence they fall by thousands an easy prey to cholera, as happened in Turkey a few years ago. The fast of Lent among tho followers of the Pope of Rome is, though in a less degree, liable to the same censure. Why, instead of these unwholesome observances, do not the priests, whether of Mecca or of Rome, preach unto the people temperance and regularity of living? Ah, I forgot, the priests both of Mecca and of Rome can always grant *dispensations* and *indulgences* to such good people as can adduce *weighty* reasons to that effect.

fair one entered from the [garden] door adorned like the full moon, wearing a rich dress, enriched with pearls, and covered from head to feet with an embroidered veil; she stepped along the garden walk, and stood [at a little distance from me]. By her coming, the beauties of that garden, and the joy of my heart revived. After strolling for a few minutes about the garden, she sat down in the alcove on a richly-embroidered *masnad*. I ran, and like the moth that flutters around the candle, offered my life as a sacrifice to her, and like a slave stood before her with folded arms. At this moment the eunuch appeared, and began to plead for my pardon and restoration to her favour. Addressing myself to him, I said, I am guilty, and culpable; whatever punishment is fixed on me, let it be executed. The lady, though she was displeased, said with *hauteur*, "The best thing that can be done for him now is that he should receive a hundred bags of gold pieces, and having got his property all right, let him return to his native country."

On hearing these words, I became a block of withered wood; if any one had cut my body, not a drop of blood would have issued; all the world began to appear dark before my sight; a sigh of despair burst involuntarily from my heart, and the tears flowed from my eyes. I had at that time no hope from any one except God; driven to utter despair, I ventured to say, "Well, [cruel fair,] reflect a moment, that if to this unfortunate wretch there had been a desire for worldly wealth, he would not have devoted his life and property to you. Are the acknowledgments due to my services, and my having devoted my life to you, flown all of a sudden from this world, that you have shown such disfavour to a wretch like me? It is all well; to me life is no longer of any use; to the helpless, half-dead lover there is no resource against the faithlessness of the beloved one."

On hearing these words, she was greatly offended, and frowning with anger, she exclaimed, "Very fine indeed! What, thou art my lover! Has the frog then caught cold?[158] O fool, for one in thy situation to talk thus is an idle fancy; little mouths should not utter big words: no more—be silent—repeat not such presumptuous language; if any other had dared to behave so improperly, I vow to God, I would have ordered his body to be cut in pieces, and given to the kites [of the air]; but what can I do?—Your services ever come to my recollection. Thou hadst best now take the road [to thy home;] thy fate had decreed thee food and drink only until now in my house!" I then weeping, said, if it has been written in my destiny that I am not to attain the desires of my heart, but to wander miserably through woods and over mountains, then I have no remedy left. On hearing these words, she became vexed and said, "These hints and this flattering nonsense are not agreeable to me; go and repeat them to those who are fit to hear them." Then getting up in the same angry mood, she returned to her house. I beseeched her to hear me, but she disregarded what I said. Having no resource, I likewise left the place, sad and hopeless.

In short, for forty days this same state of things continued. When I was tired of pacing the lanes of the city, I wandered into the woods, and when I became restless

[158] As frogs live in wet, they are not supposed to be extremely subject to catch cold; the simile is introduced to ridicule the extravagant idea of a merchant's son presuming to be in love with a princess. The simile is a proverb.

there, I returned to the lanes of the city like a lunatic. I thought not of nourishment during the day, or sleep at night; like a washerman's dog, that belongs neither to the house nor the *ghat*[159] The existence of man depends on eating and drinking; he is the worm of the grain. Not the least strength remained in my body. Becoming feeble, I went and lay down under the wall of the same mosque; when one day the eunuch aforementioned came there to say his Friday prayers, and passed near me; I was repeating at the time, slow from weakness, this verse:

> "Give me strength of mind to bear these pangs of the heart, or give me death;
> Whatever may have been written in my destiny, O God! let it come soon."

Though in appearance my looks were greatly altered, and my face was such that whoever had seen me formerly would not have recognised me to be the same person; yet the eunuch, hearing the sounds of grief, looked at me, and regarding me with attention, pitied me, and with much kindness addressed me, saying, "At last to this State thou hast brought thyself." I replied, what was to occur has now happened; I devoted my property to her welfare, and I have sacrificed my life likewise; such has been her pleasure; then what shall I do?

On hearing this, he left a servant with me, and went into the mosque; when he finished his prayers, and [heard] the *Khutba,*[160] he returned to me, and putting me into a *miyana*[161] had me carried along to the house of that indifferent fair, and placed me outside the *chik* [of her apartment]. Though no trace of my former self remained, yet as I had been for a long while constantly with the lovely fair one, [she must have recognised me]; however, though knowing me perfectly, she acted as a stranger, and asked the eunuch who I was. That excellent man replied, "This is that unfortunate, ill-fated wretch who has fallen under the displeasure and reprehension of your highness; for this reason his appearance is such; he is burning with the fire of love; how much soever he endeavours to quench the flame with the water of tears, yet it burns with double force. Nothing is of the least avail; moreover he is dying with the shame of his fault." The fair lady jocosely said, "Why dost thou tell lies? I received from my intelligencers,[162] many days ago, the news of his arrival in his own country; God knows who this is of whom you speak." Then the eunuch, putting his hands together, said, "If security be granted to my life,[163] then I will be so bold as to address your highness." She answered, "Speak;

[159] Washermen in India, in general, wash their linen at the *ghats,* and their dogs of course wander thither from home after them, and back again. This is one of their proverbs, and answers to ours of "Kicked from piller to post."

[160] The *Khutba* is a brief oration delivered after divine service every Friday (the *Musalman* Sabbath,) in which the officiating priest blesses *Muhammad,* his successors, and the reigning sovereign.

[161] A kind of sedan chair, or *palki.*

[162] The *Khabar-dars* are a species of spies stationed in various parts of oriental kingdoms in order to forward intelligence to head quarters.

[163] A mode of humble address, when the inferior presumes to state something contrary to what the superior maintains or desires; and as human life in India was, in olden times, not only precarious, but considered as insignificant, the oriental slave acts prudently

your life is secure." The eunuch said, "Your highness is by nature a judge of merit; for God's sake lift up the screen from between you, and recognise him, and take pity on his lamentable condition. Ingratitude is not proper. Now whatever compassion you may feel for his present condition is amiable and meritorious—to say more would be [to outstep] the bounds of respect; whatever your highness ordains, that assuredly is best."

On hearing this speech [of the eunuch], she smiled and said, "Well, let him be who he will, keep him in the hospital; when he gets well, then his situation shall be inquired into." The eunuch answered, "If you will condescend to sprinkle rose-water on him with your own royal hands, and say a kind word to him, then there may be hopes of his living; despair is a bad thing; the world exists through hope." Even on this, the fair one said nothing [to console me]. Hearing this dialogue, I also continued becoming more and more tired of existence. I fearlessly said, "I do not wish to live any longer on these terms; my feet are hanging in the grave, and I must soon die; my remedy is in the power of your highness; whether you may apply it or not, that you only know." At last the Almighty[164] softened the heart of that stony-hearted one; she became gracious and said, "Send immediately for the royal physicians." In a short time they came and assembled [around me]; they felt my pulse and examined my urine with much deliberation; at last it was settled in their prægnosis, that "this person is in love with some one; except the being united with the beloved object, there is no other cure; whenever he possesses her he will be well." When from the declaration of the physicians my complaint was thus confirmed, the fair lady said, "Carry this young man to the warm bath, and after bathing him and dressing him in fine clothes, bring him to me." They instantly carried me out, and after bathing me and clothing me well, they led me before the lovely angel; then that beautiful creature said with kindness, "Thou hast constantly, and for nothing, got me censured and dishonoured; now what more dost thou wish? Whatever is in thy heart, speak it out quite plainly?"

O, *Darweshes!*[165] at that moment my emotions were such that [I thought] I should have died with joy, and- swelled so greatly with pleasure, that my *jama*[166] could hardly contain me, and my countenance and appearance became changed; I praised God, and said to her, this moment all the art of physic is centered in you, who have restored a corpse like me to life with a single word; behold, from that time to this, what a change has taken place in my circumstances [by the kindness you have shewn]." After saying this, I went round her three times,[167] and standing before her, I said, "your commands are that I should speak whatever I have in my heart; this boon is more precious to your slave than the empire of the seven climes; then be generous and accept this wretch! keep me at your feet and elevate me,"

by begging his life before he presumes to be candid.

[164] Literally, "He who is the changer of hearts."

[165] Here the first *Darwesh* addresses himself directly to the other three, who were his patient listeners.

[166] The *jama* is an Asiatic dress, something like a modern female gown, only much more full in the skirts. It is made of white cloth or muslin.

[167] A superstitious custom in India; it implies that the person who goes round, sacrifices his life at the shrine of the love, prosperity and health of the beloved object.

On hearing this ejaculation, she became thoughtful for a moment; then regarding me askance, she said, "Sit down; your services and fidelity have been such that whatever you say becomes you; they are also engraven on my heart. Well; I comply with your request."

The same day, in a happy hour, and under a propitious star the *kazi*[168] quite privately performed the marriage rites. After so much trouble and afflictions, God shewed me this happy day, when I gained the desires of my heart; but in the same degree that my heart wished to possess this angelic lady, it felt equally anxious and uneasy to know the explication of those strange events [which had occurred]; for, up to that day I knew nothing about who she was; or who was that brown, handsome negro, who on seeing a bit of paper, delivered to me so many bags of gold; and how that princely entertainment was prepared in the space of one *pahar*; and why those two innocent persons were put to death after the entertainment; and the cause of the anger and ingratitude she showed me after all my services and kindnesses; and then all at once to elevate this wretch [to the height of happiness.]. In short, I was so anxious to develop these strange circumstances and doubts, that for eight days after the marriage ceremonies, notwithstanding my great affection for her, I did not attempt to consummate the rites of wedlock. I merely slept with her at night, and got up in the morning "re non effectâ."

One morning I desired an attendant to prepare some warm water in order that I might bathe.[169] The princess smiling, said, "Where is the necessity for the hot water?" I remained silent; but she was perplexed [to account] for my conduct; moreover, in her looks the signs of anger were visible; so much so, that she one day said to me, "Thou art indeed a strange man; at one time so warm before, and now so cold! what do people call this [conduct]? If you had not manly vigour, then why did you form so foolish a wish? I then having become fearless, replied, "O, my darling, justice is a positive duty; no person ought to deviate from the rules of justice. She replied, "What further justice remains [to be done]? whatever was to happen has taken place." I answered, in truth, that which was my most earnest wish and desire I have gained; but, my heart is uneasy with doubts, and the man whose mind is filled with suspicions is ever perplexed; he can do nothing, and becomes different from other human creatures. I had determined within myself that after this marriage, which is my soul's entire delight, I would question your highness respecting sundry circumstances which I do not comprehend, and which I cannot unravel; that from your own blessed lips I might hear their explanation; then my heart would be at ease." The lovely lady frowning, said, "How pretty! you have already forgotten [what I told you]; recollect, many times I have desired you not to search into my concerns, or to oppose what I say; and is it proper in you to take, contrary to custom, such liberties?" I laughing replied, as you have pardoned me much greater liberties, forgive this also. That angelic fair, changing

[168] The *kazi* is the judge and magistrate in Asiatic cities; he performs the rites of marriage, settles disputes, and decides civil and criminal causes. As the *Muhammadan* laws are derived from their religious code, the *Kuran*, the *kazi* possesses both secular and ecclesiastical powers.

[169] All good *Musalmans* bathe after performing the rites of Venus, hence the purport of the princess's *simple question* is obvious enough.

her looks and getting warm, became a whirlwind of fire, and said; "You presume too much; go and mind your own affairs; what advantage can you derive from [the explanation of) these circumstances?" I answered, "the greatest shame in this world is the exposure of our person; but we are conversant with one another [in that respect], hence as you have thought it right to lay aside this repugnance with me, then why conceal any other secrets from me?"

Her good sense made her comprehend my hint, and she said, "This is true; but I am very apprehensive if I, wretched, should divulge my secrets; it may be the cause of great trouble." I answered, what strange apprehensions you form! do not conceive in your heart such an idea of me, and relate without restraint all the events of your life; never, never, shall they pass from my breast to my lips; what possibility, then, of their reaching the ear of another?" When she perceived that, without satisfying my curiosity she should have no rest, being without resource, she said, "Many evils attend the explanation of these matters, but you are obstinately bent upon it. Well, I must please you; for which reason I am going to relate the events of my past life—take care; it is equally necessary for you to conceal them [from the world]; my information is on this condition."

In short, after many injunctions, she began the relation [of her life] as follows:—"The unfortunate wretch before you is the daughter of the King of Damascus; he is a great sovereign among sultans; he never had any child except me. From the day I was born I was brought up with great delicacy and tenderness, in joy and happiness under the eye of my father and mother. As I grew up I became attached to handsome and beautiful women; so that I kept near my person the most lovely young girls of noble families, and of my own age; and handsome female servants of the like age, in my service. I ever enjoyed the amusements of dancing and singing, and never had a care about the good or evil of the world. Contemplating my own condition thus free from care, except the praises of God, nothing else occupied my thoughts.

"It so happened that my disposition became suddenly of itself so changed, that I lost all relish for the company of others, nor did the gay assembly afford me any pleasure; my temper became melancholic, and my heart sad and confused; no one's presence was agreeable to me, nor did my heart feel inclined for conversation. Seeing this sad condition of mine, all the female servants were overwhelmed with sorrow and fell at my feet [begging to know the cause of my gloom]. This faithful eunuch, who has long been in my secrets, and from whom no action of my life is concealed, seeing my melancholy, said, 'If the princess would drink a little of the exhilarating lemonade,[170] it is most probable that her cheerful disposition would be restored; and gladness return to her heart.' On hearing him say so, I had a desire [to taste it], and ordered some to be prepared immediately.

"The eunuch went out [to make it up], and returned, accompanied by a young boy, who brought a goblet of the lemonade, carefully prepared and cooled in ice. I drank it, and perceived it produced the good effect ascribed to it; for this piece of

[170] Called *warku-l-khiyal;* it is made from the leaves of the *charas,* a species of hemp; it is a common inebriating beverage in India; the different preparations of it is called *ganja, bhang,* &c.

service I bestowed on the eunuch a rich *khil'at,*[171] and desired him to bring me a goblet of the same every day at the same hour. From that day it became a regular duty, that the eunuch came, accompanied by the boy who brought the lemonade, and I drank it. When its inebriating quality took effect, I used in the elevation of my spirits to jest and laugh with the boy, and beguile my time. When his timidity wore off, he began to utter very agreeable speeches, and related many pleasant anecdotes; moreover, he began to heave sighs and sobs. His face was handsome and worth seeing; I began to like him beyond control. I, from the affections of my heart, and the relish I felt for his playful humour, every day gave him rewards and gratuities; but the wretch always appeared before me in the same clothes that he had been accustomed to wear, and they even were dirty and soiled.

"One day I said to him, you have received a good deal [of money] from the treasury, but your appearance is as wretched as ever; what is the cause of it? have you spent the money, or do you amass it?" When the boy heard these encouraging words, and found that I enquired into his condition, he said with tears in his eyes, 'Whatever you have bestowed on this slave, my preceptor has taken from me; he did not give me one *paisa*[172] for myself; with what shall I make up other clothes, and appear better dressed before you? it is not my fault, and I cannot help it.' At this humble statement of his, I felt pity for him; I instantly ordered the eunuch to take charge of the boy from that day, to educate him under his own eye, and give him good clothes, and not to allow him to play and skip about with other boys; moreover, that my wish was, he should be taught a respectful mode of behaviour, to fit him for my own princely service, and to wait on me. The eunuch obeyed my orders, and perceiving how my inclinations leaned, he took the utmost care of him. In a little time, from ease and good living, his colour and sleekness changed greatly, like a snake's throwing off its slough; I restrained my inclinations as much as I could, but the [handsome] form of that rogue[173] was so engraven on my heart, that I fondly wished to keep him clasped to my bosom, and never take my eyes off him for a moment.

"At last, I made him enter into my companionship, and dressing him in a variety of rich clothes and all kinds of jewels, I used to gaze at him. In short, by being always with me, my longing eyes were satisfied and my heart comforted; I every moment complied with his wants and wishes; at last, my condition was such, that if on any urgent occasion he was absent for a moment from my sight, I became quite uneasy. In a few years he became a youth, and the down appeared on his cheeks; his body and limbs were well formed! then there began to be a talk about him out of doors among the courtiers. The guards of all descriptions began to forbid him from coming and going within the palace. At length, his entrance into it was quite stopped, and without him I had no rest; a moment [of absence on his part,] was an age [of pain on mine]. When I heard these tidings of despair, I was as

[171] Literally a "weighty *khil'at,*" owing to the quantity of embroidery on it. The perfection of these oriental dresses is, to be so stiff as to stand on the floor unsupported.

[172] The *paisa* is the current copper coin of India; it is the 64th part of a rupee, and is in value as nearly as possible ¾ of our halfpenny, or a farthing and a-half.

[173] The word *kafir* denotes literally, "infidel," or "heathen." It is here used as a term of endearment, just as we sometimes use the word "wicked rogue."

distracted as if the day of judgment had burst over me; and such was my condition that I could not speak a word [to express my wishes]: nor yet could I live separated from him. I had no means of relief; O God, what could I do; a strange kind of uneasiness came over me, and in consequence of my distraction I addressed myself to the same eunuch [who was in all my secrets], and said to him, 'I wish to take care of this youth. In fact, the best plan is for you to give him a thousand gold pieces, to set him up in a jeweller's shop in the *chauk*, that he may from the profit of his trade live comfortably; and to build him a handsome house near my residence; to buy him slaves, and hire him servants and fix their pay, that he may in every way live at his ease.' The eunuch furnished him with a house, and set up a jeweller's shop for him to carry on the traffic, and prepared everything that was requisite. In a short time, his shop became so brilliant and showy, that whatever rich *khil'ats* or superb jewels were required for the king and his nobles, could only be procured there; and by degrees his shop so flourished, that all the rarities of every country were to be found there; and the daily traffic of all other jewellers became languid in comparison with his. In short, no one was able to compete with him in the city, nor was his equal [to be found] in any other country.

"He made a great deal of money[174] by his business; but [grief for his] absence daily preyed on my mind, and injured my health; no expedient could be hit upon by which I might see him, and console my heart. At last, for the purpose of consultation, I sent for the same experienced eunuch, and said to him, 'I can devise no plan by which I may see the youth for a moment, and inspire my heart with patience. There remains only this method, which is to dig a mine from his house and join the same to the palace.' I had no sooner expressed my wish, than such a mine was dug in a few days, so that on the approach of evening the eunuch used to conduct the young man through that same passage, in silence and secrecy [to my apartment]. We used to pass the whole night in eating and drinking, and every enjoyment; I was delighted to meet him, and he was rejoiced to see me. When the morning star appeared, and the *muwazzin*[175] gave notice [of the time for morning prayers], the eunuch used to lead the youth by the same way to his house. No fourth person had any knowledge of these circumstances; [it was known] only to the eunuch and two nurses who had given me milk, and brought me up.

"A long period passed in this manner; but it happened one day that when the eunuch went to call him, according to custom, then he perceived that the youth was sitting sorrowful and silent. The eunuch asked him, 'Is all well to-day? why are you so sad? Come to the princess; she has sent for you.' The youth made no

[174] Literally, "*lakhs* of rupees." In India money accounts are reckoned by hundreds, thousands, *lakhs* and *crores*, instead of hundreds, thousands, and millions, as with us. A hundred thousands make a *lakh*, and a hundred *lakhs*, a *crore*. As the Indian mode of reckoning, though simple enough, is apt to perplex the beginner, let us take for example the number 123456789, which we thus point off,—123,456,789; but in India it would be pointed as follows:—12,34,56,789, and read 12 *crores*, 34 *lakhs*, fifty-six thousand seven hundred and eighty-nine.

[175] The *muwazzin* is a public crier, who ascends the turret or minaret of a mosque and calls out to the inhabitants the five periods of prayers; more especially the morning, noon and evening prayers.

reply whatever, nor did he move his tongue. The eunuch returned alone with a similar face, and mentioned to me the young man's condition. As the devil was about to ruin me, even after this conduct I could not banish him from my heart; if I had known that my love and affection for such an ungrateful wretch would have at last rendered me infamous and degraded, and would have destroyed my fame and honour; then I should have at that moment shrunk back from such a proceeding, and should have done penance; I never again should have pronounced his name, neither should I have devoted my heart to the shameless [fellow]. But it was to happen so; for this reason I took no heed of his improper conduct, and his not coming I imagined to be the affectation and airs of those [who are conscious of being] beloved; its consequences I have sadly rued, and thou art now also informed of these events without hearing or seeing them; or else where were you, and where was I? Well, what has happened is past. Bestowing not a thought on the conceited airs of that ass, I again sent him word by the eunuch, saying, 'if thou wilt not come to me now, by some means or other I will come to thee; but there is much impropriety in my coming there;—if this secret is discovered, thou wilt have cause to rue it; so do not act in a manner that will have no other result than disgrace; it is best that thou comest quickly [to me], otherwise imagine me arrived [near thee]. When he received this message, and perceived that my love for him was unbounded, he came with disagreeable looks and affected airs.

"When he sat down by me, I asked him, 'what is the cause of your coolness and anger to-day; you never showed so much insolence and disrespect before, you always used to come without making any excuses.' To this he replied, 'I am a poor nameless wretch; by your favour, and owing to you, I am arrived to such power, and with much ease and affluence I pass my days. I ever pray for your life and prosperity; I have committed this fault in full reliance on your highness's forgiveness, and I hope for pardon. As I loved him from my soul and heart, I accepted his well-turned apology, and not only overlooked his knavery, but even asked him again with affection, what great difficulty has occurred that you are so thoughtful? mention it, and it shall be instantly removed.'

"In short, in his humble way, he replied, 'Everything is difficult to me; before your highness, all is easy,' At last, from the purport of his discourse and conversation, it appeared that an elegant garden, with a grand house in it, together with reservoirs, tanks and wells, of finished masonry, was for sale, situated in the centre of the city and near his house; and that with the garden a female slave was to be sold, who sung admirably and understood music perfectly. But they were to be sold together, and not the garden alone, 'like the cat tied to the camel's neck;'[176] and that whoever purchased the garden must also buy the slave; the best of it was, the price of the garden was five thousand rupees, and the price of the slave five hundred thousand. [He concluded saying], 'Your devoted slave cannot at present

[176] This is a proverb, founded on a short story, viz.: "A certain Arab lost his camel; he vowed, if he found it, to sell it for a dinar, merely as a charitable deed. The camel was found, and the Arab sorely repented him of his vow. He then tied a cat on the camel's neck, and went through the city of *Baghdad,* exclaiming, 'O, true believers, here is a camel to be sold for a *dinar,* and a cat for a thousand *dinars;* but they cannot be sold the one without the other.'"

raise so large a sum.' I perceived that his heart was greatly bent on buying them, and that for this reason he was thoughtful, and embarrassed in mind; although he was seated near me, yet his looks were pensive and his heart sad: as his happiness every hour and moment was dear to me, I that instant ordered the eunuch to go in the morning and settle the price of the garden and the slave, get their bills of sale drawn up, and deliver them to this person, and pay the price to their owner from the royal treasury.

"On hearing this order, the young man thanked me, tears of joy came upon his face; and we passed the night as usual in laughing and delight; in the morning he took leave. The eunuch, agreeably to my orders, bought and delivered over to him the garden and the slave. The youth continued his visits at night, according to custom [and retired in the morning]. One day in the season of spring, when the whole place was indeed charming, the clouds were gathering low, and the rain drizzling fell, the lightning also continued to flash [through the murky clouds], and the breeze played gently [through the trees]—in short, it was a delightful scene. When in the *taks*[177] the liquors of various colours, arranged in elegant phials, fell upon my sight; my heart longed to take a draught. After I had drank two or three cupfulls, instantly the idea of the newly purchased garden struck me. An irrepressible desire arose within me, when in that state, that for a short time I should enjoy a walk in that [garden]. When the stream of misfortune flows against us, we struggle in vain against the tide.[178] I involuntarily took a female servant with me, and went to the young man's house by the way of the mine; from thence I proceeded to the garden, and saw that the delightful place was in truth equal to the Elysian fields. As the raindrops fell on the fresh green leaves of the trees, one might say they were like pearls set in pieces of emerald, and the carnation of the flowers, in that cloudy day, appeared as beautiful as the ruddy crepuscle after the setting sun; the basons and canals, full of water, seemed like sheets of mirrors, over which the small waves undulated.

"In short, I was strolling about in every direction in that garden, when the day vanished and the darkness of night became conspicuous. At that moment, the young man appeared on a walk [in the garden]; and on seeing me, he approached with respect and great warmth of affection, and taking my hand in his, led me to the pavilion.[179] On entering it, the splendour of the scene made me entirely forget all the beauty of the garden. The illuminations within were magnificent; on every side, gerandoles, in the shape of cypresses, and various kinds of lights in variegated lamps were lighted up; even the *shabi barat*, with all its moonlight and its illuminations, would appear dark [in comparison to the brightness which shone in the pavilion]; on one side, fire-works[180] of every description were displayed.

[177] *Taks* are small recesses in the walls of apartments in Asia, for holding flower-pots, phials of wine, fruits, &c.

[178] In the original it is a proverb, "When evil comes, the dog will bite even the man that is mounted on a camel," said of a person who is extremely unfortunate.

[179] The term *barah-dari* is applied either to a temporary pavilion, or a permanent summer-house; it is so called from the circumstance of its having "twelve doors," in honour of the twelve *Imams*.—Vide note 9, page 3.

[180] The various kinds of fire-works here enumerated admit not of translation.—Vide

"In the meantime, the clouds dispersed, and the bright moon appeared like a lovely mistress clothed in a lilac-coloured robe, who suddenly strikes our sight. It was a scene of great beauty; as the moon burst forth, the young man said, 'Let us now go and sit in the balcony which overlooks the garden.' I had become so infatuated, that whatever the wretch proposed I implicitly obeyed; now he led me such a dance, that he dragged me up [to the balcony.] That building was so high, that all the houses of the city and the lights of the *bazar*, appeared as if they were at the foot of it. I was seated in a state of delight, with my arms round the youth's neck; meanwhile, a woman, quite ugly, without form or shape, entered as it were from the chimney, with a bottle of wine in her hand; I was at that time greatly displeased at her sudden entrance, and on seeing her looks, my heart became alarmed. Then, in confusion, I asked the young man, 'who is this precious hag; from whence have you grubbed her up?' Joining his hands together, he replied, 'This is the slave who was bought with the garden through your generous assistance.' I had perceived that the simpleton had bought her with much eager desire, and perhaps his heart was fixed on her; for this reason, I, suppressing my inward vexation, remained silent; but my heart from that moment was disturbed and displeasure affected my temper; moreover, the wretch had the impudence to make this harlot our cup-bearer. At that moment I was drinking my own blood with rage, and was as uneasy as a parrot shut up in the same cage with a crow: I had no opportunity of going away, and did not wish to stay. To shorten the story, the wine was of the strongest description, so that on drinking it a man would become a beast. She plied the young man with two or three cups in succession of that fiery liquor, and I also bitterly swallowed half a cupfull at the importunity of the youth; at last, the shameless harlot likewise got beastly drunk, and took very unbecoming liberties with that vile youth; and the mean wretch also, in his intoxication, having become regardless, began to be disrespectful, and behave indecently.

"I was so much ashamed, that had the earth opened at the moment I would have willingly jumped into it; but in consequence of my passion for him, I, infatuated, even after all these circumstances, remained silent. However, he was completely a vile wretch, and did not feel the value of my forbearance. In the fervour of intoxication, he drank off two cups more, so that his little remaining sense vanished, and he completely drove from his heart all respect for me. Without shame, and in the rage of lust, the barefaced villain consummated before me his career of infamous indecency with his hideous mistress, who, in that posture, began to play off all the blandishments of love, and kissing and embracing took place between the two. In that faithless man no sense of honour remained; neither did modesty exist in that shameless woman; 'As the soul is, so are the angels.'[181] My state [of mind] at the time was like that of a songstress who having [lost the musical time,] sings out of tune. I was invoking curses on myself for having come there, saying that I was properly punished for my folly. At last, how could I bear it? I was on fire from head to foot, and began to roll on live coals. In my rage and wrath I recollect-

vocabulary.

[181] A proverb meaning that people or things are well matched; as the soul, at the hour of death, is committed to the charge of good or evil angels, according to its dessert.

ed the proverb, that 'It is not the bullock that leaps, but the sack;[182] whoever has seen a sight like this?' in saying this to myself, I came away thence.

"That drunkard in the depravity of his heart thought, if I was offended now, what then would be his treatment the next day, and what a commotion I should raise. So he imagined it best to finish my existence [whilst he had me in his power.] Having formed this resolution in his mind with the advice of the hag, he put his *patka*[183] round his neck and fell at my feet, and taking off his turban from his head, began to supplicate [my forgiveness] in the humblest manner. My heart was infatuated towards him; whithersoever he turned I turned; and like the handmill I was entirely under his control. I implicitly complied with all he desired; some way or other he pacified me, and persuaded me to retake my seat. He again took two or three cupfulls of the fiery liquor, and he induced me to drink some also. I, in the first place, was already inflamed with rage, and secondly, after drinking such strong liquor I soon became quite senseless—no recollection remained. Then that unfeeling, ungrateful, cruel wretch wounded me with his sword; yea, further, he thought he had completely killed me. At that moment, my eyes opened, and I uttered these words, 'Well, as I have acted, so I have been rewarded; but do thou screen thyself from the consequences of shedding unjustly my blood. Let it not so happen that some tyrant should seize thee; do thou wash off my blood from thy garment; what has happened is past.'

"Do not divulge this secret to any one; I have not been wanting to thee even with loss of life. Then placing him under the protection of God's mercy, I fainted [from the loss of blood], and knew nothing of what afterwards happened. Perhaps, that butcher, conceiving me dead, put me into the chest, and let me down over the walls of the fortress, the same as you yourself saw, I wished no one ill; but these misfortunes were written in my destiny, and the lines of fate cannot be effaced. My eyes have been the cause of all these calamities: if I had not had a strong desire to behold beautiful persons, then that wretch would not have been my bane.[184] God so ordained that He made thee arrive there; and, He made thee the means of saving my life. After undergoing these disgraces, I am ashamed to reflect that I should yet live and show my face to any one. But what can I do? the choice of death is not in our hands; God, after killing me, hath restored me to life; let us see what is written in my future fate. In all appearance, your exertions and zeal have been of use, so that I have been cured of such wounds. Thou hast been ready to promote my wishes with thy life and property, and whatever were thy means, thou hast offered [them cheerfully]. In those days, seeing thee without money and sad, I wrote the note to *Sidi Bahar*, who is my cashier. In that note, I mentioned that I was in health and safety in such a place, and I said, "convey the intelligence of me unfortunate to my excellent mother."

"The *Sidi* sent by thee those trays of gold for my expenses; and when I sent thee

[182] A proverb applied to those who act in a manner utterly at variance with their condition.

[183] The *patka* is a long and narrow piece of cloth or silk, which is wrapped round the waist; among the rich a *shawl* is the general *patka*. The act of throwing one's *patka* round the neck and prostrating one's self at another's feet, is a most abject mark of submission.

[184] Literally, "a collar or yoke, round my neck."

to the shop of *Yusuf* the merchant, to purchase *khil'ats* and jewels, I felt confident that the weakminded wretch, who soon becomes friends with every one, conceiving you a stranger, would certainly form an intimacy with you, and indulging his conceit, invite you to a feast and entertainment. This stratagem of mine turned out right, and he did exactly what I had imagined in my heart. Then, when you promised him to return, and came to me and related the particulars of his insisting upon it, I was heartily pleased with the circumstance; for I knew that if you went to his house, and there ate and drank, you would invite him in return, and that he would eagerly come; for this reason, I sent thee back quickly to him. After three days, when you returned from the entertainment, and, quite abashed, made me many apologies for staying away so long, to make you easy in your mind, I replied, 'it is of no consequence; when he gave you leave then you came away; but to be without delicacy is not proper, and we should not bear another's debt of gratitude without an idea of paying it; now do you go and invite him also, and bring him along with you.' When you went away to his house, I saw that no preparations could be got ready for the entertainment at our house, and if he should all at once come, what could I do? but it fortunately happened that from time immemorial, the custom of this country has been for the kings to remain out for eight months in the year, to settle the affairs of the provinces, and collect the revenues, and for four months, during the rains, to stay [in the city] in their auspicious palaces. In those days, the king, this unfortunate wretch's father, had gone into the provinces some two or four months previously to arrange the affairs of the kingdom.

"Whilst you were gone to bring the young merchant [to the entertainment], *Sidi Bahar* imparted the particulars of my present situation to the queen (who is the mother of me impure). Again I, ashamed of my guilty conduct, went to the queen and related to her all that happened to me. Although she, from motherly affection and good sense, had used every means to conceal the circumstance of my disappearance, saying, 'God knows what may be the end of it;' she conceived it wrong to make public my disgrace for the present, and for my sake she had concealed my errors in her maternal breast; but she had all along been in search of me.

"When she saw me in this condition, and heard all the circumstances [of my misfortune], her eyes filled with tears, and she said, 'O unfortunate wretch! thou hast knowingly destroyed the honour and glory of the throne; a thousand pities that thou hadst not perished also; if instead of thee I had been brought to bed of a stone, I should have been patient; even now [it is not too late to] repent; whatever was in thy unfortunate fate has happened; what wilt thou do next? Wilt thou live or die?' I replied, with excessive shame, that in this worthless wretch's fate it was so written, that I should live in such disgrace and distress after escaping such various dangers; it would have been better to have perished; though the mark of infamy is stamped on my forehead, yet I have not been guilty of such an action as can disgrace my parents.

"The great pain I now feel is, that those base wretches should escape my vengeance, and enjoy their crime in each other's company, whilst I have suffered such affliction from their hands: it is a pity that I can do nothing [in order to punish them]. I hope one favour [from your majesty], that you would order your steward to prepare all the necessary articles for an entertainment at my house, that I may, under the pretence of an entertainment, send for those two wretches, and punish them for their deeds and also inflict vengeance for myself. In the same manner that he lifted his hand upon me and wounded me, may I be enabled to cut them to pieces; then my heart will be soothed; otherwise I must continue glowing in this fire of resentment, and ultimately I must be burnt to cinders. On hearing this speech, my excellent mother became kind from maternal fondness, and concealed my guilt in her own breast, and sent all the necessaries for the entertainment by the same eunuch who is in my secrets. Every necessary attendant came also, and each was ready in his own appropriate occupation. In the time of evening, you brought the [base villain who is now dead]; I wished the harlot should likewise come.

"For this reason I earnestly desired you to send for her; when she also came and the guests were assembled, they all became thoroughly intoxicated and senseless by drinking largely of wine; you also got drunk along with them, and lay like a corpse. I ordered a *Kilmakini*[185] to cut off both their heads with a sword; she instantly drew her sword and cut off both their heads, and dyed their bodies with their blood. The cause of my anger towards thee was this, that I had given thee permission for the entertainment, but not to become an associate in wine-drinking, with people thou hadst only known for a few days. Assuredly this folly on thy part was anything but pleasing to me; for when you drank till you became senseless, then what hopes of aid from you remained? But the claims of thy services so cling around my neck, that, notwithstanding such conduct, I forgive thee. And now, behold, I have related to thee all my adventures from the beginning to the end; do you yet desire in your heart any other [explanations]? In the same manner that I have, in compliance with your wishes, granted all you requested, do you also in like manner perform what I desire; my advice on this occasion is, that it is no longer proper either for you or me to remain in this city. Henceforward you are master."

O devoted to God![186] the princess having spoken thus far, remained silent. I, who with heart and soul considered her wishes paramount to everything, and was entangled in the net of her affections, replied, "whatever you advise, that is best, and I will without hesitation carry the same into effect." When the princess found me obedient, and her servant, she ordered two swift and high-mettled horses (which might vie with the wind in speed), to be brought from the royal stables, and kept in readiness. I went and picked out just such beautiful and high spirited horses as she required, and had them saddled and brought [to our house]. When a few hours of the night remained, the princess put on men's clothes, and arming herself with the five weapons,[187] mounted on one of the horses; I got on the other,

---

[185] The *Mughal* princes in the days of their splendour had guards of *Kalmuc*, or *Kilmak*, women for their seraglios; they were chosen for their size and courage, and were armed; other Tartar women were likewise taken, but they all went by the general name of *Kilmakini*.

[186] Here the first *Darwesh* resumes his address to his three companions.

[187] In a note to my edition of Mr. F. Smith's translation of the *Baghobahar*, 1851, I inserted the following "petition." "May I request some friend in India, for auld lang syne, to ask any intelligent *munshi* the exact meaning of *panchon hathiyar bandhna*, showing him at the same time the original where the expression occurs." To this request I received, a few

completely armed, and we set out in the same direction.

When night was over, and the dawn began to appear, we arrived on the banks of a certain lake; alighting from our horses, we washed our hands and faces; having breakfasted in great haste, we mounted again and set off. Now and then the princess spoke, and said, "I have for your sake left fame, honour, wealth, country and parents all behind me; now, may it not so happen, that you also should behave to me like that faithless savage." Sometimes I talked of different matters to beguile the journey, and sometimes replied to her questions and doubts, saying "O princess, all men are not alike; there must have been some defect in that base villain's parentage, that by him such a deed was done; but I have sacrificed my wealth and devoted my life to you, and you have dignified me in every way. I am now your slave without purchase, and if you should make shoes of my skin and wear them, I will not complain." Such conversation passed between us, and day and night to travel onward was our business. If through fatigue we sometimes dismounted somewhere, we then used to hunt down the beasts and birds of the woods, and having lawfully slain them, and applied salt from the salt-cellar, and having struck fire with steel[188] (from a flint), we used to broil and eat them. The horses we let loose [to graze], and they generally found sufficient to satisfy their hunger from the grass and leaves.

One day we reached a large even plain, where there was no trace of any habitation, and where no human face could be seen; even in this [solitary and dreary scene], owing to the princess's company, the day appeared festive and the nights joyful. Proceeding on our journey, we came suddenly to a large river, the sight of which would appal the firmest heart.[189] As we stood on its banks, as far as the eye could reach, nothing was to be seen but water; no means of crossing was to be found. O God [cried I], how shall we pass this sea! we stood reflecting on this sad obstacle for a few moments, when the thought came into my mind to leave the princess there, and to go in search of a boat; and that until I could find some means to pass over, the princess would have time to rest. Having formed this plan, I said, "O princess, if you will allow me, I will go and look out for a ferry or ford." She replied, "I am greatly tired, and likewise hungry and thirsty; I will rest here a little, whilst thou findest out some means to pass over [the river]."

On that spot was a large *pipal*[190] tree, forming a canopy [of such extent], that if

---

months ago, a very kind and satisfactory reply from Lieut. J.C. Bayley, 36th Regt., M.N.I., which I have the pleasure here to insert; and at the same time, I beg to return my best thanks to that gentleman. "The *five weapons* are, 1st, the *talwar* or sword; 2nd, the *pesh-kabz* or dagger; 3rd, the *tabar* or battle-axe; 4th, the *barchhi* or lance; 5th, the *tir o kaman* or the bow and arrows. The phrase, *panchon hathiyar bandhna* is very nearly equivalent to our expression, 'to be armed cap à pié.'" I may add to Lieut. B.'s obliging account that in more recent times, the "bow and arrows" are very naturally superseded by "a pair of pistols." Still the meaning of the phrase is the same in either case.

[188] The word *chikmak* or *chikmak,* is wrongly called "a flint" in the dictionaries. It merely denotes the piece of steel used in striking a fire. The flint is called *chikmak ka pathar.*

[189] Literally, "at the seeing of which the liver would be turned into water."

[190] The *pipal* or "ficus religiosa," is a large tree venerated by the *Hindus;* it affords a most agreeable shade, as its leaves are large, in the shape of a heart. Many writers confound

a thousand horsemen sheltered themselves under its wide-spread branches, they would be protected from the sun and rain. Leaving there the princess, I set out, and was looking all around to find somewhere or other on the ground, or the river, some trace of a human being. I searched much, but found the same nowhere. At last, I returned hopeless, but did not find the princess under the tree; how can I describe the state of my mind at that moment! my senses forsook me, and I became quite distracted. Sometimes I mounted the tree, and looked for her in every individual leaf and branch; sometimes, letting go my hold, I fell on the ground, and went round the roots of the tree as one who performs the *tasadduk*[191]. Sometimes I wept and shrieked at my miserable condition; now I ran from west to east, then from north to south. In short, I searched everywhere,[192] but could not find any trace of the rare jewel [I had lost]; when, at last, I found I could do nothing, then weeping and throwing dust over my head, I looked for her everywhere.

This idea came into my mind, that perhaps some of the *jinns* had carried her away, and had inflicted on me this wound; or else that some one had followed her from her country, and finding her alone, had persuaded her to return to Damascus. Distracted with these fancies, I threw off and cast away my clothes, and becoming a naked *fakir*, I wandered about in the kingdom of Syria from morn until eve, and at night lay down to rest in any place [I could find]. I wandered over the whole region, but could find no trace of my princess, nor hear any thing of her from any one, nor could I ascertain the cause of her disappearance. Then this idea came into my mind, that since I could find no trace of that beloved one, even life itself was a weariness. I perceived a mountain in some wilderness; I ascended it, and formed the design of throwing myself headlong [from its summit], that I might end my wretched existence in a moment, by dashing my head to pieces against the stones, then would my soul be freed from a state of affliction.

Having formed this resolution within myself, I was on the point of precipitating myself [from the mountain], and had even lifted up my foot, when some one laid hold of my arm. In the meanwhile, I regained my senses, and looking round, I saw a horseman clothed in green, with a veil thrown over his face, who said to me, "Why dost thou attempt to destroy thy life; it is impious to despair of God's mercy; whilst there is breath, so long there is hope. Three *Darweshes* will meet thee a few days hence, in the empire of *Rum*, who are equally afflicted with thyself, entangled in the same difficulties, and who have met with adventures similar to thine; the name of the king of that country is *Azad Bakht*; he is also in great trouble; when he meets you and the other three *Darweshes*, then the wishes and desires of the heart of each of you will be completely fulfilled."

I instantly laid hold of the stirrup [of this guardian angel,] and kissed it, and exclaimed, "O messenger of God, the few words you have pronounced have consoled my afflicted heart; but tell me, for God's sake, who you are, and what is

---

it with the "*ficus Indicus*" or "*baniyan* tree," or rather, they devise an imaginary tree compounded of the two species, investing it with the heart-shaped leaves of the former, and the dropping and multiplying stems of the latter.

[191] Respecting the ceremony called the *tasadduk*, vide note 167, p. 35.

[192] Literally, "much dust did I sift the dust."

your name." He replied, "My name is *Murtaza 'Ali,*[193] and my office is this, that to whomsoever there occurs a danger or difficulty, I am at hand to afford relief." Having said this much, he vanished from my sight. In short, having set my heart at ease from the happy tidings I received from my spiritual guide *[Murtaza 'Ali]*, "the remover of difficulties," I formed the design of [proceeding to] Constantinople. On the road I suffered all those misfortunes which were decreed me by fate; with the hopes of meeting the princess. Through the assistance of God, I am come here, and by good fortune I have become honoured by your presence. The promised meeting has taken place between us, and we have enjoyed each other's society and conversation; now it only remains for us to be known to, and acquainted with, the king *Azad Bakht*.

Assuredly after this, we five shall attain the desires of our hearts. Do you also beseech the blessings of God, and say amen. O ye holy guides! such have been the adventures which have befallen this bewildered wanderer, which have been faithfully related in your presence; now let us look forward [to the time] when my trouble and sorrows will be changed into joy and gladness by the recovery of the princess. *Azad Bakht,* concealed in silence in his corner, having heard with attention the story of the first *Darwesh,* was greatly pleased; then he betook himself to listen to the adventures of the next *Darwesh.*

---

[193] *Murtaza 'Ali,* the son-in-law of the prophet; one of his surnames is *Mushkil-kusha,* or " the remover of difficulties." The *Saiyids,* who pretend to be descended from *'Ali,* wear green dresses, which is a sacred colour among the *Muhammadans.*

ADVENTURES OF THE SECOND DARWESH.

When it came to the turn of the second *Darwesh* to speak, he placed himself at his ease,[194] and said—

> "O friends, to this *fakir's* story listen a little;—
> I will tell it to you,—from first to the last, listen;
> Whose cure no physician can perform;
> My pain is far beyond remedy,—listen."

O ye clothed in the *dalk!*[195] this wretch is the prince of the kingdom of Persia; men skilled in every science are born there, for which reason the [Persian] proverb "*Isfahan nisfi Jahan,*"[196] or "*Ispahan* is half the world," has become well known. In the seven climes, there is no kingdom equal to that ancient kingdom; the star of that country is the sun, and of all the seven constellations it is the greatest.[197] The climate of that region is delightful, and the inhabitants are of enlightened minds, and refined in their manners. My father (who was the king of that country), in order to teach me the rules and lessons of government, made choice of very wise tutors in every art and science, and placed them over me for my instruction from my infancy. So, having received complete instruction in every kind [of knowledge], I am now learned. With the favour of God, in my fourteenth year I had learned every science, polite conversation, and polished manners; and I had acquired all that is fit and requisite for kings to know; moreover, my inclinations night and day, led me to associate with the learned, and hear the histories of every country, and of ambitious princes and men of renown.

One day, a learned companion, who was well versed in history, and had seen [a great deal of] the world, said to me, "That though there is no reliance on the life of man, yet such excellent qualities are often found in him, that owing to them, the name of some men will be handed down with praise on people's tongues to the day of judgment." I begged of him to relate circumstantially a few instances

---

[194] The phrase *char-zanu ho-baithna,* signifies "to sit down with the legs crossed in front as our tailors do when at work." It is the ordnary mode of sitting among the Turks.

[195] The *dalk,* or *dilk,* is a garment made of patches and shreds worn by *darweshes;* the epithet *dolk-posh,* "a *dalk* wearer," denotes a "darwesh," or "mendicant."

[196] *Ispahan* was once a fine city. In the time of the Chevalier Chardin, nearly two centuries ago, it was pronounced by that traveller to be the largest in the world. It is now about the size of Brighton; yet a few weeks ago, we saw in the "Illustrated London News," an account of it by a *Frenchman* (a fire-side traveller), who declares it to be, still, "the largest city in the world!"

[197] The *Muhammadans* divide the world into seven climes, and suppose that a constellation presides over the destiny of each clime.

on that score, that I might hear them, and endeavour to act accordingly. Then that person began to relate as follows, some of the adventures of *Hatim Ta'i*. "That there lived in the time of *Hatim*, a king of Arabia, named *Naufal*, who bore great enmity towards *Hatim*, on account of his renown, and having assembled many troops, he went up to give him battle. *Hatim* was a God-fearing and good man; he thus conceived, that, "If I likewise prepare for battle, then the creatures of God will be slaughtered, and there will be much bloodshed; the punishment of heaven for which will be recorded against my name." Reflecting on this, he quite alone, taking merely his life with him, fled and hid himself in a cave in the mountains. When the news of *Hatim's* flight reached *Naufal*, he confiscated all the property and dwellings of *Hatim*, and proclaimed publicly, that whoever would look out for him and seize him, should receive from the king's treasury five hundred pieces of gold. On hearing this [proclamation], all became eager, and began to make diligent search for *Hatim*.

"One day, an old man and his wife, taking two or three of their young children with them, for the purpose of picking up wood, strayed near the cave where *Hatim* was concealed; and began to gather fuel in that same forest. The old woman remarked, 'If our days had been at all fortunate, we should have seen and found *Hatim* somewhere or other, and seizing him, we should have carried him to *Naufal*; then he would give us five hundred pieces of gold, and we should live comfortably, and be released from this toil and care,' The old woodman said, 'What art thou prating about? it was decreed in our fate, that we should pick up wood every day, place it on our heads, and sell it in the *bazar*, and [with its produce] procure bread and salt; or one day the tiger of the woods will carry us off: peace, mind thy work; why should *Hatim* fall into our hands, and the king give us so much money?' The old woman heaved a cold sigh, and remained silent.

"*Hatim* had heard the words of the two [old people], and conceived it unmanly and ungenerous to conceal himself to save his life, and not to conduct those helpless ones to the object of their desire. True it is, that a man without pity is not a human being, and he in whose heart there is no feeling is a butcher.

> 'Man was created to exercise compassion,
> Otherwise, angels were not wanting for devotion.'

In short, *Hatim's* manly mind would not allow him to remain concealed, after what he had with his own ears heard [from the woodman]; he instantly came out, and said to the old man, 'O friend, I myself am *Hatim*, lead me to *Naufal*; on seeing me, he will give thee whatever amount of money he has promised.'[198] The old woodman replied, 'It is true that my welfare and advantage certainly consist in doing so, but who knows how he will treat thee; if he should put thee to death, then what shall I do? This, on my part, can never be done—that I should deliver over thee to thine enemy for the sake of my own avarice. In a few days I shall spend the [promised] wealth, and how long shall I live? I must die at last; then what answer shall I give to God?' *Hatim* implored him greatly, and said, 'Take me along with

[198] The Arabic phrase *lantarani*, a corruption of *la-an-tarani*, literally signifies "egad, if you saw me [do so and so];" hence *lantarani-wala* is equivalent to our terms, "an egregious egotist," or "great boaster."

thee—I say so of my own pleasure; I have ever desired that, should my wealth and life be of use to some one or other [of my fellow creatures], then so much the better.' But the old man could not in any way be persuaded to carry *Hatim* along with him, and receive the [proclaimed reward. At last, becoming hopeless, *Hatim* said, 'If you do not carry me in the way I wish, then I will go of myself to the king, and say, this old man concealed me in a cave in the mountains,' The old man smiled and said, 'If I am to receive evil for good, then hard will be my fate.' During this conversation, other men arrived, and a crowd assembled [around them]; perceiving the person they saw to be *Hatim*, they instantly seized him and carried him along; the old man also, a little in the rear, followed them in silent grief. When they brought *Hatim* before *Naufal*, he asked, 'Who has seized and brought him here?' A worthless, hard-hearted [boaster] answered, 'Who could have performed such a deed except myself? This achievement belongs to my name, and I have planted the standard [of glory] in the sky.' Another vaunting fellow clamoured, 'I searched for him many days in the woods, and caught him at last, and have brought him here; have some consideration for my labour, and give me what has been promised.' In this manner, from avidity for the [promised] pieces of gold, every one said he had done the deed. The old man, in silence, sat apart in a corner, and heard all their boastings, and wept for *Hatim*. When each had recounted his act of bravery and enterprise, then *Hatim* said to the king, 'If you ask for the truth, then it is this; that old man, who stands aloof from all, has brought me here; if you can judge from appearances, then ascertain the fact, and give him for my seizure what you have promised; for in the whole body the tongue[199] is a most sacred [member]. It is incumbent upon a man to perform what he has promised; for in other respects God has given tongues to brutes likewise; then what would have been the difference between a man and other animals?'

"*Naufal* called the old wood-cutter near him, and said, 'Tell the truth; what is the real state of the matter; who has seized and brought *Hatim* here?' The honest fellow related truly all that had occurred from beginning to end, and added, '*Hatim* is come here of his own accord for my sake.' *Naufal*, on hearing this manly act of *Hatim's*, was greatly astonished, and exclaimed, 'How surprising is thy liberality! even thy life thou hast not feared to risk [for the good of others]!' With regard to all those who laid false claims to having seized *Hatim*, the king ordered them to have their hands tied behind their backs, and instead of five hundred pieces of

[199] A novice in the language would say, "Here a distinction seems to be drawn between the words *zaban* and *jibh*. Both signify 'tongue,' but the former applies to men and the latter to animals." To this profound bit of criticism I should reply—Not so fast, Mr. Novice; a distinction there is, but that is not it. The word *zaban* in Persian and *Hindustani* means both the fleshy member of the body, called the tongue, and also language or speech, just like our word "tongue," which has both significations. In the former sense it applies alike to man and beast; in the latter it is mere truism to say that it applies to man only. *Jibh*, in *Hindi* and *Hindustani*, means the tongue only in the sense of the member of the body, never in the sense of speech; hence it is equally applicable to man or brute. Ask any physician who has practised in India the *Hindustani* for "show the tongue," he will tell you *jibh dikla,o*, or *zaban dikla,o*; and if he was a man of discernment, he would use *jibh* with a *Hindu*, and *zaban* with a *Musalman*; but I believe he would be perfectly understood, whichever word he used to either party.

gold, to receive each five hundred strokes of a slipper on their heads, so that their lives might perish [under the punishment]. Instantly, the strokes of the slippers began to be laid on in such a style, that in a short time their heads became quite bald. True it is, that to tell an untruth is such a guilt, that no other guilt equals it; may God keep every one free from this calamity, and not give him a propensity for telling lies; many people persevere in uttering falsehoods, but at the moment of detection they meet with their dessert.

"In short, *Naufal* having rewarded all of them according to their desserts, thought it contrary to gentlemanly conduct and manliness of character to harbour enmity and strife towards a man like *Hatim*, from whom multitudes received happiness, and who, for the sake of the necessitous, did not even spare his own life, and was entirely devoted to the ways of God. He instantly seized *Hatim's* hand with great cordiality and friendship, and said to him, 'Why should it not be the case?[200] such a man as you are can perform such an action.' Then the king, with great respect and attention, made *Hatim* sit down near him, and he instantly restored to him the lands and property, and the wealth and moveables, he had confiscated; and bestowed on him anew the chieftainship of the tribe of *Ta,i*, and ordered the five hundred pieces of gold to be given to the old man from the treasury, who, blessing [the king], went away."

When I had heard the whole of this adventure of *Hatim's*, a spirit of rivalry came into my mind; and this idea occurred to me, viz., "*Hatim* was the only chief of his own tribe [of Arabs]. He, by one act of liberality has gained such renown, that to this day it is celebrated; whilst I am, by the decree of God, the king of all *Iran*; and it would be a pity if I were to remain excluded from this good fortune. It is certain that in this world no quality is greater than generosity and liberality; for whatever a man bestows in this world, he receives its return in the next. If any one sows a single seed, then how much does he reap from its produce! With these ideas impressed upon my mind, I called for the lord of the buildings, and ordered him to erect, as speedily as possible, a grand palace without the city, with forty high and wide gates.[201] In a short time, even such a grand palace as my heart wished for, was built and got ready, and in that place every day at all times, from morning till night, I used to bestow pieces of silver and gold on the poor and helpless; whoever asked for anything in charity, I granted it to the utmost of his desire.

In short, the necessitous entered [daily] through the forty gates, and received whatever they wanted. It happened one day that a *fakir* came in from the front

---

[200] The case is *Hatim's* philanthropy in respect to the old woodman, which on the part of any other than *Hatim* might seem super-human.

[201] It is related by grave historians, that *Hatim* actually built an alms-house of this description. On *Hatim*'s death, his younger brother, who succeeded him, endeavoured to act the generous in the above manner. His mother dissuaded him, saying, "Think not, my son, of imitating *Hatim*: it is an effort thou canst not accomplish;" and in order to prove what she said, the mother assumed the garb of a *fakir*, and acted as above related. When she came to the first door the second time, and received her son's lecture on the sin of avarice; she suddenly threw off her disguise, and said, "I told thee, my son, not to think of imitating *Hatim*. By *him* I have been served three times running, in this very manner, without ever a question being asked."

gate and begged some alms. I gave him a gold piece; then the same person entered through the next gate, and asked two pieces of gold; though I recollected him [to be the same *fakir*], I passed over [the circumstance] and gave them. In this manner he came in through each gate, and increased a piece of gold in his demand each time; and I knowingly appeared ignorant [of the circumstance], and continued supplying him according to his demand. At last he entered by the fortieth gate, and asked forty pieces of gold—this sum I likewise ordered to be given him. After receiving so much, the *fakir* re-entered from the first gate and again begged alms: his conduct appeared to me highly impudent, and I said, hear, O avaricious man, what kind of a *fakir* art thou, that dost not even know the meaning of the three letters which compose the word [Arabic: faqr] *fakr* (poverty); a *fakir* ought to act up to them. He replied, "Well, generous soul, explain them yourself." I answered, "[Arabic: f] *fe* means *faka* (fasting); [Arabic: q] *kaf* signifies *kina'at* (contentment); and [Arabic: r] *re* means *riyazat* (devotion);[202] whoever has not these three qualities, is not a *fakir*. All this which you have received, eat and drink with it, and when it is done, return to me, and receive whatever thou requirest. This charity is bestowed on thee to relieve immediate wants and not for the purpose of accumulation. O avidious! from the forty gates thou hast received from one piece of gold up to forty; add up the amount, and see by the rule of arithmetical progression how many pieces of gold it comes to; and even after all this, thy avarice hath brought thee back again through the first gate. What wilt thou do after having accumulated so much money? A [real] *fakir* ought only to think [of the wants] of the passing day; the following day the great Provider [of necessaries] will afford thee a new pittance. Now evince some shame and modesty; have patience, and be content; what sort of mendicity is this that thy spiritual guide hath taught thee?"

On hearing these reproaches of mine, he became displeased and angry, and threw down on the ground all [the money] he had received from me, and said, "Enough, sir, do not be so warm; take back your gifts and keep them, and do not again pronounce the word generosity. It is very difficult to be generous; you are not able to support the weight of generosity, when will you attain to that station?[203] you are as yet very far from it. The word [Arabic: sakhy] *Sakhi* (generous), is also composed of three letters; first act up to the meaning of those three letters, then you will be called generous." On hearing this I became uneasy, and said to the *fakir*, well, holy pilgrim, explain to me the meaning of those three letters. He replied, "from [Arabic: s] *sin* is derived *sama,i* (endurance); from [Arabic: kh] *khe* comes *khaufi Ilahi* (fear of God); and from [Arabic: y]*ye* proceeds *yad* (remembrance of one's birth and death). Until one is possessed of these three qualities, he should not mention the name of generosity; and the generous man has also this happiness, that although he acts amiss [in other points], yet he is dear to his Maker [on account of his generosity]. I have travelled through many countries, but except the princess of *Basra*, I have not seen a [person really] generous. The robe of generosity God hath shaped out on [the person] of that woman; all others desire the name,

[202] This and the following *jeu de mots* cannot be easily explained to a person who does not understand a little Arabic or Persian.

[203] The original is, "as yet *Dilli* is a long way off," a proverb like that of the Campbells—"It is a far cry to Loch Awe."

but do not act up to it." On hearing this, I made much entreaty, and conjured him [by all that was sacred] to forgive my rebuke, and take whatever he required. He would not, on any account, accept my proffered gifts, but went away repeating these words, "Now if thou wert to give all thy kingdom, I would not spit upon it, nor would I even **."[204] The pilgrim went away, but having heard such praises of the princess of *Basra*, my heart became quite restless, and no way could I be easy. Now this desire arose within me, that by some means or other I must go to *Basra* and take a look at her.

In the meantime, the king, my father, died, and I ascended the throne. I got the empire, but the idea [I had formed of going to *Basra]*] did not leave me. I held a consultation with the *wazir* and nobles, who were the support of the throne, and the pillars of the empire, saying, I wish to make a journey to *Basra*. Do ye remain steady in your respective stations; if I live, then the duration of the journey will be short; I will soon be back. No one seemed pleased at the idea of my going; in my helplessness, my heart continued to become more and more sorrowful. One day, without consulting any one, I privately sent for the resourceful *wazir*, and made him regent and plenipotentiary [during my absence], and placed him at the head of the affairs of the empire. I then put on the ochre-coloured habit [of a pilgrim], and, assuming the appearance of a *fakir*, I took the road to *Basra* alone. In a few days, I reached its boundaries, and [constantly] began to witness this scene; wherever I halted for the night, the servants of the princess advanced to receive me, and made me halt at some elegant house, and they used to provide me in perfection with all the requisites of a banquet, and to remain in attendance on me all night with the utmost respect. The following day, at the next stage, I experienced the same reception. In this comfort I journeyed onwards for months; at last I entered [the city of] *Basra*. I had no sooner entered it, than a good-looking young man, well dressed, and well-behaved, who carried wisdom in his looks, came up to me, and said with extreme sweetness of address, "I am the servant of pilgrims; I am always on the look out to conduct to my house all travellers, whether pilgrims or men of the world, who come to this city; except my house alone, there is no other place here for a stranger to put up at; pray, holy sir, come with me, bestow honour on my abode, and render me exalted.

I asked him, "what is the noble name of your honour?" He replied, "they call the name of this nameless one *Bedar Bakht*." Seeing his good qualities and affable manners, I went along with him and came to his house. I saw a grand mansion fitted up in a princely style—he led me to a grand apartment, and made me sit down; and sending for warm water, he caused [the attendants] to wash my hands and feet; and having caused the *dastar-khwan*[205] to be spread, the steward placed

[204] The expression in the original is so *plain* as to need no translation.

[205] Some would-be knowing critics inform us that "*Dastar-khwan*" literally signifies the "turband of the table"!!! How they manage to make such a meaning out of it is beyond ordinary research; and when done, it makes nonsense. They forget that the Orientals never made use of tables in the good old times. The *dastar-khwan* is, in reality, both table and table-cloth in one. It is a round piece of cloth or leather spread out on the floor. The food is then arranged thereon, and the company squat round the edge of it, and, after saying *Bism-Illah*, fall to, with what appetite they may; hence the phrase *dastar-khwan par baithna*,

before me alone a great variety of trays and dishes, and large quantities of fruit and confectionery.[206] On seeing such a grand treat, my very soul was satiated, and taking a mouthful from each dish, my stomach was filled; I then drew back my hand from eating.[207]

The young man became very pressing, and said, "Sir, what have you eaten? all the dinner remains as it were for a deposit;[208] eat some more without ceremony." I replied, there is no shame in eating; God prosper your house, I have eaten as much as my stomach can contain, and I cannot sufficiently praise the relish of your feast, and even now my tongue smacks with their flavour, and every belch[209] I make is absolutely perfumed, now pray take them away. "When the *dastar-khwan* was removed, they spread a carpet of *kashani* velvet, and brought to me ewers and basins of gold, with scented soap and warm water, wherewithal I might wash my hands; then *betel* was introduced, in a box set with precious stones, and spices of various kinds; whenever I called for water to drink, the servants brought it cooled in ice. When the evening came, camphorated candles were lighted up in the glass shades; and that friendly young man sat down near me and entertained me with his conversation. When one watch of the night had elapsed, he said to me, "be pleased to sleep in this bed, in front of which are curtains and screens." I said, O, Sir, for us pilgrims a mat or a deer-skin is sufficient; this [luxury] God has ordained for you men of the world.

He replied, "All these things are for pilgrims; they do not in the least belong to me." On his pressing me so urgently, I went and lay down on the bed which was softer than even a bed of flowers. Pots of roses and baskets of flowers were placed on both sides of the bedstead, and aloes and other perfumes were burning; to whichever side I turned, my senses were intoxicated with fragrance; in this state I slept. When the morning came, [the attendants] placed before me for breakfast, almonds, pistachio nuts, grapes, figs, pears, pomegranates, currants, dates, and *sharbat* made of fruit. In this festive manner I passed three days and nights. On the fourth day I requested leave to depart. The young man said, with joined hands,

---

to sit on, (not *at*,) the table. The wise critics seem to be thinking of our modern mahogany, which is a very different affair.

[206] In the original, an infinite variety of dishes is enumerated, which are necessarily passed over in the translation, simply, because we have no corresponding terms to express them in any Christian tongue. They would puzzle the immortal Ude himself, or the no less celebrated Soyer, the present autocrat of the culinary kingdom. But my chief reason for passing them over so lightly is the following, viz.: I have fully ascertained from officers home on furlough, that these passages are never read in India, nor is the student ever examined in them. They can interest only such little minds as are of the most contemptibly frivolous description. A man may be a first-rate English or French scholar, yea, an accomplished statesman, without being conversant with the infinite variety of dishes, &c., set down on the *carte* of a first-rate Parisian restaurateur.

[207] The Asiatics eat with the right hand, and use no knives or forks; so to draw back the hand from eating is to leave off eating. Of course, spoons are used for broths, &c, which cannot be eaten by the hand.

[208] As it were intended to be stored up and not eaten.

[209] This exceedingly plain expression is, so far from seeming gross or indelicate, considered as a very high compliment among Orientals.

"Perhaps I have been deficient in my attentions to you, for which reason you are displeased." I replied with astonishment, for God's sake, what a speech is this? the rules of hospitality [require one to stay] three days—these have I fulfilled; to remain longer would be improper; and besides this, I have set out to travel, and if I remain merely at one place, then it will not suit; for which reason I beg leave to depart; in other respects, your kindness is such that my heart does not wish to be separated from you.

He then said, "Do as you please; but wait a moment, that I may go to the princess and in her presence mention [the circumstance]; and as you wish to depart [be it known to you], that all the wearing apparel and bedding, also the vessels of silver and gold, and the jewelled vessels in this guest's apartment, are your property; whatever directions you may give for the purpose of taking them away, an arrangement [to that effect] shall be made." I answered, "cease[210] to talk in this manner; I am a pilgrim, and not a strolling bard; if such avarice had a place in my heart, then why should I have turned pilgrim; and where would be the evil of [my leading] a worldly life?" That kind young man replied, "If the princess should hear of this circumstance [of your refusal], she will discharge me from my employment, and God knows what other punishment I shall receive; if you are so indifferent [to possess them], then lock up all these articles in a room, and put your seal on the door, and you may hereafter dispose of them as you please."

I would not accept [his offer], and he would not submit [to me]. At last, this plan was adopted, I locked them all up in a room, and put my seal on the door, and waited [with impatience] for leave of departing. In the meantime a confidential eunuch, having on his head an aigrette, and a short robe round his loins, and a golden mace studded with gems in his hand, accompanied by several other respectable attendants, filling [various] offices, came near me with this splendour and pomp. He addressed me with such kindness and complaisance that I cannot express it, and added, "O, sir, if shewing kindness and benevolence, you do me the favour to dignify my humble dwelling with your presence, then it will not be far from courtesy and condescension.

Perhaps the princess will hear that a traveller had been here, and no one had received him with courtesy and politeness; and that he had gone away as he came; for this reason God knows what punishment she will inflict on me, or how far her displeasure will be raised; yea more, it is a matter affecting my life," I refused to listen to his request, but through dint of solicitations he overcame my resistance, and conducted me to another house, which was better than the first Like the former host, he entertained me twice a day for three days and nights, with the same kind of meals, and in the morning and afternoon sherbet, and fruits for passing away the time, and he told me that I was the master of all the rich gold and silver dishes, carpets, &c, and that I might do with them whatever I pleased.

On hearing these strange proposals, I was quite confounded, and wished that I might by some means take my leave and escape from this place. On perceiving my [embarassed] countenance, the eunuch said, "O creature of God, whatever your wants or wishes may be, impart them to me, that I may lay them before the

[210] Literally, "recite the *la haul*," &c, vide note 14, p. 4.

princess." I replied, "in the garb of a pilgrim, how can I desire the riches of this world, which you offer me unasked, and which I refuse?" He then said, "The desire of worldly goods forsakes the heart of no one, for which reason some poet has composed these verses:—

"I have seen [ascetics] with nails unpared;
I have seen [others] with hair thickly matted;
I have seen *jogis*[211] with their ears split,
Having their bodies covered with ashes;
I have seen the *maunis*[212] who never speak;
I have seen the *sevras*[213] with heads shaved;
I have seen [the people] sporting,
In the forest of *Ban-khandi*;
I have seen the brave, I have seen heroes;
I have seen the wise and the foolish, all;
I have seen those filled with delusion,
Continuing in forgetfulness amidst their wealth;
I have seen those [who were] happy from first to last.
I have seen those [who were] afflicted from their birth;
But never have I seen those [men]
In whose minds avarice did not exist."

On hearing these [lines], I replied, what you say is true, but I want nothing; if you will permit, I will write out a note and send it which will express my wish, and which you will convey to the presence of the princess, it will be [doing me] a great favour, as if I had received all the riches in the world. The eunuch said, "I will do it with pleasure, there is no difficulty in it." I immediately wrote a note to the following purport:—first, I began with the praise of God; I then related my circumstances and situation, saying, "that this creature of God had, some days since, arrived in the city, and from the munificence of her government, had been taken care of in every way; that I had heard such accounts of her highness's generosity and munificence, as had raised in me an ardent desire to see her, and that I had found those qualities four-fold greater than they had been represented. Your nobles now tell me to set forth before you whatever wants or wishes I may have; for this reason I beg to represent to you without ceremony the wishes of my heart. I am not in want of the riches of this world. I am also the king of my own country; my sole reason for coming so far and undergoing such fatigues, was the ardent desire I had to see you, which motive only has conducted me here in this manner quite alone. I now hope through your benevolence to attain the wishes of my heart; I shall then be satisfied. Any further favours will rest with your pleasure; but if the request of this wretch is not granted, then he will wander about in this same manner, encountering hardships, and sacrifice his restless life to the passion he feels for you. Like *Majnun* and *Farhad*,[214] he will end his life in some forest or mountain."

[211] *Jogis* are *Hindu* ascetics, or fanatics; some of them let the nails grow through the palm of their hands by keeping their fists shut, &c.

[212] The *maunis* are *Hindu* ascetics who vow everlasting silence.

[213] The *sevras* are mendicants of the *Jain* sects.

[214] *Majnun* is a mad lover of eastern romance, who pined in vain for the cruel *Laili*.

Having written my wishes, I gave the note to the eunuch; he carried it to the princess. After a short while, he returned and called me, and conducted me to the door of the seraglio. On arriving there, I saw an elderly and respectable woman dressed in jewels, sitting on a golden stool, and many eunuchs and other servants richly clothed, were standing before her with arms across. I imagining her to be the superintendent of affairs, and regarding her as a venerable [person], made her my obeisance; the old lady returned my salute with much civility, and said, "Come and sit down, you are welcome; it is you who wrote an affectionate note to the princess." I feeling ashamed, hung down my head and remained sitting silent.

After a short pause, she said, "O, young man, the princess has sent you her *salam*,[215] and said thus, 'There is nothing wrong in my taking a husband; you have solicited me [in marriage]; but to speak of your kingdom, and to conceive yourself a king in this mendicant state, and to be proud of it, is quite out of place; for this reason, that all men among each other are certainly equal; although superior consideration ought to be due to those who are of the religion of *Muhammad*. I also have wished for a long while to marry, and as you are indifferent to worldly riches, to me likewise God has given such wealth as cannot be counted. But there is one condition, that first of all you procure my marriage portion.'[216] The marriage-gift of the princess," added the old lady, "is a certain task to perform, if yon can fulfil it." I replied, "I am ready in every way, and I shall not be sparing of my wealth or life; tell me what the task is, that I may hear it. The old woman then said, "Remain here to-day, and tomorrow I will tell it to you." I accepted [her proposal] with pleasure, and taking my leave, I came out.

The day had in the meantime passed away, and when the evening came, a eunuch called upon me, and conducted me to the seraglio. On entering, I saw that the nobles, the learned, the virtuous, and the sages of the divine law were present. I likewise joined the assembly and sat down. In the meantime the cloth for the repast was spread, and eatables of every variety, both sweet and salt, were laid out. They all began to eat, and with courtesy solicited me to join them. When dinner was over, a female servant came out from the interior [of the seraglio] and asked, "Where is *Bahrawar*? call him." The servants in waiting brought him immediately; his appearance was very respectable, and many keys of silver and gold were suspended from his waist. After saluting me, he sat down by me. The same female servant said, "O, *Bahrawar*, whatever thou hast seen, relate it fully [to this stranger]."

Bahrawar, addressing himself to me, began the following narration:—"O, friend! our princess possesses thousands of slaves, who are established in trade; among them I am one of the humblest of her hereditary servants. She sends them to different countries with goods and merchandise, worth *lakhs* of rupees, of which

Farhad is equally celebrated as an unhappy *amant* who perished for *Shirin*.

[215] The word *salam*, "salutation," is used idiomatically in the sense of our terms "compliments" or "respects," &c. And in that sense it has now become, in India, adopted into the English language.

[216] The marriage portion here alluded to is not to be taken in the vague sense we attach to the term. The word *mahar* denotes a present made to, or a portion settled on, the wife at or before marriage.

they have the charge; when these return [from the respective countries to which they were sent to trade], then the princess, in her own presence, inquires of them the state and manners of such country, and hears [their different accounts]. Once it so happened that this meanest [of her slaves] went to the country and city of *Nimroz*[217] to trade, and perceiving that all the inhabitants were dressed in black, and that they sighed and wept every moment, and it appeared to me that some sad calamity had befallen them. From whomsoever I asked the reason [of these strange circumstances], no one would answer my inquiry. One day, the moment the morning appeared, all the inhabitants of the city, little and great, young and old, poor and rich, issued forth. They went out and assembled on a plain; the king of the country went there also mounted on horseback, and surrounded by his nobles; then they all formed a regular line, and stood still.

"I also stood among them to see the strange sight, for it clearly appeared that they were waiting for [the arrival of] some one. In an hour's time a beautiful young man, of an angelic form, about fifteen or sixteen years of age, uttering a loud noise, and foaming at the mouth, and mounted on a dun bull, holding something in one hand, approached from a distance, and came up in front of the people; he descended from the bull, and sat down [oriental fashion] on the ground, holding the halter of the animal in one hand, and a naked sword in the other; a rosy-coloured, beautiful [attendant] was with him; the young man gave him that which he held in his hand; the slave took it, and went along showing it to all of them from one end of the line to the other; but such was the nature [of the object], that whoever saw it, the same involuntarily wept aloud and bitterly [at the strange sight]. In this way he continued to show it to every one, and made every one weep; then passing along the front of the line, he returned to his master again.

"The moment he came near him, the young man rose up, and with the sword severed the attendant's head [from his body], and having again mounted his bull, galloped off towards the quarter from whence he had come. All [present] stood looking on. When he disappeared from their sight, the inhabitants returned to the city. I was anxiously asking every one I met the real meaning of this strange occurrence; yea, I even held out the inducement of money and beseeched and flattered them to get an explanation, who the young man was, and why he committed the deed [I had seen], and from whence he came, and where he went, but no one would give me the slightest information on the subject, nor could I comprehend it. When I returned here, I related to the princess the astonishing circumstance I had seen. Since then, the princess herself has been amazed [at the strange event], and anxious to ascertain its real cause. For which reason she has been fixed on this very point as her marriage portion, that whatever man will bring her a true and particular account of that strange circumstance, she will accept him [in marriage]; and he shall be the master of all her wealth, her country, and herself."

[*Bahrawar* concluded by saying], "You have now heard every circumstance; reflect within yourself if you can bring the intelligence [which is required] respecting the young man, then undertake the journey towards the country of *Nimroz*,

[217] *Nimroz* is that part of Persia which comprehends the provinces of *Sijistan* and *Mikran*, towards the south-east.

and depart soon, or else refuse [the conditions and the attempt], and return to your home." I answered, "If God please, I will soon ascertain all the circumstances [relating to the strange event], and return to the princess with success; or if my fate be unlucky, then there is no remedy; but the princess must give me her solemn promise she will not swerve from what she engages [to perform]. And now an uneasy apprehension arises in my heart; if the princess will have the benevolence to call me before her, and allow me to sit down outside the *parda,* and hear with her own ears the request I have made, and favour me with an answer from her own lips; then my heart will be at ease, and every thing will be possible for me." These my requests the female servant related to the fairy-formed princess. At last, by way of condescension, she ordered me to be called before her.

The same female returned, and conducted me to the apartment where the princess was; what [a display of beauty] I saw! Handsome female slaves and servants, and armed damsels, from *Kilmak, Turkistan, Abyssinia, Uzbak Tartary and Kashmir,* were drawn up in two lines, dressed in rich jewels, with their arms folded across, and each standing in her appropriate station. Shall I call this the court of Indra? or is it a descent on the part of the fairies? an involuntary sigh of rapture escaped [from my breast], and my heart began to palpitate; but I forcibly restrained myself. Regarding them all around, I advanced on; but my feet became each as heavy as a hundred *mans.*[218] Whenever I gazed on one of those lovely women, my heart was unwilling to proceed farther. On one side [of the saloon] a screen was suspended, and a stool set with precious stones was placed near it, as well as a chair of sandal-wood; the female servant made me a sign to sit down on the [jewelled] stool; I sat down upon it, and she seated herself on the [sandal-wood chair]; she said, "Now, whatever you have to say, speak it fully and from the heart."

I first extolled the princess's excellent qualities, also her justice and liberality; I then added, that "ever since I have entered the limits of this country, I saw at every stage accommodations for travellers and lofty buildings; and found everywhere servants of all grades appointed to attend upon travellers and necessitous persons. I have likewise spent three days at every halting place, and the fourth day, when I wished to take my leave, no one said with good will, "You may depart;" and whatever articles and furniture had been [applied to my use] at those places, such as chequered carpets,[219] &c., &c., I was told that they were all mine, and that I might either take them away or lock them up in a room, and put my seal on it; that, should it be my pleasure, whenever I came back I might take them away. I have done so; but the wonder is, that if a lonely pilgrim like me has met with such a [princely] reception, then there must be thousands of such pilgrims who will resort to your dominions; and if every one is hospitably received in the same manner [as myself], sums incalculable must be spent. Now, whence comes the great wealth of which there is such an expenditure, and of what nature is it? The treasures of *Karun* would not be equal to it; and if we look at the princess's territories, it would appear that their revenues would hardly suffice to defray the

[218] The *man,* commonly called "maund," a measure of weight, about eighty pounds avoirdupois.

[219] It is needless here to enumerate the stores of various articles detailed in the original, as they will all be found in the vocabulary.

kitchen charges, setting the other expenses aside. If the princess would condescend to explain this [seeming wonder] with her own lips, then, my mind being set at ease, I shall set out for the country of *Nimroz;* and reaching it by some means or other, after having learned all the particulars [of the strange circumstance], I will return, if God should spare my life, to the presence of the princess, and attain the desires of my heart."

On hearing these words, the princess herself said, "O youth, if you have a strong desire to know the exact nature of these circumstances, then stay here today also. I will send for you in the evening, and the account of my vast riches shall be unfolded to you without any reservation." After this assurance, I retired to my place of residence, and waited anxiously, (saying,) "when will the evening arrive, that my curiosity may be gratified?" In the meantime a eunuch brought some covered trays on the heads of porters, and laid them before me, and said, "The princess has sent you a dinner[220] from her own table; partake of it." When he uncovered the trays before me, the rich fragrance [of the meats] intoxicated my brains, and my soul became satiated. I ate as much as I could, and sent away the rest, and returned my grateful thanks [to the princess.] At last, when the sun, the traveller of the whole day, wearied and fatigued, reached his home, and the moon advanced from her palace, attended by her companions, then the female servant came to me and said, "Come, the princess has sent for you."

I went along with her; she led me to the private apartment; the effect of the lights was such that the *shabi kadr*[221] was nothing to it. A *masnad,* covered with gold, was placed on rich carpets, with a pillow studded with jewels; over it an awning of brocade was stretched, with a fringe of pearls on [silver] poles studded with precious stones; and in front of the *masnad* artificial trees formed of various jewels, with flowers and leaves attached, (one would say they were nature's own production,) were erected in beds of gold; and on the right and left, beautiful slaves and servants were in waiting with folded arms and down-cast eyes, in respectful attitude. Dancing women and female singers, with ready-tuned instruments, attended to begin their performances. On seeing such a scene and such splendid preparations, my senses were bewildered. I asked the female servant [who came with me] "there is here such gay splendour in the scene of the day, and such magnificence in that of the night, that the day may very justly be called *'Id,* and the night *shabi barat;* moreover, a king who possessed the whole world could not exhibit greater splendour and magnificence. Is it always so at the princess's court? The servant replied, "The princess's court ever displays the same magnificence you see now; there is no abatement [or difference], except that it is sometimes greater: sit you here; the princess is in another apartment,—I will go and inform her of your arrival."

Saying this, the nurse went away and quickly returned; he desired me to come

[220] Literally, "her own leavings." In the East it considered a very high compliment on the part of a person of rank to present his guest with the remnants of his own dish.

[221] Literally, "night of power or grandeur," would in that place be "without grandeur." The *shabi kadr,* or as the Arabs have it, *lailatu-l-kadri,* is a sacred festival held on the 27th of *Ramazan,* being, according to the *Musalmans,* the night on which the *Kur,an* was sent down from heaven.

to the princess. The moment I entered her apartment I was struck with amazement. I could not tell where the door was, or where the walls, for they were covered with Aleppo mirrors, of the height of a man, all around, the frames of which were studded with diamonds and pearls. The reflection of one fell on the other, and it appeared as if the whole room was inlaid with jewels. At one end a *parda* was hung, behind which the princess sat. The female servant seated herself close to the *parda*, and desired me to sit down also; then she began the following narrative, according to the princess's commands—"Hear, O intelligent youth! The sultan of this country was a potent king; he had seven daughters born in his house. One day, the king held a festival, and these seven daughters were standing before him [superbly dressed], with each sixteen jewels, twelve ornaments, and in every hair an elephant pearl. Something came into the king's mind, and he looked towards his daughters and said, 'If your father had not been a king, and you had been born in the house of some poor man, then who would have called you princesses? Praise God that you are called princesses; all your good fortune depends on my life.'

"Six of his daughters being of one mind, replied, 'Whatever your majesty says, is true, and our happiness depends on your welfare alone.' But the princess now present, though she was younger [than all her sisters], yet even in sense and judgment, even at that age, she was superior to them, all. She stood silent, and did not join her sisters in the reply they made; for this reason, that to say so was impious. The king looked towards her with anger, and said, 'Well, my lady, you say nothing; what is the cause of this?' Then the princess, tying both her hands with a handkerchief, humbly replied, 'If your majesty will grant me safety [of my life], and pardon my presumption, then this humble slave will unfold the dictates of her heart.' The king said, 'Speak what thou hast to say.' Then the princess said, 'Mighty king, you must have heard, that the voice of truth is bitter; for which reason, disregarding life at this moment, I presume to address your majesty; whatever the great Writer has written in [the book of] my destiny, no one can efface, and in no way can it be evaded. "Whether you bruise your feet [by depending on your own exertions], or lay your head on the carpet [in prayer], your fate [written] on the forehead, whatever it be, shall come to pass."

"'That Almighty Ruler, who has made you a king, He indeed also has made me a princess. In the arsenal of his omnipotence, no one has power. You are my sovereign and benefactor, and if I should apply the dust which lies under your auspicious feet, as a colyrium [for my eyes], then it would become me; but the destinies of every one are with every one.' The king, on hearing this [speech], became angry; the reply displeased him highly, and he said with wrath, 'What great words issue from a little mouth! Now let this be her punishment, that you strip off whatever jewels she has on her hands and feet, and let her be placed in a sedan-chair, and set down in such a wilderness, where no human traces can be found; then we shall see what is written in her destinies.'

"According to the king's commands, at that midnight hour, when it was the very essence of darkness, the princess (who had been reared with such delicacy and tenderness), and had seen no other place except her own apartments, was carried by the porters in a litter, and set down in a place where not even a bird ever flapped its wing, much less did human creatures there exist; they left her there and returned. The princess's heart was all at once in such a state [as cannot be conceived]; reduced to what she was, from what she had been! Then in the threshold of God, she offered up her prayers, and said, "Thou art so mighty [O Lord], that what thou hast wished, Thou hast done; and whatever Thou willest, Thou dost; and whatever Thou mayest wish, that Thou wilt do: whilst life remains in my nostrils, I shall not be hopeless of [thy protection']. Impressed with these thoughts, she fell asleep. When the morn appeared, the eyes of the princess opened; she called for water to perform her ablutions. Then, all at once, the occurrences of last night came to her recollection; she said to herself, 'Where art thou, and where this speech?'[222] Saying this to herself, she got up, and performed the *tayammum*,[223] said her prayers, and poured forth the praises of her Maker! O youth, the heart is torn with anguish to reflect on the princess's sad condition at that time. Ask that innocent and inexperienced heart what it felt.

"In short, she sat in the litter, and putting her trust in God, she repeated to herself at that moment these verses:—

"When I had no teeth, then thou gavest milk;
When thou hast given teeth, wilt thou not grant food!
He who takes care of the fowls of the air,
And of all the animals of the earth,
He will also take care of thee.
Why art thou sad, simple-minded one!
By being sorrowful thou'lt get nothing;
He who provides for the fool, for the wise, and for the whole world,
Will likewise provide for thee.'

"It is true, that when no resource remains, then God is remembered, or else every one in his own plans, thinks himself a *Lukman*, and a *Bu' Ali Sina*.[224] Now listen to the surprising ways of God. In this manner three days clear passed away, during which a grain of food did not enter the princess's mouth; her flower-like frame became quite withered as a [dry] thorn; and her colour, which hitherto shone like gold, became yellow as turmeric; her mouth became rigid, and her eyes were petrified, but still a faint respiration remained passing and re-passing. Whilst there is life, there is hope. In the morning of the fourth day, a hermit appeared of bright countenance, in appearance like *Khizr*,[225] and of an enlightened heart. See-

[222] Meaning that, under present circumstances, her commands were altogether out of place.

[223] It is incumbent on good Mussulmans to wash the hands and face before prayers. Where water is not to be had, this ceremony, called *tayammum* is performed by using sand instead.

[224] *Lukman* is supposed to be the Greek slave Æsop, the author of the Fables. *Bu 'Ali Sina* is the famous Arab physician and philosopher, by mediæval writers erroneously called Avicenna.

[225] *Khizr* or *Khwaja Khizr* is the name of a saint or prophet, of great notoriety among the *Muhammadans*. The legends respecting his origin and life are as numerous as they are absurd and contradictory. Some say he was grand *Vizir* to Solomon, others to Alexander the Great. They all agree, however, that he discovered the water of immortality, and that in

ing the princess in that state, he said, 'O daughter, though your father is a king, yet these [sorrows] were decreed in thy destiny. Now, conceive this old hermit your servant, and think day and night of your Maker. God will do what is right.' And whatever morsels the hermit had in his wallet, he laid them before the princess; then he went in search of water; he saw a well, but where were the wheel and bucket by means of which he might draw the water? He pulled off some leaves from a tree, and made a cup, and taking off his sash, he fastened the cup to it, and drew up some water, and gave it to the princess. At last she regained her senses. The holy man, seeing her helpless and solitary state, gave her every consolation, and cheered her heart; and he himself began to weep. When the princess saw his sympathetic grief, and [heard] his kind assurances, she became easy in her mind. From that day, the old man made this an established rule, that in the morning he went to the city to beg, and brought to the princess whatever scraps or morsels he received.

"In this way a few days passed. One day the princess designed to put some oil in her hair, and comb it; just as she opened the plaits of her hair a pearl round and brilliant dropped out. The princess gave it to the hermit, and desired him to sell it in the city, and bring her the amount. He sold that pearl, and brought back the money received for it to the princess. Then the princess desired that a habitation fit for her residence might be erected on that spot. The hermit replied, 'O daughter, do you dig the foundation for the walls, and collect some earth; I will, some of these days, bring some water, knead the clay [for the bricks], and erect a room for you.' The princess, on his advice, began to dig the ground; when she had dug a yard in depth, behold, under the soil a door appeared. The princess cleared away the earth [which lay before it]; a large room filled with jewels and gold pieces appeared: she took four or five handfuls of gold and closed the door, and having filled up the place with earth, made level its surface. In the meantime the hermit returned. The princess said to him, "bring good masons and builders, and workmen of every kind, expert and masters in their craft, so that a grand palace may be erected on this spot equal to the palace of *Kasra*,[226] and superior to the palace of *Ni'man*;[227] and that the fortifications of the city, a fort, a garden, a well, and an unrivalled caravanserai [be built as soon as possible]; but first of all, draw out the plans on paper and bring them to me for approval."

"The hermit brought clever, skilful, intelligent workmen, and had them ready. The erection of the different buildings was soon begun according to the princess's directions, and clever and trusty servants for every office were chosen and entertained. The news of the erection of such princely buildings by degrees reached the king, the shadow of Omnipotence, who was the princess's father. On hearing it, he became greatly surprised, and asked every one, 'Who is this person who has begun to erect such edifices?' No one knew anything of the matter to be able to give a reply. All put their hands on their ears and said, 'No one of your slaves

consequence of having drunk thereof, he still lives and wanders about on the earth.

[226] *Kasra* is the title of the King of Persia, hence the Greek forms Cyrus and Chosroes, and most probably the more modern forms Caesar, Kaisar, and Czar. The form *Kisra* used in the text is generally applied to *Naushirwan*.—Vide note 45, page 9.

[227] *Ni'man*, also *Nu'man*, the name of an ancient king of *Hirat*, in Arabia.

knows who is the builder of them.' Then the king sent one of his nobles with this message, 'I wish to come and see those buildings, and to know also of what country you are the princess, and of what family; for I wish much to ascertain all these circumstances.'

"When the princess received this agreeable intelligence, she was greatly pleased in her mind, and wrote the [following letter]: 'To the protector of the world, prosperity! On hearing the intelligence of your majesty's visit, to my humble mansion, I am infinitely rejoiced; and it has been the cause of respect and dignity to me, the meanest [of your slaves]. How happy is the fate of that place where your majesty's footsteps are impressed, and on the inhabitants of which the shadow of the skirt of your prosperity is cast; may they both be dignified with the look of favour! This slave hopes that to-morrow, being Thursday, is a propitious day, and to me, it is more welcome than the day of *Nau Roz*,[228] your majesty's person resembles the sun; by condescending to come here, be pleased to bestow, with your light, value and dignity on this worthless atom, and partake of whatever his humble slave can provide; this will be the essence of benevolence and courtesy, on the part of your majesty: to say more would exceed the bounds of respect.' To the nobleman who brought the message she made some presents, and dismissed him [with the above reply.]

"The king read the letter, and sent word, saying, 'We have accepted your invitation, and will certainly come.' The princess ordered the servants and all the attendants to get ready the necessary preparations for an entertainment, with such propriety and elegance, that the king, on seeing [the banquet] and eating thereof, might be highly pleased; and that all who came with the king, great and little, should be well entertained and return content. From the princess's strict directions, the dishes, of every kind, both salt and sweet, were so deliciously prepared, that if the daughter of a *Brahman*[229] had tasted them, she would have become a *Musalman*.[230] When the evening came, the king went to the princess's palace, seated on an uncovered throne; the princess, with her ladies in waiting, advanced to receive him; when she cast her eyes on the king's throne, she made the royal obeisance with such proper respect, that on seeing it, the king was still more surprised; with the same profound respect she accompanied the king to the throne, set with jewels, which she had erected for him. The princess had prepared a platform of 125,000 pieces of silver;[231] a hundred and one trays of jewels and of gold pieces, and woollen shiffs, shawls, muslins, silk and brocades; two elephants and ten

[228] The first day of the new year, which is celebrated with great splendour and rejoicings.

[229] The *Brahmans*, erroneously called Bramins, do not eat meat.

[230] Literally, "she would have repeated the *Kalima*," or "Confession of Faith" of the followers of *Muhammad*, which is as follows:—"There is no God but God, and *Muhammad* is his prophet." Some profane wags have parodied this creed into a Jewish one, viz.—"There ish no God but the monish, and shent per shent (cent. per cent.) ish hish prophet" (profit.)

[231] The common mode to present large sums in specie to princely visitors, is to form a platform with the money, spread the *masnad* on it, and place the visitor on the rich seat. Mr. Smith states that he had himself seen *Asafu-d-Daula*, the then *Nawwab* of Lucknow, receive a lack of rupees in this way from *Almas*, one of his eunuchs.

horses, of *'Irak* and *Yaman*, with caparisons set with precious stones, were likewise prepared [for the royal acceptance]. She presented these to his majesty, and stood before him herself with folded arms. The king asked with great complacency, 'Of what country are you a princess, and for what reasons are you come here?'

"The princess, after making her obeisance, replied, 'This slave is that offender who in consequence of the royal anger was sent to this wilderness, and all these things which your majesty sees are the wonderful works of God.' On hearing these words, the king's blood glowed (with paternal warmth), and rising up, he pressed the princess fondly to his bosom, and seizing her hand, he ordered her to be seated on a chair that he had placed near the throne; but still the king was astonished and surprised [at all he saw], and ordered that the queen, along with the princesses, should come thither with all speed. When they arrived, the mother and sisters recognised [the princess], and, embracing her with fondness, wept over her, and praised God. The princess presented her mother and sisters with such heaps of gold and jewels, that the treasures of the world could not equal them in the balance. Then the king, having made them all sit in his company, partook of the feast [which had been prepared].

"As long as the king lived, the time passed in this manner; sometimes the king came [to visit the princess], and sometimes carried the princess with him to his own palaces. When the king died, the government of the kingdom descended to this princess; for, except herself, no other person [of her family] was fit for this office. O, youth, the history [of the princess] is what you have heard. Finally, heaven-bestowed wealth never fails, but the intentions of the possessor must [at the same time] be just; moreover, how much soever is spent [out of this providential wealth] so much also is the increase: to be astonished at the power of God, is not right in any religion." The female servant, after finishing this narrative, said, "Now if you still intend to proceed to the country of *Nimroz*, and if you are determined in your mind to bring the requisite intelligence, then depart soon." I replied, I am going this moment, and if God pleases I shall be back very soon. At last, taking leave [of the princess] and relying on the protection of God, I set out for that quarter.

In about a year's time, after encountering many difficulties, I arrived at the city of *Nimroz*. All the inhabitants of that place that I saw, noble or common, were dressed in black, and whatever I had heard, that I fully perceived. After some days the evening[232] of the new moon occurred. On the first day of the month, all the inhabitants of the city, little and great, children, nobles, prince, women and men, assembled on a large plain. I also, bewildered and distracted in my condition, went along with the vast concourse; separated from my country and possessions, in the garb of a pilgrim, I was standing to behold the strange sight, and to see what might result from the mysterious scene. In the meantime, a young man advanced from the woods, mounted on a bull, foaming at the mouth, and roaring and shouting [in a frightful manner]. I, miserable, who had undergone such labour, and overcome so many dangers, and had come there to ascertain the circumstances, yet on seeing

[232] *Chand-rat*, is applied to the night on which the new moon is first visible, which night, together with the following day till sunset, constitutes the *pahli tarikh*, or *ghurra*, that is the first of the lunar month.

the young man I was quite confounded and stood silent with astonishment. The young man, according to his usual custom, did what he used to do, and returned [to the woods]; and the concourse of people from the city likewise returned thither. When I had collected my senses, I then repented [saying to myself], "What is this you have done? Now it is your lot to wait anxiously for another whole month." Having no remedy, I returned with the rest; and I passed that month like the month of *Ramazan,*[233] counting one day after another. At last the new moon appeared, and was hailed by me as *'Id.*[234] On the first of the month, the king and the inhabitants again assembled on that same plain; then I determined, that this time, let what will happen, I would be resolute, and propound this mysterious circumstance.

Suddenly the young man appeared, mounted, according to custom, on a yellow bull, and, dismounting, sat down [on the ground]; in one hand he held a naked sword, and in the other the bull's halter; he gave the vase to his attendant, who, as usual, showed it to every one, and carried it back [to his master]. The crowd, on seeing the vase, began to weep; the young man broke the vase, and struck such a blow on the slave's neck as to sever his head from his body, and, he himself remounting the bull, returned [towards the woods]. I began to run after him, with all speed, but the inhabitants laid hold of my hand, and exclaimed, "What is this you are going to do? why, knowingly, art thou about to perish? If thou art so tired of life, there are a great many ways of dying, by which thou mayest end thy existence." How much soever I beseeched them [to let me go], and even had recourse to main force, in order that by some means I might escape from their hands, yet I could not release myself. Three or four men clung fast to me, and having seized me, led me towards the city. I again suffered for another whole month in a strange state of disquietude.

When that month passed also, and the last day of it had elapsed, all the inhabitants assembled on the plain on the following morning in the same manner. I, apart from all, arose at the hour of [morning] prayer. I went before all the others [were astir] into the woods, and there lay concealed, exactly on the road by which the young man was to pass; for no one could there restrain me [from executing my project]. The young man came in the usual manner, performed the same acts [already described], re-mounted, and was returning. I followed him, and eagerly running up, I joined him. The young man, from the noise of my steps, perceived that some body was coming after him. All at once, turning round the halter of his bull, he gave a loud shout, and threatened me; then drawing his sword, he advanced towards me, and was about to strike. I bent down with the utmost respect, and made him my *salam,* and joining both my hands together, I stood in silence. That person being a judge of respectful behaviour [restraining his blow], said to me. "O pilgrim, thou wouldest have been killed for nothing, but thou hast escaped—thy life is prolonged; get away. Where art thou going?" He then drew

[233] *Ramazan* is the ninth *Muhammadan* month, during which they keep Lent. Vide note, p. 32.

[234] The *'Id* is the grand festival after the Lent of *Ramazan* is over. There is another *'Id,* called *Al-Kurban,* in commemoration of Abraham's meditated sacrifice of his son Isaac, or as the *Muhammadans* believe of his son Ishmael.

a jewelled dagger, having a tassel set with pearls, from his waist, and threw it towards me, and added, "At this moment I have no money about me to give thee; carry this [dagger] to the king, and thou wilt get whatever thou askest." To such a degree did my fear and dread of him prevail, that I had not power to speak or ability to move; my voice was choked, and my feet became heavy.

After saying this, the brave young man, roaring aloud, went on. I said to myself, "let what will happen, to remain behind now is, in thy case, folly thou wilt never again get such an opportunity [to execute thy project]. Regardless, therefore, of my life,[235] I also went on. He again turned round and forbade me in great wrath [to follow him], and seemed determined to put me to death. I stretched forth my neck, and conjuring him [by all that was sacred], I said, "*O Rustam*[236] of these days, strike such a blow that I may be cut clean in two; let not a fibre remain together, and let me be released from this wandering and wretched state; I pardon you my blood." He replied, "O demon-faced! why dost thou for nothing bring thy blood on my head, and makest me criminal; go thy own way; what! is thy life become a burden to thee?" I did not mind what he said, but advanced; then he knowingly appeared not to regard me, and I followed him. Proceeding on about two *kos*, we passed the wood, and came to a square building; the young man went up to the door and gave a frightful scream; the door opened of itself; he entered, and I remained altogether outside. O God, [said I] what shall I now do? I was perplexed; at last, after a short delay, a slave came out and brought a message, saying, "Come in, he has called you to his presence; perhaps the angel of death hovers over your head; what evil fortune has befallen you?" I replied, "Verily it is good fortune;" and without fear, I entered along with him into the garden.

At last, he led me to a place where [the young man was sitting]; on seeing him, I made him a very low[237] *salam*; he beckoned me to sit down; I sat down with respect. What do I see but the young man sitting alone on a *masnad*, with the tools of a goldsmith lying before him; and he had just finished a branch of emeralds. When the time came for him to rise up, all the slaves that were around the place concealed themselves in [different] rooms; I also from fear hid myself in a small closet. The young man rose up, and having fastened the chains of all the apartments, he went towards the corner of the garden, and began to beat the bull he usually rode. The noise of the animal's roaring reached my ear, and my heart quaked [with fear]; but as I had ran all these risks to develop this mystery, I forced the door, though trembling with fear, and under the screen of the trunk[238] of a tree, I stood and saw [what was going on]. The young man threw down the club with which he was beating [the bull], and unlocked a room and entered it. Then, instantly coming out, he stroked the bull's back with his hand, and kissed its mouth; and having given it some grain and grass, he came towards me. On perceiving this, I ran off

[235] Literally, "having washed my hands of my life."

[236] *Rustam*, a brave and famous hero of Persia, whose Herculean achievements are celebrated in the *Shah-Nama*.

[237] Literally, "a *salam* as low as the carpet;" or as we say, "a bow to the ground."

[238] The various editions of the text read *tunna*, "a particular kind of tree." In one of my MSS., however, the reading is *tane*, the inflected form of *tana*, the "trunk of a tree," which is better sense.

quickly, and hid myself in the room.

The young man unfastened the chains of all the rooms, and the whole of the slaves came out, bringing with them a small carpet, a wash-hand basin, and a water pot. After washing his hands and face, he stood up to pray; when he had finished his prayers, he called out, "Where is the pilgrim?" On hearing myself called, I ran out and stood before him; he desired me to sit down; after making him a *salam*, I sat down; the dinner was served; he partook of it, and gave me some, which I also ate. When the dishes were removed, and we had washed our hands, he dismissed his slaves and told them to go to rest. When no one [except ourselves] remained in the apartment, he then spoke to me, and asked, "O friend, what great misfortune has befallen thee that thou goest about seeking thy death?" I related in full detail all the adventures of my life, from beginning to end, and added, that, "from your goodness, I have hopes of obtaining my wishes." On hearing this, he heaving a deep sigh, went raving mad, and began to say, "O God! who except thee is acquainted with the tortures of love! He whose chilblain has not yet broken out, how can he know the pains of others? he only knows the degree of this pain who has felt the pangs of love!

'The anguish of love, you must ask of the lover,
Not of him who feigns, but of the true lover.'"

A moment after, coming to himself, he heaved a heart-burning sigh; the room resounded with it; then I perceived that he was likewise tortured with the pangs of love, and was suffering from the same malady [as myself]. On this discovery, I plucked up courage and said, "I have related to you all my own adventures; now do me the favour to impart to me the past events [of your life]; I will then first of all assist you as far as I can, and by exerting myself obtain for you the desires of your heart." In short, that true lover, conceiving me his companion and fellow-sufferer, began the relation of his adventures in the following manner. "Hear, O friend! I whose heart is tortured with anguish, am the prince of this country of *Nimroz*; the king, that is to say, my father, at my birth, collected together all the fortune tellers, astrologers and learned men, and ordered them to cast and examine my horoscope, to fix my nativity, and to state in full to his majesty whatever was to befall me every individual moment, and hour, and *pahar*, and day, and month, and year, [of my life]. They all assembled according to the king's order, and consulting together, they, from their mystical science, ascertained my future fate, and said, 'By the blessing of God, the prince has been begotten and born under such a propitious planet, and in such a lucky moment, that he ought to be equal to Alexander in extent of dominion, and in justice equal to *Naushirwan*. He will be, moreover, proficient in every science, and every [branch of] learning, and towards whatever subject his heart is inclined, he will accomplish it with perfection. He will in generosity and bravery acquire such renown, that mankind will no longer remember *Hatim* and *Rustam*; but until [he attains] the age of fourteen, he is exposed to great danger if he sees the sun or moon; yea, it is to be feared he may become a mad demoniac, and shed the blood of many; and restless [of living in society], he will fly to the woods, and associate with beasts and birds; great and strict pains must be taken that he should never behold the sun by day or the moon by night, or cast a look even towards the heavens. If this period [of fourteen years] pass away without danger and in safety, then for the rest of his life he will reign in peace and prosperity.'

"On hearing this [prognostication], the king ordered this garden to be laid out, and caused to be built in it many apartments of various kinds. He gave an order for me to be brought up in a vault, lined [on the inside] with felt, so that not a single ray of light from the sun or moon might penetrate [into my apartment]. I had a wet nurse and all other kinds of female servants and attendants attached to me, and was brought up in this grand palace with this [imagined] security. A learned tutor, who was skilled in public affairs, was appointed to [superintend] my education; so that I might acquire every science and art, and the practice of the seven varieties of penmanship; and my father always looked after me; the occurrences of every day and every moment were told to the king. I considered that same place as the whole world, and amused myself with toys and flowers; and I had procured for me every delicacy the world [could produce] for my food; whatever I desired I had. By the age of ten years, I had acquired every species of learning, and every useful accomplishment.

"One day, beneath that dome, an astonishing flower appeared from the skylight, which increased in size as I gazed upon it; I wished to seize it with my hands, but as I stretched them towards it, it ascended [and eluded my grasp]. I, having become astonished, was looking steadfastly at it, when the sound of a loud laugh reached my ear; I raised my head to look [towards the dome from which the noise proceeded]. Then I saw that a face, resplendent as the full moon, having rent the felt, continued issuing forth. On beholding it, my reason and senses vanished. On coming to myself, I looked up, and saw a throne of jewels raised on the shoulders of fairies; a person was seated on it, with a crown of precious stones on her head, and clothed in a superb dress; she held in her hand a cup made of ruby, and seated, was drinking wine. The throne descended by slow degrees from its height, and rested on [the floor of] the dome. Then the fairy called me, and placed me beside her [on the throne]; she began to make use of expressions of endearment, and having pressed her lips to mine, she made me drink a cup of rosy wine, and said, 'The human race is faithless, but my heart loves thee.' The expressions she uttered were so endearing and so fascinating, that in a moment my heart was enraptured, and I felt such pleasure as if I had tasted the supreme joys of life, and thus I conceived that I had only on that day entered the world [of enjoyment].

"The result is my present state! but no one [on earth] hath ever seen, or heard such ecstatic pleasure! In that zest, with our hearts at ease, we both were seated, when all at once our joys were dashed to pieces! Now listen to the unlooked-for circumstance [which produced this sudden change]. At the moment, four fairies descended from the heavens, and whispered something in that beloved one's ear. On hearing it, her colour changed, and she said to me, 'O my beloved, I fondly wished to pass some moments with you, and regale my heart, and to repeat my visits in the same manner, or to take thee with me. But fate will not permit two persons [like us] to remain in one place in peace and felicity; farewell, my beloved! may God protect you!' On hearing these [dreadful words], my senses vanished, and my bliss fled from my grasp.[239] I cried, 'O my charmer, when shall we meet again? what dreadful words of wrath are these which you have made me hear? If you will return quickly, then you will find me alive, otherwise you will regret the delay; or else tell me your name and place of residence, that I may from those directions, by diligent search, conduct myself to you.' On hearing this she said, 'God forbid [you should do so]; may the ears of Satan be deaf; may your age amount to a hundred and twenty years;[240] if we live we shall meet again; I am the daughter of the king of the *Jinns*, and I dwell in the mountain of *Kaf*.[241] On saying this, she caused the throne to ascend,[242] and it ascended in the same manner as it had descended.

"Whilst the throne was in sight, our eyes were fixed on each other; when it disappeared from my eyes, my state became such as if the shadow of a fairy had fallen on me; a strange sort of gloom was spread over my heart, and my understanding and consciousness left me; the world appeared dark under my eyes; distracted and confused, I wept bitterly, and scattered dust over my head, and tore my clothes; I became regardless of food and drink, nor cared for good or evil.

'What various evils result from this same love!
In the heart are produced sadness and impatience.'[243]

"My misfortune was soon known to my nurse and preceptor; with fear and trembling they went before the king, and said, 'Such is the state of the prince of the people of the world; we do not know how this disaster has suddenly and of itself fallen upon him, so that rest, food, and drink have all [on his part] been abandoned.' [On hearing these sad tidings] the king immediately came to the garden [where I resided], accompanied by the *wazir*, intelligent nobles, wise physicians, true astrologers, learned *mullas*, holy devotees, and men abstracted from worldly

[239] Literally, "the parrot of my hand flew away."

[240] The *Muhammadans* reckon a hundred and twenty years as the *'umri tabi'i*, or the natural period of man's life.

[241] The mountain of *Kaf*, is the celebrated abode of the *jinns*, *paris*, and *divs*, and all the fabulous beings of oriental romance. The *Muhammadans*, as of yore all good Christians, believe that the earth is a flat circular plane; and on the confines of this circle is a ring of lofty mountains extending all round, serving at once to keep folks from falling off, as well as forming a convenient habitation for the *jinns*, &c., aforesaid. The mountain, (I am not certain on whose trigonometrical authority) is said to be 500 *farasangs* or 2000 English miles in height.

[242] With regard to the plain, simple sentence, "*yih kahkar takht uthaya*," we have somewhere seen the following erudite criticism, viz.:—"With deference to *Mir Amman*, this is bad grammar. The nominative to *kahkar* and *uthaya* ought to be the same!!!" Now, it is a great pity that the critic did not favour us here with his notions of *good* grammar. Just observe, O reader, how the expression stands in the text: "*yih kahkar takht uthaya*," and you will naturally ask, "where is the fault in the grammar?" The nominative, or rather the agent, is *pari ne*, hence the translation, "the fairy, having thus spoken, took up the throne." The poor critic seems to confound "*uthaya*" with "*utha*."

[243] One of the would-be poets of our day has translated the above most elegantly and literally, as follows:—

"What mischiefs through this love arise!
What broken hearts and miseries!"

affairs. On seeing my distracted, sighing, weeping condition, his mind became also distracted; he wept, and with fond affection clasped me to his breast, and gave orders for my proper treatment. The physicians wrote out their prescriptions, in order to strengthen my heart and cure my brain, and the holy priests wrote out charms[244] and amulets, some to be swallowed, and others to be worn on my person, and having each repeated prayers [of exorcism], they began to blow upon me; the astrologers said this misfortune had happened owing to the revolution of the stars [for the averting] of it, give pious donations. In short, every one advised according to his science; but what was passing within me, my heart alone experienced; no one's assistance or remedy was of avail to my evil destiny; day after day my lunacy increased, and my body became emaciated from the want of nourishment. There remained for me only to shriek and moan, day and night. Three years passed away in this state. In the fourth year, a merchant, who was on his travels, arrived, and brought with him into the royal presence rare and valuable articles of different countries; he met with a gracious reception.

"The king favoured him greatly, and after inquiries respecting his health, he said to him, 'You have seen many countries; have you anywhere seen a truly learned physician, or have heard of such from any one?' The merchant replied, 'Mighty sire, this slave has travelled a great deal; in the middle of the [Ganges] river in *Hindustan* there is a small mountain; there a *Jata-dhari Gusa,in*[245] has built a large temple to *Mahadev,*[246] together with a place of worship, and a garden of great beauty, and in that [mountain-island] he lives; and his custom is this, that once a year on the day of *Shevrat,*[247] he comes out of his dwelling, swims in the river, and enjoys himself. After washing himself, when he is returning to his abode, then the sick and afflicted of various countries and regions, who come there from afar, assemble near his door. Of these a numerous crowd is formed.

"'The holy *Gusa,in* (who ought to be called the Plato[248] of these days), moves along examining the urine, and feeling the pulse of each, and giving each a recipe.

[244] The *Muhammadans* have great confidence in charms which are written on slips of paper, along with numerous astrological characters. They consist chiefly of quotations from the *Kuran,* and are often diluted in water, and drank as medicine in various distempers. As the Indian ink and paper can do no harm, and often act as an emetic, they are probably more innocent than the physic administered by eastern physicians, who are the most ignorant of their profession. The fact is, that the soi disant "teachers" of mankind, in all ages and countries—the African fetish, the American Indian sachem, the *Hindu jogi,* the *Musalman mulla,* and the Romish priest and miracle-monger—have all agreed on one point, viz., to impose on their silly victims a multitude of unmeaning ceremonies, and absurd mummeries, in order to conceal their own contemptible vacuity of intellect.

[245] The *Jata-dhari Gusa,in* is a sect of fanatic *Hindu* mendicants, who let their hair grow and matted, and go almost naked.

[246] *Mahadev* is a *Hindu* idol; the emblem of the creative power, and generally and naturally represented by the Lingum.

[247] *Shevrat* is a *Hindu* festival, which corresponds nearly with the Mahometan *shabi barat.*

[248] Plato is supposed by the *Muhammadans* to have been not only a profound philosopher, but a wise physician. In short, it is too general an idea with them, that a clever man must be a good doctor.

God has given him such healing power, that, on taking his medicines, their effects are instantaneous, and the disease utterly vanishes. These circumstances I have seen with my own eyes, and adored the power of God which has created such beings! If your majesty orders it, I will conduct the prince of the people of the world to that [wonderful man], and show the prince to him; I firmly hope he will soon be completely cured; moreover, this scheme is externally beneficial, for from inhaling the air of various places, and from the diet and drink of different countries [through which we shall pass], the prince's mind will be restored to cheerfulness.' The merchant's advice seemed very proper to the king, and being pleased, he said, 'Very well; perhaps the holy man's treatment may prove efficacious, and this melancholy may be removed from my son's mind.' The king appointed a confidential nobleman, who had seen the world, and had been tried on [various] occasions, together with the merchant, to attend me, and he furnished us with the requisite equipment. Having seen us embark on boats of every variety, together with our baggage, he dismissed us. Proceeding onwards, stage after stage, we arrived at the place [where the holy *Gusa,in* lived]. From change of air, and from living on a different diet, my mind became somewhat composed; but there still remained the same state of silence; and I wept incessantly. The recollection of the lovely fairy was not for a moment effaced from my mind; if I spoke sometimes, it was only to repeat these lines:—

'I know not what fairy-faced one has glanced over me,
But my heart was sound and tranquil not long ago.'

At last, when two or three months had passed away, nearly four thousand sick had assembled on the rock, and all said, 'If God please, the *Gusa,in* will shortly come out of his abode, and bestow on us his advice, and we shall be perfectly cured.' In short, when that day arrived, the *Gusa,in* appeared in the morning, like the sun, and bathed and swam in the river; he crossed over it and returned, and rubbed ashes of cow-dung over his body, and hid his fair form like a live coal under the ashes. He made a mark with sandal wood on his forehead, girded on his *langoti,*[249] threw a towel over his shoulders, tied his long hair up in a knot, twisted his mustachios, and put on his shoes. It appeared, from his looks, that the whole world possessed no value to him. Having put a small writing desk set with gems under his arm, and looking at each [patient] in turn, he gave them his recipes, and came to me. When our looks met, he stood still, paused for a moment, and then said to me, 'Come with me.' I went along with him.

"When he had done with all the rest, he led me into the garden, and into a neat and richly-ornamented private apartment, and he said to me, 'Do you make your residence here,' and went himself to his abode. When forty days had elapsed, he came to me, and found me better comparatively with [what I had been] before. He then, smiling, said, 'Amuse yourself by walking about in this garden, and eat whatever fruits you like.' He gave me a china pot filled with *ma'jun,*[250] and add-

[249] The *langot* or *langoti* is a piece of cloth wrapped or fastened round the loins, and tucked in between the feet. It barely conceals what civilization requires should be hid from the public view.

[250] *Ma'jun* is the extract from the intoxicating plant called *charas* or *bhang,* a species of hemp; it is mixed with sugar and spices to render it palatable. The inebriation it produces

ed, 'Take without fail six *mashas*[251] from this pot every morning, fasting.' Saying this, he went away, and I followed strictly his prescription. My body perceptibly gained strength daily, and my mind composure, but mighty love was still triumphant; that fairy's form ever wandered before my eyes.

"One day I perceived a book[252] in a recess in the wall; I took it down, and saw that all the sciences relating to the future and the present world were comprised in it, as if the ocean had been compressed into a vase. I used to read it at all times; I acquired great skill in the science of physic, and the mystical art of philters. A year passed away in the meantime, and again that same day of joy returned; the *Gusa,in,* having arisen from his devotional posture, came out [of his abode]; I made him my *salam;* he gave me the writing case, and said, 'Accompany me.' I [accordingly] went along with him. When he came out of the gate a vast crowd showered blessings on him. The nobleman and the merchant, seeing me with the *Gusa,in,* fell at his feet, and began to pour forth their blessings on him, saying, "by the favour of your holiness, this much at least has been effected." The *Gusa,in* went to the *ghat* of the river, according to custom, and performed his ablutions and devotions, as he was wont to do every year; returning [from thence], he was proceeding along the line and examining the sick.

"It happened, that in the group of lunatics, a handsome young man, who had scarce strength to stand up, attracted the *Gusa,in's* attention. He said to me, 'Bring him with you.' After delivering his prescriptions of cure to all, he went into his private apartment and opened a little of the young lunatic's skull; he attempted to seize with his forceps the centipede which was curled on his brain. An idea struck me, and I spoke out, saying, 'If you will heat the forceps in the fire, and then apply it to the centipede's back, it will be better, as it will then come out of its own accord; but if you thus attempt to pull it off, it will not quit its grasp on the brain, and [the patient's] life will be endangered.'[253] On hearing this, the *Gusa,in* looked towards me; silently he rose up, and, without saying a word, he went to the corner of the garden, and seizing a tree in his grasp, he formed his long hair into a noose, and hanged himself. I went to the spot, and saw, alas! alas! that he was dead. I became quite afflicted at the strange and astonishing sight; but being helpless, I thought it best to bury him. The moment I began to take him down from the tree, two keys dropt from his locks; I took them up, and interred that treasure of excellence in the earth. Having taken with me the two keys, I began to apply them to all the locks. By chance I opened the locks of two rooms with these keys, and perceived that they were filled from the floor to the roof with precious stones; in one place I saw a chest covered with velvet, with clasps of gold, and locked. When I opened it, then

---

fills the imagination with agreeable visions, and the effects are different from those of wine or spirits.

[251] Six *mashas* amount to nearly a quarter of an ounce; a sicca rupee weighs eleven *mashas*.

[252] Literally, "a volume of a book."

[253] This exceedingly absurd story is of Rabbinical origin. I have a strong impression on my mind of having read something very like it long ago in the works of Philo Judaeus, the contemporary of Josephus.

I saw in it a book, in which was written the "Most awful of Names,"[254] and the mode of invoking the genii, and the fairies, and the holding of intercourse with spirits, and how to subdue them, also the mode of charming the sun.

"I became quite delighted at the idea of having acquired such a treasure, and began to put those [charms] in practice. I opened the garden door, and said to the nobleman, and to those who had come with me, 'Send for the vessels [which had brought us, and embark in them all these jewels, specie, merchandise, and books,' and having embarked myself in a small vessel, I proceeded from thence to the main ocean. When sailing along, I approached my own country. The intelligence reached my father. He mounted his horse, and advanced to meet us; with anxious affection he clasped me to his bosom; I kissed his feet, and said, 'May this humble being be allowed to live in the former garden?'

"The king replied, 'O my son, that garden appears to me calamitous, and I have therefore forbidden its being kept up; that spot is not at present fit for the abode of man; reside in any other abode which your heart may desire. You had best choose some place in the fort, and live under my eyes; and having there formed such a garden as you wish, continue to walk about and to amuse yourself.' I strenuously resisted and caused the former garden to be repaired once more, and having embellished it like a perfect paradise, I went to reside in it. There, at my ease, I fasted forty days for the purpose of subduing the *jinns* to my will; and having abandoned living creatures, I began to practise [my spells] on the world of spirits.

"When the forty days were completed, such a terrible storm arose at midnight, that the very strongest buildings fell down, and trees were uprooted and scattered in all directions; an army of fairies appeared. A throne descended from the air, on which a person of dignified appearance was seated, richly dressed, with a crown of pearls on his head. On seeing him, I saluted him with great respect; he returned my salutation, and said, 'O friend, why hast thou raised this commotion for nothing? what dost thou want with me?' I replied, 'This wretch has been long in love with your daughter, and for her I have every where wandered about wretched, distracted, and am dead, though alive; I am now sick of existence, and have staked my life on this deed which I have done. All my hopes now rest on your benevolence, that you will exalt this unfortunate wanderer with your favour, and that you will bestow on me life and happiness, by allowing me to behold [your fair daughter]; it will be an act of great merit.'[255]

"On hearing my wishes he said, 'Man is made of earth, and we are formed of fire; connection between two such [classes] is very difficult.' I swore an oath, saying, 'I only desire to see her, and have no other purpose.' Again the king [of the fairies] replied, 'Man does not adhere to his promises; in time of need he promises everything, but he does not keep it in recollection. I say this for thy good; for if

[254] The *Ismi A'zam,* or the "Most Mighty Name" [of God] is a magic spell or incantation which the acquirer can apply to wonderful purposes. God hath, among the *Muhammadans,* ninety-nine names or epithets; the *Ismi A'zam* is one of the number, but it is only the initiated few who can say which of the ninety-nine it is.

[255] The word *sawab* strictly means, "the reward received in the next world for virtuous actions performed in the present state of existence."

ever thou formest other wishes, then she and thou wilt be ruined and undone; moreover, it will endanger your lives.' I repeated my oaths, and added, that whatever could injure both of us, I would never do, and that all I desired was to see her sometimes. These words were passing [between us], when suddenly, the fairy (of whom we were talking) appeared before us, with much splendour, and completely adorned; and the throne of the king [of the fairies] remounted thence. I then embraced the fairy with fond eagerness, and repeated this verse:—

> 'Why should not she of the arched eyebrows come [to my house],
> She for whose sake I have fasted for forty days.'

In that state of felicity we resided together in the garden. I dreaded through fear to think of other joys; I only tasted the superficial pleasure [of her roseate lips], and constantly gazed upon her charms. The lovely fairy, seeing me so true to my oath, was surprised within herself, and used sometimes to say, 'O my beloved, you are indeed strictly faithful to your promise; but I will give you, by the way of friendship, a piece of advice; take care of your mystical book; for the *jinns*, seeing you off your guard, will purloin it some day or other.' I replied, 'I guard this book as I would my life.'

"It so happened, that one night Satan led me astray; in a fit of overpowering passion, I said to myself, 'Let happen what will, how long can I restrain myself?' I clasped the [lovely fairy] to my bosom, and attempted to revel in ecstatic joys. Instantly, a voice came forth, saying, 'Give me the book, for the great name of God is written in it; do not profane it.' In that fervour of passion, I was insensible [to every other consideration]; I took the book from my bosom and delivered it, without knowing to whom I gave it, and plunged myself into the fervid joys of love. The beautiful fairy, seeing my foolish conduct, said, 'Alas! selfish man, thou hast at last transgressed, and forgotten my admonition.'

"On saying this, she became senseless, and I perceived a *jinn* standing at the head of the bed, who held the magical book in his hand; I attempted to seize him, and beat him severely, and snatch away the book, when in the meantime another appeared, took the book from his hand, and ran off. I began to repeat the incantations I had learnt. The *jinn*, who was still standing near me, became a bull; but, alas! the lovely fairy had not in the least recovered her senses, and that same state of stupor continued. Then my mind became distracted, and all my joys were turned into bitterness. From that day, man became my aversion. I live in a corner of this garden; and for the sake of agreeably occupying my mind, I made this emerald vase, ornamented with flowers, and every month I go to the plain, mounted on that same bull, break the vase, and kill a slave, with the hope that every one may see my sad state and pity me; perhaps some creature of God may so far favour me and pray for me, that I even may regain the desire [of my heart]. O faithful friend, such as I have related to thee is the sad tale of my madness and lunacy."

I wept at hearing it, and said, "O prince, you have truly suffered greatly from love; but I swear here by God, that I will abandon my own wishes, and will now roam among woods and mountains for your good, and do all I can [to find out your beloved fairy]. Having made this promise, I took leave of the prince, and for five years wandered through the desert, sifting the dust, like a mad man, but found no trace [of the fairy]. At last, desponding of success, I ascended a mountain, and wished to throw myself down [from its summit], so that neither bone nor rib [in my frame] might remain entire. The same veiled horseman, [who saved you from destruction], came up to me and said, "Do not throw away thy life; in a few days thou wilt be in possession of the desires of thy heart." O holy *Darweshes*! I have at last seen you. I have now hopes that joy and happiness will be our lot, and all of us, now affected as we are, may attain our wished-for objects.

TALE OF AZAD BAKHT.

When the second *Darwesh* had likewise finished telling the relation of his adventures, the night ended, and the time of morning was just beginning. The king, *Azad Bakht,* silently proceeded towards his own kingly abode. On arriving at his palace, he said his prayers. Then, having gone to the bathing-house, and dressed himself superbly, he proceeded to the *Diwani 'Amm* and mounted his throne; and he issued an order, saying, "Let a messenger go and bring along with him, with respect, to our presence, four *Darweshes* who have [recently] arrived at such a place." The messenger went there according to orders, and perceived that the four *Darweshes,* after performing the necessary calls, and washed their hands and faces, were on the point of setting out on [their peregrinations], and take their different roads. The messenger said to them, "Reverend sirs, the king has called you four personages; come along with me." The four *Darweshes* began to stare at each other, and said to the messenger, "Son, we are the monarchs of our own hearts; what have we to do with a king of this world?" The messenger answered, "Holy sirs, there is no harm in it, and it is better you should go."

The four *Darweshes* then recollected that what *Maula Murtaza*[256] had said to them, that same had now come to pass; they were pleased at the recollection], and went along with the messenger. When they reached the fort and went before the king, the four *Kalandars* gave a benediction, saying, "Son, may it be well with thee." The king then retired to the *Diwani khass,* and having called two or three of his confidential nobles near him, he ordered the four *Darweshes* to be brought in. When they went there [before his majesty], he commanded them to sit down, and asked them their adventures, saying, "From whence come you, where do you intend to go, and where is the residence of your worships?"

"They replied, "May the king's age and wealth be always on the increase! we are *Darweshes,* and have in this very manner for a long while wandered and roamed about; we bear our homes on our shoulders. There is a saying, that 'a pilgrim's home is where the evening overtakes him;' and all we have seen in this versatile world is too long a tale to relate."

Azad Bakht gave them every confidence and encouragement, and having sent for refreshment, he made them breakfast before him. When they finished [their meal] the king said to them, "Relate all your adventures to me, without the least reserve; whatever services I can render you, I will not fail to do." The *Darweshes* replied that, "whatever has happened to us, we have not the strength to relate, nor will any pleasure result to the king from hearing it; therefore pardon us." The king

[256] The veiled horseman who rescued the first and second *Darweshes* from self-destruction.

then smiled, and said, "Where you were sitting on your couches last night and relating each his own adventures, there I was likewise present; moreover, I have heard the adventures of two of you; I now wish that the two who remain would also relate theirs; and stay with me a few days in perfect confidence, for 'the foot-steps of the *Darwesh* scare away evil.'"[257] On hearing these words from the king, they began to tremble in consequence of their fear; and having hung down their heads, they remained silent—they had not the power to speak.

When *Azad Bakht* perceived that now through fear their senses no longer remained with them, so as to enable them to tell anything, he said [to revive their spirits] "There is no person in this world to whom rare and strange incidents have not occurred; although I am a king, yet I have even seen strange scenes, which I will first of all relate to you [to inspire you with confidence and remove your fears]; do you listen to it with your minds at ease," The *Darweshes* replied, "O king, peace be on thee! such are your kindnesses towards us darweshes, condescend to relate them."

Azad Bakht began his adventures, and said,

"Hear, O pilgrims, the adventures of the king.
Whatever I have heard or seen, O hear!
I will relate to ye every thing, from end to end.
My story with heartfelt attention hear."

When my father died, and I ascended the throne, it was in the very season of youth, and all this kingdom of *Rum* was under my dominion. It happened one year, that some merchant from the country of *Badakhshan*[258] came [to my capital] and brought a good deal of merchandise. The reporters of intelligence[259] sent notice to me to this effect, that so considerable a merchant had never visited our city before: I sent for him.

"He came, and brought with him the rarities of every country, which were worthy of being offered to me, as presents. Indeed, every article appeared to be of inestimable value; above all, there was a ruby in a box, of an exceedingly fine colour, very brilliant, perfect in shape and size, and in weight [amounting to] five *miskals*.[260] Though I was a king, I had never seen such a precious stone, nor had I heard of such from any other person. I accepted it, and bestowed upon the merchant many presents and honours; I gave him passports for the roads, that throughout my empire no one should ask him any duties; that they should treat him with kindness wherever he went; that he should be waited on, and have guards for his protection, and that they should consider any loss he might expe-

[257] A Persian proverb.

[258] *Badakhshan* is a part of the grand province of *Khurasan*, and the city of *Balkh* is its metropolis, to the eastward of which is a chain of mountains celebrated for producing fine rubies.

[259] All Asiatic princes, like others nearer home, have spies, called "reporters of intelligence," who inform themselves of what passes in public. They are, as a matter of course, the pest of society, and generally corrupt.

[260] A *miskal* is four and a half *mashas*; our ounce contains twenty-four *mashas*. So the ruby weighed more than half an ounce.

rience as their own. The merchant attended at the time of audience, and was well versed in the forms of respect due to royalty; his conversation and eloquence were worth hearing. I used to send for the ruby daily from the jewel office, and look at it at the time of public audience.

One day I was seated in the *diwani 'amm,* and the nobles and officers of state were in waiting in their respective places, and the ambassadors of different sovereigns, who had come to congratulate me [on my accession to the throne], were likewise present. I then sent for the ruby, according to custom; the officer of the jewel office brought it; I took it in my hand and began to praise it, and gave it to the ambassador of the Franks [to look at it]. On seeing it, he smiled, and praised it by way of flattery; in the same manner it passed from hand to hand, and every one looked at it, and all said together, "The preponderance of your majesty's good fortune has procured you this; for otherwise, even unto this day, no monarch has ever acquired so inestimable a jewel." At that moment my father's *wazir,* who was wise, and held the same station under me, and was standing in his place, made his obeisance and said, "I wish to impart something [to the royal ear], if my life be granted."

I ordered him to speak; he said, "Mighty sire, you are king, and it is very unbecoming in kings to laud so highly a stone; though it is unique in colour, in quality, and in weight, yet it is but a stone; and at this moment the ambassadors of all countries are present in the court; when they return to their respective countries, they will assuredly relate this anecdote, saying, 'What a strange king he is, who has got a ruby from somewhere, and makes such a rarity of it, that he sends for it every day, and praising it himself the first, shows it to every one present.' Then whatever king or *raja*[261] hears this anecdote, the same will certainly laugh at it in his own court. Great sire, there is an insignificant merchant in *Naishapur,*[262] who has twelve rubies, each weighing seven *miskals,*[263] which he has sewed on a collar, and put it round his dog's neck." On hearing this, I became greatly displeased, and said with anger, put this *wazir* to death.

The executioners immediately seized hold of his hands, and were going to lead him out [to execution]. The ambassador of the king of the Franks, joining his hands [in humble supplication] stood before me. I asked him what he wanted; he replied, "I hope I may become informed of the *wazir's* fault," I answered, what can be a greater fault than to lie, especially before kings. He replied, "His falsehood has not yet been confirmed; perhaps what he has said may be true; now, to put an innocent person to death is not right." I said to him in reply, "It is not at all consistent with reason, that a merchant, who, for the sake of gain, wanders disconsolate from city to city and from country to country, and hoards up every farthing [he can save], should sew twelve rubies, which weigh seven *miskals* each, on the collar of a dog." The ambassador in answer said, "Nothing is surprising before the

[261] The word *raja* is the *Hindu* term for a prince or sovereign. In more recent times it has become a mere empty title, conferred upon rich *Hindus* by the Emperor of *Delhi.*

[262] *Naishapur* was once the richest and grandest city in the province of *Khurasan.* It was utterly destroyed by *Tuli,* the son of *Jenghis Khan* (or more correctly, *Changis Ka,an*), in A.D. 1221.

[263] Seven *miskals* are more than an ounce and a quarter.

power of God; perhaps it may be the case; such rarities often fall into the hands of merchants and pilgrims. For these two [classes of people] go into every country, and they bring away with them whatever they find rare in [their travels]. It is most advisable for your majesty to order the *wazir* to be imprisoned, if he is as guilty [as you suppose]; for *wazirs* are the intelligencers of kings, and such conduct as this appears unhandsome in the latter, that in a case, the truth and falsehood of which is as yet unascertained, to order them to be put to death, and that the services and fidelity of a whole life should be forgotten.

"Mighty sire, former kings have erected prisons for this very reason, that when the kings or chiefs may be in wrath towards any one, then they might confine him. In a few days their anger will have entirely subsided, and [the suspected one's] innocence will become manifest, and the king will be exempt from the stain of shedding innocent blood, and not have to answer for it on the day of judgment." Though I wished ever so much to refute him, yet the ambassador of the Franks[264] gave such just replies, that he reduced me to silence. Then I said, well, I agree to what you say, and I pardon him his life. But he shall remain imprisoned; if in the space of a year his words are proved to be true, that such rubies are round the neck of a dog, then he shall be released; otherwise, he shall be put to death with many torments. I accordingly ordered the *wazir* to be carried to prison. On hearing this order, the ambassador made me his humble obeisance,[265] and performed his parting salute.

When this news reached the *wazir's* family, weeping and lamentations took place, and it became a house of mourning. The *wazir* had a daughter of the age of fourteen or fifteen years, very handsome and accomplished, perfect in writing and reading. The *wazir* loved her greatly, and was extremely fond of her; so much so, that he had erected an elegant apartment for her behind his own *diwan khana;* and had procured for her the daughters of noblemen as her companions, and handsome female servants waited on her; with these she passed her time in laughter and joy, and playing and romping about.

It happened that on the day the *wazir* was sent to prison, the girl was sitting with her young companions, and was celebrating with [infantile] pleasure the marriage of her doll; and with a small drum and timbrel she was making preparation for the night vigils; and having put on the frying pan, she was busy making up sweetmeats, when her mother suddenly ran into her apartment, lamenting and beating [her breasts], with dishevelled tresses and naked feet. She struck a blow on her daughter's head, and said, "Would that God had given me a blind son instead of thee; then my heart would have been at ease, and he would have been the friend of his father." The *wazir's* daughter asked, "What use would a blind son have been to you? whatever he could do, I can do likewise." The mother replied, "Dust be on thy head! such a calamity hath fallen on thy father, that he is confined in the prison for having used some improper expressions before the king." The daughter asked,

[264] The term Farang, vulgarly Frank, was formerly applied to Christian Europe in general, with the exclusion of Russia.

[265] Literally, "kissed the ground of obeisance," a Persian phrase, expressive of profound respect.

"What were the expressions? let me hear them." Then her mother answered, "Your father said that there is a merchant in *Nishapur*, who has fixed twelve inestimable rubies on his dog's collar: the king would not believe him, but conceived him a liar, and has imprisoned him. If he had had to-day a son, he would have exerted himself by every means to ascertain the truth of the circumstance; he would have assisted his father, besought the king's forgiveness, and have got my husband released from prison."

The *wazir's* daughter said [in reply], "O mother, we cannot combat against fate; man under sudden calamity ought to be patient, and place his hopes in the bounty of God. He is merciful, and does not hold any one's difficulties to be irremovables; weeping and lamentations are improper. God forbid that our enemies should misrepresent [the motive of our tears] to the king, and the teller of tales calumniate us, for that would be the cause of farther displeasure. On the contrary, let us offer up our prayers for the king's welfare; we are his born slaves, and he is our master; even as he is wroth, so will he be gracious." The girl, from her good sense, thus made her mother comprehend these things, so that she became somewhat patient and tranquil, and returned in silence to her palace. When the night arrived, the *wazir-zadi*[266] sent for her foster father, [or nurse's husband], and fell at his feet and beseeched him greatly, and weeping, said, "I have formed a resolution to wipe off the reproach my mother has cast on me, so that my father may regain his freedom. If you will be my companion, then I will set out for *Niashapur*, and having seen the merchant [who has such rubies round his dog's neck], I will do all in my power [to the end that] I may release my father."

The man indeed made some excuses at first; at length after much discussion, he agreed [to her request]. Then the *wazir-zadi* said, "Make the preparations for the Journey in secrecy and silence, and buy some articles of trade fit to be presented as offerings to kings, and procure as many slaves and servants as may be required; but do not let this circumstance be revealed to any one." The foster father agreed [to the project], and set about [the necessary] preparations. When all the materials were got ready, he loaded the camels and mules, and set out; the *wazir's* daughter also put on the dress of a man, and joined him. No one in the house knew anything whatever [of the departure]. When the morning came, it was mentioned in the *wazir's* family, that the *wazir-zadi*, had disappeared, and that it was uncertain where she was gone.

At last, the mother, from fear of scandal, concealed the circumstance of her daughter's disappearance; and there [on the journey] the *wazir-zadi* gave herself out as a "young merchant." Travelling onwards stage by stage, they arrived at *Naishapur*; and with great pleasure they went and put up at the *caravan-serai* and unloaded all their merchandise. The *wazir-zadi* I remained there that night; in the morning she went to the bath; and put on a rich dress, according to the costume of the inhabitants of *Rum*, and went out to ramble through the city. Proceeding along, she reached the *chauk*, and stood where the four great streets crossed each other; and a jeweller's shop appeared on one side, where a great deal of jewels were exposed [for sale], and slaves wearing rich dresses were in waiting, with crossed

[266] "The minister's daughter," afterwards called "the young merchant."

arms; and a man, who was their chief, of about fifty years[267] of age, dressed like rich persons in a short-sleeved jacket, was seated there, with many elegant companions near him, seated likewise on stools, and conversing among themselves.

The *wazir-zadi* (who had represented herself as a merchant's son,[268]) was greatly surprised at seeing the jeweller; and, on reflection, she became pleased in her own heart, saying, "God grant this be no delusion! it is most probable that this is the very merchant, the anecdote of whom my father mentioned to the king. O, great God, enlighten me as to his circumstances." It happened, that on looking around her, she saw a shop, in which two iron cages were suspended, and two men were confined in them. They looked like *majnun* in appearance, only skin and bones remained; the hair of their heads and their nails were quite overgrown, and they sat with their heads reclined on their breasts; two ugly negroes, completely armed, were standing on each side [of the cages]. The young merchant was struck with amazement, and exclaimed, "God bless us." When she looked round the other way, she saw another shop, where carpets were spread, on which an ivory stool was placed, with a velvet cushion, and a dog sat thereon, with a collar set with precious stones around his neck, and chained by a chain of gold; and two young handsome servants waited on the dog. One was shaking [over him] a *morchhal*[269] with a golden handle, set with precious stones, and the other held an embroidered handkerchief in his hand, with which he [from time to time] wiped the dog's mouth and feet. The young merchant, having looked at the animal with great attention, perceived on its collar the twelve large rubies, as she had heard [them described]. She praised God, and began to consider thus: "By what means can I carry those rubies to the king, and show them to him, and get my father released?" She was plunged in these perplexing reflections; meanwhile, all the people in the square and on the road, seeing her beauty and comeliness, were struck with astonishment, and remained utterly confounded. All the people said one to another, "Even unto this day, we have never seen a human being of this form and beauty." The *khwaja*[270] also perceived her, and sent a slave, saying, "Go thou and entreat that young merchant to come to me."

The slave went up to her and delivered his master's message, and said, "If you will have the kindness, then my master is desirous of [seeing] your honour; pray

[267] The phrase *pachas ek* means "about fifty." It is strange that a certain critic on this work, (who has a prodigiously high opinion of himself,) should have rendered the above passage, "whose age was about forty or fifty years!" Most assuredly, the merest tyro in *Hindustani* can tell him that it cannot have such a latitude as to mean "about forty or fifty." He might just as correctly have said "about fifty or sixty." The phrase *pachas ek*, as I have stated, means simply "about fifty," i.e., it may be *one* year more or less.

[268] In the text, the *wazir-zadi* is henceforth called *saudagar-bacha* or the young merchant, being the character under which she, for some time, figures.

[269] *Morchhals*, vulgarly called *chowrees*, are fly-flaps, to drive away those troublesome companions; the best kind is made of the fine white long tail of the mountain cow; the others of the long feathers from, the peacock's tail, or the odoriferous roots of a species of grass called *Khas*. They are likewise a part of the paraphernalia of state in India.

[270] The title *khwaja* means "chief," or "master;" it is generally applied to rich merchants, &c., such as we would call "men of respectability." The idiomatic London English for it is "governor," or (as it is pronounced) "guv'ner".

come and have an interview with him." The young merchant indeed wished this very thing, and said in reply, "Very well."[271] The moment she came near the *khwaja*, and he had a full view of her, the dart of attachment pierced his breast; he rose up to receive her respectfully, but his senses were utterly bewildered. The young merchant perceived that "now he is entangled in the net" [of my charms]. They mutually embraced one another; the *khwaja* kissed the young merchant's forehead, and made him sit down near him; and asked with much kindness, "inform me of your name and lineage? whence have you come, and where do you intend to go?" The young merchant replied, "This humble servant's country is *Rum*, and Constantinople has been for ages the birth-place [of my ancestors.] My father is a merchant; and as he is now from old age unable to travel [from country to country on his mercantile concerns] on this account he has sent me abroad to learn the affairs of commerce. Until now I had not put my foot out of our door; this is the very first journey that has occurred to me. I had not courage[272] to come here by sea, I therefore travelled by land; but your excellence and good name is so renowned in this country of *'Ajam*[273] that to have the pleasure only of meeting you I have come so far. At last, by the favour of God, I have had the honour of [sitting in] your noble presence, and have found your good qualities exceed your renown; the wish of my heart is accomplished; God preserve you in safety, I will now set out from hence."

On hearing these [last words], the *khwaja's* mind and senses were quite discomposed, and he exclaimed, "O, my son, do not speak to me of such a thing;" stay some days with me in my humble abode; pray tell me where are your goods, and your servants?" The young merchant replied, "The traveller's abode is the *sara,e*;[274] leaving them there, I came to see you." The *khwaja* said, "It is unbecoming [a person of your consideration] to dwell in the *sara,e* I have some reputation in this city, and much celebrity; send quickly for your baggage, &c.; I will prepare a house for your goods; let me see whatever commodities you have brought; I will so manage it, that you will get here great profit on them. At the same time, you will be at your ease, and saved the danger and fatigue [of travelling any farther for a market], and by staying with me a few days you will greatly oblige me." The young merchant pretended[275] to make some excuses, but the *khwaja* would not accept them, and ordered one of his agents, saying, "Send quickly some burden-bearers, and bring

[271] Literally, "What difficulty" (is there in so doing).

[272] The city of *Naishapur* being some 270 miles inland, it would not be easy for the young merchant to reach it by sea. Asiatic story-tellers are not at all particular in regard to matters of geography.

[273] *'Ajam* means, in general, Persia; the Arabs use it in the same sense as the Greeks did the word "barbarian;" and all who are not Arabs they call *'Ajami*; more especially the Persians.

[274] *Sara,e, sera,i* or *caravanserai*, are buildings for the accommodation of travellers, merchants, &c., in cities, and on the great roads in Asia. Those in Upper *Hindustan*, built by the emperors of *Dilli*, are grand and costly; they are either of stone or burnt bricks. In Persia, they are mostly of bricks dried in the sun. In Upper *Hindustan* they are commonly sixteen to twenty miles distant from each other, which is a *manzil* or stage. They are generally built of a square or quadrangular form with a large open court in the centre, and contain numerous rooms for goods, men, and beasts.

[275] Literally, made excuses from the surface of his heart," i.e., not serious excuses.

the goods, &c., from the *caravanserai* and lodge them in such a place."

The young merchant likewise sent a slave of his own with [the agent] to bring the property and merchandise; and he himself remained with the *khwaja* until the evening. When the time of [the afternoon] market had elapsed, and the shop was shut, the *khwaja* went towards his house. Then one of the two slaves took the dog up under his arm, and the other took up the stool and carpet; and the two negro slaves placed the two cages on the heads of porters, and they themselves, accoutred with the five weapons,[276] went alongside of them. The *khwaja* took hold of the young merchant's hand, and conversing with him, reached his house.

The young merchant saw that the house was grand, and fit for kings or nobles [to reside in]. Carpets were spread on the border of a rivulet, and before the *masnad* the different articles for the entertainment were laid out. The dog's stool was placed there also, and the *khwaja* and young merchant took their seats; he presented to him some wine without ceremony; they both began to drink. When they got merry, the *khwaja* called for dinner; the *dastar-khwan*[277] was spread, and the good things of the world were laid out. First they put some meat in a dish, and having covered it with a cover of gold, they carried it to the dog, and having spread an embroidered *dastar-khwan*, they laid the dish before him. The dog descended from his stool, ate as much as he liked, and drank some water out of a golden bowl, then returned and sat on his stool. The slaves wiped his mouth and feet with a napkin, and then carried the dish and bowl to the two cages, and having asked for the keys from the *khwaja,* they opened the locks.

They took out the two men [who were confined in the cages], gave them many blows with a great stick, and made them eat the leavings of the dog and drink the same water; they again fastened the doors [of the cages] and returned the keys to their master. When all this was over, the *khwaja* began to eat himself. The young merchant was not pleased at these circumstances, and did not touch the victuals from disgust. How much soever the *khwaja* pressed him, yet he flatly refused. Then the *khwaja* asked the reason of this, saying, "Why do you not eat?" The young merchant replied, "This conduct of yours appears disgusting to me, for this reason that man is the noblest of God's creatures, and the dog is decidedly impure. So to make two of God's own creatures eat the leavings of a dog, in what religion or creed is it lawful? Do not you think it sufficient that they are your prisoners? otherwise they and you are equal. Now, I doubt if you are a *Musulman*; who knows what you are? Perhaps you worship the dog; it is disgusting to me to eat your dinner, until this doubt is removed from my mind."

The *khwaja* answered, "O, son, I comprehend perfectly all that you say, and am generally censured for these reasons; for the inhabitants of this city have fixed upon me the name of dog-worshipper, and call me so, and have published it [everywhere]; but may the curse of God alight on the impious and the infidel!" The *khwaja* then repeated the *kalima,*[278] and set the young merchant's mind at ease. Then the young merchant asked, thus, "If you are really a *Musalman* in your heart,

[276] That is, "completely armed." Vide note 187, page 45.

[277] On the exact meaning of *dastar-khwan,* see note 205, page 54.

[278] The *Musalman* confession of faith, see note 230, page 65.

then what is the reason of this? By so acting, get yourself generally censured?" The *khwaja* said in reply, "O, son, my name is reprobated, and I pay double taxes in the city, that no one may know this secret [motive of my conduct]. It is a strange circumstance, which, whoever hears, will get nothing by the recital but grief and indignation. You must likewise pardon me [from relating it]; for I shall not have strength of mind to recount it, nor will you have the composure of mind to listen to it." The young merchant thought within himself, "I have only to mind my own business; why should I to no purpose press him further on the subject?" She accordingly replied to the *khwaja*, "Very well; if it is not proper to be related, do not mention it." He then began to partake of the dinner, and having lifted a morsel, began to eat. The space of about two months[279] the young merchant passed with the *khwaja*, with such prudence and circumspection, that no one found out by any chance that he was a woman [in disguise]. All thought that this [individual] was a male, and the *khwaja's* affection for him increased daily, so that he could not allow him to be a moment absent from his sight.

One day, in the midst of a drinking feat, the young merchant began to weep. On seeing it, the *khwaja* comforted her, and began to wipe away his tears with his handkerchief, and asked him the cause of his weeping. He answered, "O, father, what shall I say? would to God that I had never attained access to your presence, and that your worship had never shown me that kindness which you are shewing. I am now distressed between two difficulties; I have no heart to be separated from your presence, nor is there a possibility of my staying here. Now, it is necessary for me to go; but in separating from you, I do not perceive hopes of life."

On hearing these words, the *khwaja* involuntarily wept so loudly, that he was nearly choked, and exclaimed, "O, light of my eyes! are you so soon tired of your old friend, that you think of going away and leaving him in such affliction? banish from your heart the idea of departing; as long as I have to live, remain here; I shall not live a day in your absence, and must [in such case] die before my appointed hour. The climate of this kingdom of Persia is very fine and congenial [to your health], you had best despatch a confidential servant, and send for your parents and property here; I will furnish whatever equipages and conveyances you require; when your parents and all their household come here, you can pursue your commercial concerns at your ease. I also have in my life gone through many hardships, and have wandered many countries. I am now old and have no issue; I love you dearer than a son, and make you my heir and head manager. Be you, on the other hand, careful and attentive to my concerns. Give me a bit of bread to eat whilst I live; when I die, be pleased to bury me, and then take [possession of] all my wealth and effects."

To this the young merchant replied, "It is true, you have, more than a father, shewn to me kindness and affection, so that I have forgotten my parents; but this humble culprit's father only allowed a year's leave; if I exceed it, then he in his extreme old age will weep himself to death; finally, a father's approbation is meritorious before God, and if mine should be displeased with me, then I fear he may

[279] The idiom *"do mahine ek,"* about two months, similar to the phrase, *"pachas ek baras," v.* note 269, page 83.

curse me, and I shall be an outcast from God's grace in this world and the next. Now such is your worship's kindness, that you will give me leave to obey my father's commands, and fulfil the duties [of a son] towards a parent; I shall, while life lasts, bear on my neck the gratitude I owe for your kindness. If I am ever [so fortunate as] to reach my native country, I will still ever think of your goodness with my heart and soul. God is the Causer of causes; perhaps some such cause may again occur, that I may have occasion to pay you my respects. In short, the young merchant urged such persuasive and feeling arguments to the *khwaja*, that he, poor man, being helpless, yielded to their force.[280] Inasmuch as he was now completely fascinated, he began to say in reply, "Well, if you will not stay here, I will myself go with you. I consider you equivalent to my own life: hence, if my life goes with you, of what use is a lifeless body? If you are determined to go, then proceed, and take me with you." Saying this to the young merchant, he began his preparations likewise for the journey, and gave orders to his agents to get ready quickly the necessary conveyances.

When the news of the *khwaja's* departure became public, the merchants of that city on hearing it, began likewise their preparations to set out with him. The dog-worshipping *khwaja* took with him specie and jewels to a great amount, servants and slaves without number, and rich rarities and property worthy of a king, and having pitched his tents of various sorts outside of the city, he went to them. All the other merchants took articles of merchandise with them according to their means, and joined the *khwaja;* they became for themselves a [regular] army.

One day, having fixed on a lucky moment for departure, they set out thence on their journey. Having laden thousands of camels with canvas sacks filled with goods, and the jewels and specie on mules, five hundred slaves from the steppes of *Kapchak*, from *Zang*, and from *Rum*,[281] completely armed, men used to the sword, mounted on horses of Arabia, of Tartary, and of *Irak*, accompanied [the caravan]. In the rear of all came the *khwaja* and the young merchant, richly dressed, and mounted on sedans; a rich litter was lashed on the back of a camel, in which the dog reposed on a cushion, and the cages of the two prisoners were slung one on each side of another, across a camel, and thus they marched onwards. At every stage they came to, all the merchants waited on the *khwaja* and on his *dastar-khwan* they ate of his food and drank of his wine. The *khwaja* offered up his grateful thanks to the Almighty for the happiness of having the young merchant with him, and proceeded on, stage by stage. At last, they reached the environs of Constantinople in perfect safety, and encamped without the city. The young merchant said [to the *khwaja*], "O, father, if you grant me permission, I will go and see my parents, and prepare a house for you, and when it is agreeable to you, you will be pleased to enter the city."

The *khwaja* replied, "I am come so far for your sake, well, go quickly and see [your parents], and return to me, and give me a place to live in near your own." The young merchant having taken leave [of the *khwaja*], came to his own house. All the people of the household of the *wazir* were surprised, and exclaimed, "What

[280] Literally, "began to smack his lips;" denoting his satisfaction.

[281] Tartar, African, and Turkish slaves.

man has entered [the house]!" The young merchant, that is, the *wazir's* daughter, ran and threw herself at her mother's feet, and wept and said, "I am your child." On hearing this, the *wazir's* wife began to reproach her, by saying, "O, wanton girl, thou hast greatly dishonoured thyself; thou hast blackened thine own face, and brought shame on thy family; we had imagined thee lost, and, after weeping for thee, had with resignation given thee up; be gone hence."

Then the *wazir-zadi* threw the turban off her head and said, "O, dear mother, I did not go to an improper place, and have done nothing wrong; I have contrived the whole of this scheme according to your wishes to release my father from prison. God be praised, that through the good effect of your prayers, and through His grace, I, having accomplished the entire object, am now returned; I have brought that merchant with me from *Naishapur,* along with the dog (around whose neck are those rubies), and have returned with the innocence you bestowed[282] on me. I assumed the appearance of a man for the journey; now one day's work remains; having done that, I will get my father released from prison, and return to my home; if you give me leave, I will go back again, and remain abroad another day, and then return to you." When the mother thoroughly comprehended that her daughter had acted the part of a man, and had preserved herself in all respects pure and virtuous, she offered up her grateful acknowledgments to God, and, rejoicing [at the event], clasped her daughter to her bosom and kissed her lips; she prayed for her and blessed her, and gave her leave to go, saying, "Do what thou thinkest best, I have full confidence in thee."

The *wazir-zadi* having again assumed the appearance of a man, returned to the dog-worshipping *khwaja.* He had been in the meantime so much distressed at her absence, that through impatience he had left his encampment. It so happened, that as the young merchant was going out in the vicinity of the city, the *khwaja* was coming from the opposite direction; they met each other in the middle of the road. On seeing him, the *khwaja* exclaimed, "O, my child! leaving this old man by himself, where wast thou gone?" The young merchant answered, "I went to my house with your permission, but the desire I had to see you again would not allow me to remain [at home], and I am returned to you." They perceived a shady garden close to the gate of the city on the sea shore; they pitched their tents and alighted there. The *khwaja* and the young merchant sat down together, and began to eat their *kababs,* and drink their wine. When the time of evening arrived, they left their tents, and sat out on high seats to view the country. It happened that a royal chasseur passed that way; he was astonished at seeing their manners and their encampment, and said to himself, "Perhaps the ambassador of some king is arrived;" he stood [and amused himself by] looking on.

One of the *khwaja's* messengers called him forward, and asked him who he was. He replied, "I am the king's head chasseur." The messenger mentioned him to the *khwaja,* who ordered a negro slave, saying, "Go and tell the chasseur that we are travellers, and if he feels inclined to come and sit down, the coffee and pipe are ready."[283] When the chasseur heard the name of merchant, he was still more

[282] Literally, "I have not proved false in what you have entrusted to me."

[283] The coffee and pipe are always presented to visitors in Turkey, Arabia, and Persia,

astonished, and came with the slave to the *khwaja's* presence; he saw [on all sides] the air of propriety and magnificence, and soldiers and slaves. To the *khwaja* and the young merchant he made his salutations, and on seeing the dog's state and treatment, his senses were confounded, and he stood like one amazed. The *khwaja* asked him to sit down, and presented him coffee; the chasseur asked the *khwaja's* name and designation. When he requested leave to depart, the *khwaja* having presented him with some pieces [of cloth] and sundry rarities, dismissed him. In the morning, when the chasseur attended the king's audience, he related to those present the circumstances of the *khwaja*; by degrees it came to my knowledge; I called the chasseur before me, and asked about the merchant.

He related whatever he had seen. On hearing of the dog's exalted state, and the two men's confinement in the cage, I was quite indignant, and exclaimed, that reprobate of a merchant deserves death! I ordered some of my executioners, saying, "Go immediately, and cut off and bring me the heretic's head." By chance, the same ambassador of the Franks was present at the audience; he smiled, and I became still more angry, and said, "O, disrespectful; to display one's teeth[284] without cause in the presence of kings, is remote from good manners; it is better to weep than laugh out of season." The ambassador replied, "Mighty sire, several ideas came across my mind, for which reason I smiled; the first was, that the *wazir* had spoken truth, and would now be released from prison; secondly, that your majesty will be unstained with the innocent blood of the *wazir*; and the third was, that the asylum of the universe, without cause or crime, ordered the merchant to be put to death. At all these circumstances I was surprised, that without any inquiry your majesty should, on the tale of an idle fellow, order people to be put to death. God in reality knows what is the merchant's real case; call him before the royal presence and inquire into his antecedents; if he should be found guilty, then your majesty is master; whatever treatment you please, that you can administer to him.

When the ambassador thus explained [the matter to me], I also recollected what the *wazir* had said, and ordered the merchant, together with his son, the dog, and the cages, to be brought in my presence immediately. The messengers set off quickly [on the errand], and in a short time brought them all. I summoned them before me. First came the *khwaja* and his son [the young merchant], both richly dressed. All present were astonished and bewildered on beholding the young merchant's extreme beauty; he brought in his hand a golden tray, loaded with precious stones, (the brilliancy of every one of which illuminated the room,) and laid it before my throne, made his obeisance and stood [in respectful silence]. The *khwaja* also kissed the ground, and offered up his prayers [for my prosperity]; he spoke with such sweet modulation, as if he were the nightingale of a thousand melodies. I greatly admired his elegant and decorous speech; but, assuming a face of anger, I exclaimed, "O, you Satan in human form! what net is this that thou hast spread, and in thine own path what pit hast thou dug? What is thy religion, and what rite is this I see? Of what prophet's sect are thou a follower? If thou wast an

and they are considered as indispensable in good manners.

[284] "*Dant kholne*" is fully explained in my Grammar, page 129. It appears to have sadly puzzled a learned critic, to whom I have occasionally alluded.

infidel, even then what sense is there in thy conduct? what is thy name, that thou actest thus?

The *khwaja* calmly replied, "May your majesty's years and prosperity ever increase; this slave's religious creed is this, that God is one: he has no equal, and I repeat the confession of faith of *Muhammad* the pure (the mercy of God be shown to him and his posterity; may he be safe!) After him, I consider the twelve *Imams* as my guides; and my rite is this, that I say the five regulated prayers and I observe fasts, and I have likewise performed the pilgrimage, and from my wealth, I give the fifth in alms, and I am called a *Musalman*. But there is a reason, which I cannot disclose, that I appear to possess all those bad qualities which have raised your majesty's indignation, and for which I am condemned by every one of God's creatures. Though I am [ever so much] called a dog-worshipper, and pay double taxes, all this I submit to; but the secrets of my heart I have not divulged to any one." On hearing this excuse, my anger became greater, and I said, thou art beguiling me with words; I will not believe them until thou explainest clearly the reasons which have made thee deviate from the right path, that my mind may be convinced of their truth; then thy life will be saved; or else, as a retribution [for what thou hast done], I will order thy belly to be ripped up, that the exemplary punishment may deter others in future from transgressing the religion of *Muhammad*.

The *khwaja* replied, "O king, do not spill the blood of this unfortunate wretch, but confiscate all the wealth I have, which is beyond counting or reckoning, and having made me and my son a votive offering to your throne, release us, and spare us our lives." I smiled, and said, O fool! dost thou exhibit to me the temptation of thy wealth? Thou canst not be released, except thou speakest the truth. On hearing these words, the tears streamed profusely from the *khwaja's* eyes; he looked towards his son and heaved a deep sigh, and said [to him] "I am criminal in the king's eyes; I shall be put to death; what shall I do now? to whom shall I entrust thee?" I threatened him, and said, O dissembler! cease; thou hast made too many excuses [already]; what thou hast to say, say it [quickly].

Then, indeed, that man having advanced forward, came near the throne and kissed the foot of it, and poured forth my praise and eulogy, and said, "O king of kings, if the order for execution had not been issued in my case, I would have borne every torture, and would not have disclosed my story; but life is dear above every [consideration]; no one of his own accord jumps into a well; to preserve life, then, is right; and the abandoning of what is right is contrary to the mandates of God. Well, if such is the royal pleasure, then be pleased to hear the past events of this feeble old man. First, order the two cages, in which the two men are confined, to be brought and placed before your majesty. I am going to relate my adventures; if I falsify any circumstance, then ask them to convict me, and let justice be done." I approved of his proposal and sent for the cages, took them both out, and made them stand near the *khwaja*.

The *khwaja* said, "O king! this man, who stands on the right hand of your slave is my eldest brother, and he who stands on my left is my second[285] brother. I am

[285] Literally, "middle brother;" as there were three in number, of course the "second" and "middle" are identical.

younger than they; my father was a merchant in the kingdom of Persia, and when I was fourteen years of age, he died. After the burial ceremony was over, and the flowers had been removed [from the corpse on the *Siyum*],[286] my two brothers said to me one day, 'Let us now divide our father's wealth, whatever there is, and let each do [with his share] what he pleases.' On hearing [this proposal], I said, O brothers! what words are these! I am your slave, and do not claim the rights of a brother. Our father, on the one hand, is dead, but you both are alive and in the place of that father. I only want a dry loaf [daily] to pass through life, and to remain alert in your service. What have I to do with shares or divisions? I will fill my belly with your leavings, and remain near you. I am a boy, and have not learnt even to read or write? what am I able to do? At present do you confer instruction upon me.

"On hearing this, they replied, 'Thou wishest to ruin and beggar us also along with thyself.' I was silent, and retired to a corner and wept; then I reasoned with myself and said, my brothers, after all, are my elders; they are reproving [me for my good, and] with a view to my education, that I may learn some [profession]. In these reflections I fell asleep. In the morning, a messenger from the *kazi* came and conducted me to the court of justice; I saw that both my brothers were there in waiting. The *kazi* asked me, 'Why dost not thou accept thy share of thy father's property?' I repeated to him what I had at home said [to my brothers]. The latter said, 'If he speaks this sentiment from his heart, then let him give us a deed of release, saying he has no claims on our father's wealth and property.' Even then I thought, that as they both were my elders, they advised for my good; that if I got my share of my father's property I might improperly spend it. So, according to their desire, I gave them a deed of release, with the *kazi's* seal. They were satisfied, and I returned home.

"The second day after this, they said to me, 'O brother, we require the apartment in which you live; do you hire another place for your residence, and go and stay there.' 'Twas then I perceived that they were not pleased that I should even remain in my father's house; I had no remedy, and determined to leave it. O protector of the world! when my father was alive, whenever he returned from his travels, he used to bring the rarities of different countries, and give them to me by way of presents; for this reason, that every one loves most the youngest child. I from time to time sold these [presents], and raised a small capital of my own; with this [sum] I carried on some traffic. Once, my father brought for me a female slave from Tartary, and he once brought thence some horses, from which he gave me also a promising young colt; and I used to feed it from my own little property.

"At last, seeing the inhumanity of my brothers, I bought a house, and went and resided there; this dog also went along with me. I purchased the requisite articles for housekeeping, and bought two slaves for attendance; with the remainder of my capital I opened a shop as a cloth merchant, and placing my confidence in God, I sat down quietly [in it], and felt contented with my fate. Though my brothers had behaved unkindly to me, yet, since God was gracious, my shop in three years' time

[286] The *Siyum* are the rites performed for the dead on the third day after demise; it is called the *tija* in *Hinduwi*.

increased so greatly, that I became a man of credit. Whatever rarities [in the way of clothes or dresses] were required in every great family, went from my shop only. I thereby earned large sums of money, and began to live in affluent circumstances. Every hour I offered up my prayers to the pure God, and lived at my ease; and often used to repeat these verses on my [prosperous] circumstances:—

'Why should not the prince be displeased?
I have nothing to do with him.
Except thyself, O, mighty Prince,[287]
What other [sovereign] can I praise?
Why should not my brother be displeased?
Nothing can he do [to harm me];
Thou alone art my help;
Then to whom else should I go?
Why should not the friend or foe be displeas'd,
During the whole [eight] watches,
Let me fix my affections on thy feet only.
Let the world be wrathful [with me],
But thou dost far transcend [the world];
All others may kiss my thumb,
Only it is my wish that thou be not displeased.'

"It happened, that on a Friday I was sitting at home, when a slave of mine had gone to the *bazar* for necessaries; after a short time, he returned in tears. I asked him the reason, and what happened to him. He replied with anger, 'What business is it to you? do you enjoy yourself; but what answer will you give on the day of judgment?' I said, O, you Abyssinian, what demon has possessed thee? He answered, 'This is the calamity, that the arms of your two elder brothers have been tied behind their backs in the *chauk* by a Jew; he is beating them with a whip, and laughs and says, 'If you do not pay my money, I will beat you even unto the death [and if I lose my money by the act], it will be at least a meritorious deed on my part.' Such is your brother's treatment, and you are indifferent; is this right? and what will the world say?' On hearing these circumstances from the slave, my blood glowed[288] [with fraternal warmth]; I ran towards the *chauk* with naked feet, and told my slaves to hasten with money. The instant I arrived there, I saw that all that the slave had said was true; blows continued to fall on my brothers. I exclaimed to the magistrate's guards, for God's sake forbear awhile; let me ask the Jew what great fault [my brothers] have committed, in retaliation for which, he so severely punishes them.

"On saying this, I went up to the Jew and said, to-day is the sabbath day;[289] why dost thou continue to inflict stripes on them? The Jew replied, 'If you wish to take their part, do it fully, and pay me the money in their stead; or else take the road to your house.' I said, 'what is the amount? produce the bond, and I will count thee out the money.' He replied, 'that he had just given the bond to the mag-

[287] Alluding to God.

[288] Or it may mean, "my blood boiled" [with resentment].

[289] The *Muhammadan* sabbath is Friday.

istrate.' At this moment, my slaves brought two bags of money. I gave a thousand pieces of silver to the Jew, and released my brothers. Such was their condition, naked, hungry, and thirsty, I brought them with me to my own house, and caused them instantly to be bathed in the bath, and dressed in new clothes, and gave them a hearty meal. I never asked them what they had done with our father's great wealth, lest they might feel ashamed.

"O king, they are both present; ask them if I tell truth, or falsify any of the circumstances. Well, after some space of time, when they had recovered from the bruises of the beating [they had suffered], I said to them one day, 'O brothers, you have now lost your credit in this city, and it is better you should travel for some days.' On hearing this, they were both silent; but I perceived they were satisfied [with my proposal]. I began to make preparations for their journey, and having procured tents and all necessary conveyance, I purchased for them merchandise to the amount of 20,000 rupees. A *kafila*[290] of merchants was going to *Bukhara*;[291] I sent them along with it.

"After a year, that caravan returned, but I heard no tidings of my brothers; at last, putting a friend on his oath, I asked him [what had become of them]. He replied, 'When they went to *Bukhara*, one of them lost all his property at the gambling house, and is now a sweeper at the same house, and keeps clean and plastered the place of gambling, and waits on the gamblers who assemble there; they, by way of charity, give him something, and he remains there as a scullion. The other brother became enamoured of a *boza-vendor's*[292] daughter, and squandered all his property [on her], and now he is one of the waiters at the *boze-khana*.[293] The people of the *kafila* do not mention these circumstances to you for this reason, that you would become ashamed [at hearing them].

"On hearing these circumstances from that person, I was in a strange state; hunger and sleep vanished through anxiety; taking some money for [the expenses of] the road, I set out instantly for *Bukhara*. When I arrived there, I searched for them both, and I brought them to the house [I had taken]. I had them bathed and clothed in new dresses, and, from fear of their being abashed with shame, I said not a word to them [of what had happened]. I again purchased some goods for merchandise for them, and returned with them home. When we arrived near *Naishapur*, I left them in a village with all the goods and chattels, and came [secretly] to my house, for this reason, that no one might be informed of my return. After

[290] A *kafila* means a company of merchants who assemble and travel together for mutual protection. It is synonymous with caravan.

[291] *Bukhara* is a celebrated city in Tartary; it was formerly the capital of the province called *Mawaralnahr*, or *Transoxiana*, before the Tartar conquerors fixed on *Samarkand*. It lies to the northward of the river *Oxus* or *Gihun*, which divides Tartary from Persia, or as the Persian geographers term it, *Iran*, from *Turan*. *Bukhara* is celebrated by Persian poets for its climate, its fruits, and its beautiful women.

[292] The *boza* is an intoxicating drink made of spirits, the leaves of the *charas* plant, *tari*, and opium. *Tari*, erroneously called *todee*, is the juice of the palm tree.

[293] Literally, ale-house, or tippling-house. One is strongly led to believe that this is the origin of our cant word *boozing-ken*, imported from the East by the gipsies some four or five centuries ago.

two days, I gave out publicly that my brothers were returned from their journey, and that I would go out tomorrow to meet them. In the morning, as I wished to set out, a peasant of that village came to me, and began to make loud complaints; on hearing his voice I came out, and seeing him crying, I asked, why dost thou make a lamentation? He answered, 'Our houses have been plundered, owing to your brothers; would to God that you had not left them there!'

"I asked, what misfortune has occurred? He replied, 'A gang of robbers came at night and plundered their property and goods, and they at the same time robbed our houses.' I pitied him, and asked, where are these two now? He answered, 'They are sitting without the city, stark naked and utterly distressed.' I instantly took two suits of clothes with me and went [to them], and having clothed them, brought them to my house. The people [of the city], hearing [the circumstances of the robbery], continued coming to see them, but they did not go out through shame. Three months passed in this same manner; at last I reflected within myself, 'how long will they thus remain squatted in a corner? If it can be brought about, I will take them with me on some voyage.'

"I proposed it to my brothers, and added, 'if you please, I will go with you.' They were silent. I again made the necessary preparations for the voyage, purchased some goods for the trade, and set out and took them with me. After I had distributed the customary alms [for a prosperous voyage], and loaded the merchandise on the ship, we weighed anchor, and the vessel set sail. This dog was sleeping on the banks [of the river]; when he awoke, and saw the ship in the middle of the stream, he was surprised, and having barked and jumped into the river, he began to swim [after us]. I sent a skiff for him, at last having seized [the faithful animal], they conveyed him into the ship. One month passed in safety on the river; somehow, my second brother became enamoured of my slave girl. One day, he thus spoke to our eldest brother, that, 'to bear the load of our younger brother's favours is very shameful; what remedy shall we apply to this [evil]?' The eldest answered, 'I have formed a plan in my mind; if it can be executed, it will be a great thing.' Both at last consulted together, and settled it between them to destroy me, and seize all my property and goods.

"One day, I was asleep in the cabin, and the female slave was *shampooing*[294] me, when my second brother came in hastily and awaked me. I started up in a hurry, and came forth [on deck]. This dog also followed me. I saw my eldest brother leaning on his hands against the vessel's side, and intensely looking at the wonders of the river, and calling out to me. I went up to him and said, 'is all well?' He answered, 'Behold this strange sight; mermen are dancing in the stream, with pearl, oysters, and branches of coral in their hands.' If any other had related this circumstance so contrary to reason, I should not, indeed, have believed it. I imagined what my brother said to be true, and bent down my head to look at it. How much soever I looked, I perceived nothing, and he kept saying, 'Do you now see

[294] A grateful and luxurious operation in the warm climate of India, more especially after the fatigue of travelling. *Shampooing* is a word of uncertain etymology; the French have a better term, *masser*. The natives say it has a physical advantage, as it quickens their languid circulation; perhaps they are right.

it?' Now, had there been anything, I should have seen it. Perceiving me [by this trick] off my guard, my second brother came behind me, unperceived, and gave me such a push that, without choice, I tumbled into the water, and they began to scream and cry aloud, 'Run, run, our brother has fallen into the river.'

"In the meantime the ship went on, and the waves carried me away from it; I was plunging in the water, and drifting amidst the waves. I became at last quite exhausted; I invoked the aid of God, but nought was of any avail. All of a sudden my hand touched something; I looked at it, and saw this dog. Perhaps, when they pushed me into the river, he also jumped after me, and kept swimming close by my side. I took hold of his tail, and God made him the cause of my salvation. Seven days and nights passed in this manner; the eighth day we reached the shore. I had no strength whatever left, but throwing myself on my back, I rolled along as well as I could, and threw myself on the land. I remained senseless for one whole day; the second day the dog's barking reached my ears; I came to myself, and I thanked God [for my salvation], I began looking around me, and perceived at a distance the environs of a city; but where had I strength, that I should attempt to reach it? Having no other resource, I continued crawling along about two paces, and then rested; in this way I had finished a *kos*[295] of the road by the evening.

"Half way [to the city] I reached a mountain, and lay there all night; the next morning I reached the city; when I came to the *bazar* and saw the shops of the bakers and confectioners, my heart began to palpitate, for I had not money to buy, nor did I feel inclined to beg. In this way, I went along, saying to myself, I will ask something in the next shop. At last, strength had failed me, and my stomach[296] yearned with extreme hunger; life was nearly quitting my body. By chance, I saw two young men dressed like Persians, walking along hand in hand. On seeing them, my spirits revived, as they seemed [by their dress] to be my countrymen—perhaps some of my acquaintance—to whom, therefore, I might relate my circumstances. When they drew near, [I perceived] they were of a verity, my brothers; and on perceiving this, I was extremely rejoiced, and praised God, saying, 'God has preserved my reputation; and I have not stretched forth my hands to strangers [for subsistence].' I went up to them and saluted them, and kissed my eldest brother's hand. Immediately on seeing me, they made a great noise, and my second brother struck me so forcibly that I staggered and fell down. I seized my eldest brother's robe, thinking that he would perhaps take my part; but he gave me a violent kick.

"In short, they both thoroughly pounded me, and behaved to me as Joseph's brothers [did to him]. Though I besought them in God's name [to desist] and implored mercy, yet they felt no pity. A crowd assembled [round us]; and every one asked, 'What is this man's crime?' Then my brothers replied, 'This rascal was our brother's servant and pushed him over into the sea, and seized all his treasure and property. We have been long in search of him, and to-day he has appeared [to us] in this guise.' They then continued questioning me, saying, 'O villain! what [infernal idea] entered thy mind, that thou murderedst our brother? What injury had he

[295] A *kos* is nearly two English miles, being about fifteen furlongs.

[296] Literally, "the fire was kindled in my stomach."

done to thee? Had he behaved ill to thee, that he had made thee superintendent [of his affairs]?' They both then tore their own clothes, and wept loudly with sham grief for their brother, and continued to beat and kick me.

"In the meantime, the soldiers of the governor arrived, and having spoken to them threateningly, said, 'Why do you beat him?' And taking hold of my hand, they carried me to the magistrate. These two[297] also went with us, and repeated to the magistrate the same [tale which they had told the crowd], and having given him something by way of bribe, they demanded justice, and insisted on blood for blood. The magistrate asked me [what I had to say for myself]. Such was my condition from hunger and the blows [I had received], that I had not strength to speak; hanging down my head, I remained standing [in silence]; no answer issued from my mouth. The magistrate also became convinced that I was assuredly a murderer; he ordered me to be led to the plain, and placed on the stake.[298] O, protector of the world,[299] I had paid money, and got these [two here] released from the Jew's bondage; in return for which, they having given money, endeavoured to take away my life. They are both present; ask them if [in all I have related] I have varied a hair's breadth [from the truth]. Well, they led me out [to the plain]; when I saw the stake, I washed my hands of life.

"Except this dog, I had no one else to weep for me; his state was such that he rolled on every one's feet and barked. Some beat him with sticks, and others with stones, but he would not stir from that place. I stood with my face towards the *kibla,*[300] and addressing myself to God, I said, 'At this moment I have no one except Thee to intervene and save the innocent! Now, if Thou savest, I am saved.' After this address, I repeated the prayer of *shahadat,*[301] staggered, and then fell. By the dispensation of God, it so happened, that the king of that country was attacked with the cholic; the nobles and physicians assembled; whatever remedies they applied, produced no good. One holy man said, 'The best of all remedies is, that alms be given to the destitute, and that all prisoners should be released; for in prayer there is greater efficacy than in physic.' Instantly the royal messengers went off running towards the prisons.

"By chance, some one came to that plain [where I was], and seeing a crowd, he ascertained [from a bystander] that they were placing some person on the stake. Immediately on hearing this, he galloped up to the stake, and cut the ropes with his sword. He threatened and chastised the magistrate's soldiers, and said, "At such a time, when the king is in such a state, are you going to put a creature of God to death?' and he got me released. Upon which, these two brothers went again to

[297] Pointing to his two brothers who were present, and heard his tale.

[298] The stake was a common mode of punishment in India in former days, and, until recently, was practised among the *Sikhs, Marhattas,* and other Asiatic princes, who were independent of our government.

[299] Addressing himself to the king *Azad Bakht.*

[300] The term *kibla* signifies the "point of adoration," and is generally applied to the *Ka'ba,* or holy edifice, situated in the sacred inclosure of Mecca. To this point all *Muhammadans* must turn when they pray.

[301] The prayer of martyrdom among the *Musalmans.* It is often repeated when they go into action against Christians and Pagans

the magistrate, and urged him to put me to death. As this official had already taken a bribe from them, he [readily] acquiesced to do whatever they dictated.

"The magistrate said to them, 'Rest satisfied; I will now confine him in such a way, that he will of himself, from want of food and drink, die of sheer exhaustion, and no one will know anything about it.' They re-seized me, and kept me In a corner. About a *kos* without the city was a mountain, in which, in the time of Solomon, the *divs* had dug a deep and narrow well; it was called Solomon's prison. Whoever fell greatly under the king's wrath, was confined in that well, where he perished of himself [from hunger and thirst]. To shorten my story, these two brothers and the magistrate's soldiers carried me at night, in silence, to the mountain, and having cast me into that pit, and thus set their own minds at ease, they returned. O king, this dog went with me, and when they put me into the well, he remained lying on its brink. I lay some time senseless in the inside, and then a little consciousness returned to me; I conceived myself to be dead, and that place my grave At this time I heard the sounds of two men's voices, who were saying something to each other; I concluded that these were *Nakir* and *Munkir*,[302] who were come to question me; and I likewise heard the rustling of a rope, as if some one had let it down there. I was wondering, and began to feel about me on the ground, when some bones came into my gripe.

"After a moment, a noise like that made by the mouth when some one is masticating, struck my ears. I exclaimed, 'O creatures of God, who are ye; tell me for God's sake?' They laughed, and said, 'This is the great Solomon's prison, and we are prisoners.' I asked them, 'Am I really alive?' They again laughed heartily, and replied, 'You are as yet alive, but will soon die.' I said, 'You are eating; what would it be if you were to give me some?' They then got angry, and gave me a dry answer, but nothing else. After eating and drinking, they fell asleep. I through faintness and weakness, fell into a swoon, and wept and dreamed of God. Mighty sire, I had been seven days in the sea, and so many days since without food, owing to my brothers' false accusation; yea, instead of food, I had got a beating, and was now ingulfed in such a prison, that not the least appearance of release came even into my imagination.

"At last, life was leaving me; sometimes it came, and sometimes it left me. From time to time some person used to come at midnight, and let down by a rope some bread tied up in a handkerchief, and a jar of water, and used to call out. Those two men who were confined near me used to seize it and eat and drink. The dog constantly witnessing this circumstance, exerted his intelligence, thus, 'In the way in which this person lets down water and bread into the pit, do thou also make some contrivance whereby some food may reach this destitute one, who is thy master, then may his life be saved.' Thus having reflected, he went to the city, [and saw that] round cakes of bread piled up on the counter at a baker's shop; leaping up, he seized a cake in his mouth, and ran off with it; the people pursued him, and pelted him with clods, but he would not quit the cake; they became tired [of pursuing him], and returned; the dogs of the city ran after him; he fought arid

[302] According to the *Muhammadan* belief, *Nakir* and *Munkir* are two angels who attend at the moment of death, and call to an account the spirit of the deceased.

struggled with them, and having saved the cake, he came to the well, and threw in the bread. There was sufficient light for me to see the cake lying near me, and I heard, moreover, the dog bark. I took up the cake; and the dog, after throwing down the bread, went to look for water.

"On the outskirts of a certain village, there was an old woman's hut; jars and pots filled with water stood [at the door], and the old woman was spinning. The dog went up to the pot, and attempted to seize it; the old woman made a threatening noise, and the pot slipped from the dog's mouth and fell upon an earthenware jar which was broken; the rest of the vessels were upset and the water spilt. The old woman seized a stick, and rose up to beat [the animal]; the dog seized the skirt of her clothes, and began to rub his mouth on her feet, and wag his tail; then he ran towards the mountain; again having returned to her, he sometimes seized a rope, and sometimes having taken up a bucket in his mouth, he shewed it [to her]; and he rubbed his face against her feet, and seizing the hem of her garment, he continued pulling her. The Almighty inspired the old woman's heart with compassion, so that she took up the rope and bucket and went along with him. He keeping hold of the end of her clothes, after coming out of the hut, kept going on before her.

"At last, he guided her to the very mountain; the old woman imagined, from the dog's conduct, that his master was confined in the well, and that he, perhaps, wanted water for him. In short, conducting the old woman, he came to the mouth of the well. The old woman filled the bucket with water and let it down by a rope. I seized the vessel and ate a morsel of the cake. I drank two or three gulps of the water, and satisfied my hunger and thirst.[303] I thanked God [for this timely supply], and retired to a corner, and waited with patience for the interference of the Almighty, saying, "Now let us see what is to come about." In this manner, this dumb animal used to bring me bread, and by means of the old woman, he used to supply me with water to drink. When the bakers perceived that the dog always carried off bread [in this way], they took compassion on him, and made it a rule to throw him a cake whenever they saw him; and if the old woman neglected to carry the water, he used to break her pots; so that she, being helpless, used to let down a bucket of water every day. This faithful companion removed all my apprehensions for bread and water, and he himself always lay at the mouth of the prison. Six months passed in this manner; but what must be the condition of the man who was confined so long in such a prison, where the air of heaven could never reach him? Only my skin and bones remained; life became a torment to me, and I used to say in my heart, 'O God, it would be better if my life became extinct!'

"One night, the two prisoners were asleep; my heart overflowed [with sorrow], and I began to weep bitterly, and supplicate[304] the Almighty [to end my woes]. At the last quarter [of the night], what do I see! that, by the dispensation of God, a rope was hanging down in the well, and I heard [some one] in a low voice saying, 'O, unfortunate wretch! tie the end of the rope tightly to thy hands, and escape from this place.' On hearing these words, I in my heart imagined that my

[303] Literally, "satiated the dog of my stomach."

[304] Literally, to perform the act of "rubbing the nose on the earth," expressive of extreme humility.

brothers had at last felt compassion for me, and, from the ties of blood, had come in person to take me out. With much joy I tied the rope tightly to my waist; some one pulled me up. The night was so dark, that I could not recognise the person who had hauled me up. When I was out, he said, 'Come, be quick; this is no place to tarry.' I had no strength whatever left; but from fear I rolled down the hill as well as I could. Then I saw at the bottom two horses standing, ready saddled; that person mounted me one of them, and he mounted the other himself, and took the lead. Proceeding on, we reached the banks of a river.

"The morning appeared, and we had gone forth ten or twelve *kos* from the city. I then saw the young man [very clearly]; he was completely armed, having on a coat of mail, together with back, front, and sidepieces [of burnished steel],[305] and with iron armour on his horse; he was looking at me with great rage, and biting his lips, he drew his sword from the scabbard, and springing his horse towards mine, he made a cut at me. I threw myself off my horse [on the ground], and called out for mercy, and said, 'I am faultless; why are you about to kill me? O, kind sir, from such a prison you have taken me out, and now wherefore this unkindness?' He replied, 'Tell me the truth, who art thou.' I answered, I am a traveller, and have been involved in unmerited calamity; by your humane assistance, I have at last come out alive. And I addressed to him many other flattering expressions.

"God inspired his heart with pity. He sheathed his sword, and said, 'Well, what God wills, he does; go, I spare thee thy life; remount quickly; this is no place to delay.' We put our horses to their speed, and went forward; on the road he continued to sigh and show signs of regret. By the time of mid-day,[306] we reached an island. There the young man got off his horse, and made me also dismount; he took off the saddles and pads from the horses' backs, and let them loose to graze; he also took off his arms from his own person, and sat clown and said to me, 'O you of evil destiny, relate now your story, that I may know who you are,' I told him my name and place of residence, and whatever various misfortunes had befallen me, I related to the end.

"When the young man had heard all my history, he wept, and addressing himself to me, he said, 'O youth, hear now my story. I am the daughter of the *raja* of the land of *Zerbad*,[307] and that young man who is confined in the prison of Solomon, his name is *Bahramand*; he is the son of my father's prime minister. One day the *Maharaj* [my father] ordered that all the *rajas* and *kunwars*[308] should assemble on the plain, which lay under the lattices [of the seraglio] to shoot arrows, and play at *chaugan*,[309] so that the horsemanship and dexterity of every individual might

[305] Literally, "having fastened [on his person] the four mirrors."

[306] The term *zuhr* strictly denotes the period devoted to the mid-day prayer, which is offered up after the sun has perceptibly declined from the meridian. Vide note 51, in page 10.

[307] The name of the countries which lie, as the people of *Hindustan* term it, below Bengal, i.e., to the south-east of it; the name includes the kingdoms of Ava and Pegu.

[308] *Kunwar* is the *Hindu* name for the son of a *raja*.

[309] The *chaugan* is a Persian sport performed on horseback, with a large ball like a foot-ball, which is knocked about with a long stick like a shepherd's crook; it is precisely the game called in Scotland "shintey," and in England "hockey," only that the players are

be displayed. I was seated near the *rani*[310] my mother, behind one of the lattices of the highest story, and the female servants and slaves were in waiting around; there I was looking at the sport. The minister's son was the handsomest [man] among them; and having caracoled his horse, he performed his exercises with much address. He appeared very agreeable [in my eyes], and my heart became enamoured of him. I kept this circumstance concealed for a long while.

"'At last, when I became quite restless, I mentioned it to my hand-maid, and gave her many presents [to gain her assistance]. She contrived, by some means or other, to introduce the youth in secrecy into my apartment; he then began to love me likewise. Many days passed in these love interviews. In short, the sentinels saw him one midnight going armed into my apartment, and seized him, and informed the *raja* of the circumstance. The *raja* ordered him to be put to death; through the solicitations of all the officers of state, his life was pardoned, but he was ordered to be thrown into the prison of Solomon; and the other young man, who is a fellow-prisoner with him, is his brother, and was with him the night [he was seized]. Both were put into the well, and it is now three years since they were confined, but no one has yet found out why the youth entered the *raja's* palace. God has preserved my character [from public exposure], and in return for his goodness, I conceived it my duty to continue to supply the two prisoners with bread and water. Since their confinement I go there every eight days, and let them down eight days' provisions at once.

"'Last night, I saw in a dream that somebody advised me, saying, "arise quickly and take a horse, a dress, a rope-ladder, and some money for expenses, and go to that pit, and deliver from thence the unfortunate prisoners." On hearing this, I started up [from my sleep], and being greatly rejoiced, I dressed myself like a man, filled a casket with jewels and gold pieces, and taking this horse and some clothes with me, I went to the prison to draw them out with the rope-ladder. It was in your fate to be delivered from such a confinement in this manner; no one knows what I have done; perhaps he was some protecting angel who sent me to enlarge you. Well, whatever was in my destiny, the same has come to pass.' After finishing this relation, she took out some cakes fried in butter, some wheaten bread, some pulse, and meat curry from her handkerchief; but first, she dissolved some sugar in a cup of water, and put some spirit of *bed-mushk* in it, and gave it to me. I took it from her hand and drank it, and then ate some breakfast. After a short while, she made me wrap a piece of cloth round my waist, and led me to the river, and with scissors she cut my hair and nails and bathing me, dressed me in the clothes [she had brought], and made a new man of me. I, having turned my face to the *kibla* offered up a prayer of thanksgiving; the beautiful girl regarded what I was doing.

"When I had finished from praying, she asked me, 'What hast thou been thus doing?' I answered, 'I have been worshipping the Almighty God who has created the whole world, and who has effected my relief through a being lovely as thou art, and who has inclined thy heart to kindness towards me, and caused me to

---

mounted.

[310] *Rani* is the *Hindu* name of a *raja's* wife.

be released from such a prison. His person is without an equal,[311] to Him I have performed my devotions, and obeisance, and rendered my thanks.' On hearing these words she said, 'You are a *Musalman*.' I replied, 'Thanks be to God, I am,' 'My heart,' said she, 'is delighted with your pious expressions; instruct me also, and teach me to recite your *kalima*.' I said in my own heart, 'God be praised that she is inclined to embrace our faith.' In short, I recited [our creed], viz., 'There is no God but God, and *Muhammad* is the apostle of God,' and made her repeat it. Then mounting our horses, we two set out from thence. When we halted at night, she talked of [nothing else but] our religion and faith; and she listened and felt delighted [with my words]. In this way we journeyed on incessantly day and night, for two months.

"At last, we arrived in a country which lay between the boundaries of the kingdoms of *Zerbad* and *Sarandip*;[312] a city appeared, which was more populous than Constantinople, and the climate very fine and agreeable. On finding that the king of that country was more renowned for his justice than *Naushirwan*[313], and also for being the protector of his subjects; my heart was greatly rejoiced. Having there bought a house, we took up our residence. After some days, when we had got over the fatigues of the journey, I purchased some necessary articles, and married the young lady according to the law of *Muhammad*, and lived with her. In the space of three years, I having freely associated with the great and small of that place, established my credit, and entered into an extensive trade. At last, I surpassed all the merchants of that place. One day, I went for the purpose of paying my respects to the first *wazir*, and saw a great crowd of people assembled on a plain. I asked some one, 'Why is there such a crowd here?' I learnt that two persons had been caught in the act of adultery and theft; and perhaps they had even committed murder; they were brought here to be stoned [to death].

"On hearing this [circumstance], I recollected my own case; that once upon a time I had likewise been led in the same manner to be empaled, and that God preserved me. 'Who can these be,' [I said to myself], 'that they should have become involved in such calamity? I do not even know if they are justly [punished], or, like me, the victims of a false accusation.' Pressing through the crowd, I reached [the spot where the culprits stood], and perceived they were my brothers, who were led along with their hands tied behind their backs, and with bare heads and feet. On seeing their sad state, my blood boiled, and my liver was on fire. I gave the guards a handful of gold pieces, and besought them to delay [the execution] for a moment; and from thence, having put my horse to his utmost speed, I went to the governor's house. I presented to him, as a *nazar*, a ruby of inestimable value, and made intercession for them. He replied, 'A person has a plaint against them, and their crimes have been fully proved; the king's mandate has been issued, and

[311] Literally, "without a partner." The *Musalmans* consider our doctrine of the Trinity as a deadly error.

[312] *Sarandip* is the name for the island of Ceylon among the Arabs and Persians, as well as the *Musalmans* of India. The ancient *Hindu* name was *Lanka*, applied both to the island and its capital.

[313] The term *kisra* is evidently applied here to *Naushirwan*, not to Cyrus, as is stated in some books.

I have no alternative.'

"At last, after much entreaty and supplication [on my part], the governor sent for the complainant, and made him consent that for five thousand pieces of silver he should withdraw his charge of murder. I counted out the money, and got his written engagement [not to prosecute them again], and had them released from their dire calamity. O protector of the world! ask them if I tell truth or falsehood." Here the two brothers stood in silence, and hung down their heads like those who are ashamed. "Well, [to proceed], I got them released, and brought them to my house, had them bathed and dressed, and gave them apartments for their residence in the *diwan-khana*. I did not at that time introduce my wife to them; I myself attended to all their wants, and ate [and drank] with them, and at the hour of sleep returned to my apartment. For the space of three years [the time] thus passed in my kind treatment of them, and on their part, no evil action took place, so as to be the cause of my displeasure. When I used to go out riding any where, they remained at home.

"It happened, that my good wife went one day to the bath; when she came to the *diwan-khana,* seeing no male person there, she took off her veil; perhaps my second brother was lying down there awake, and immediately on seeing her, he became enamoured of her. He imparted [the circumstance] to our eldest brother, and they formed a plan together for murdering me. I had no knowledge whatever of this circumstance; on the contrary, I used to say to myself, 'God be praised, that this time, as yet, they have done nothing such [as they formerly did]; their conduct is now correct; perhaps they have felt the effects of shame.' One day, after dinner, my eldest brother began to weep, and to praise our native country, and to describe the delights of *Iran.*[314] On hearing this, the other brother began to sigh. I said, 'If you wish to return to] our native land; then it is well; I am devoted to your pleasure, and it is also my own wish. Now, if it please God, I will go along with you.' I mentioned the circumstance of my brothers' afflictions to my wife, and also my own intentions. That sensible woman replied, 'You may think so; but they again design to perpetrate some villany [towards you]; they are the enemies of your life; you have fostered [a brace of] serpents in your sleeve, and you still place reliance on their regard. Act as you please, but beware of those who are noxious.' At all events, the preparations for the journey were completed in a short time, and the tents pitched on the plain. A great *kafila* assembled, and they agreed to confer on me the rank of leader and *kafila-bashi.*[315] A propitious hour being ascertained, [the *kafila*] set out; but on my part, I was on my guard against my brothers, though in every way I obeyed their commands, and made everything agreeable to them.

"One day [when we arrived] at our stage, my second brother said that, 'one

[314] *Iran* is the ancient name of Persia in its more extended sense, that is, the Persian Empire. *Fars* is sometimes used in the same sense. Strictly speaking, it denotes Persia proper, which is only a province of *Iran.*

[315] The *kafila-bashi* is the head man of the *kafila,* or company of merchants, who travel in a body for mutual safety, and compose what is commonly called a caravan, properly a *karwan*; the richest and most respectable merchant of the party is generally elected *bashi*; all the rest obey his orders, and he directs the movements, &c., of the whole company, and moreover, acts, in all cases of dispute, as judge and magistrate.

farsakh[316] from this place is a running fountain like *salsabil*[317] and in the [circumjacent] plain, for miles around, lilies, and tulips, and narcissuses, and roses, grow spontaneously. In truth, it is a delightful spot to walk in; if we had our will, we would go there to-morrow, and enliven our hearts [with the sight], and recover from our fatigues.' I said, 'you are masters here; if you command it, we will halt to-morrow, and having gone to that spot, we will stroll about [and amuse ourselves].' They replied, 'what can we do better?' I gave orders, saying, 'advertise the whole *kafila* that to-morrow there will be a halt,' and I told my cook to prepare breakfast, of every variety [of dishes] for next day, as we should go on an excursion [of pleasure]. When the morning came, these two brothers put on their clothes, and having armed themselves, they reminded me to make haste, that we might arrive there in the cool [of the morning] and enjoy our walk. I ordered my horse, but they observed thus, 'The pleasure which results by viewing [the place] on foot, can the same be felt in riding?[318] Give orders to the grooms that they may lead the horses after us.'

Two slaves carried the *kaliyan*[319] and coffee-pot, and went along with us. On the road, as we proceeded, we amused ourselves by shooting arrows, and when we had gone some distance from the *kafila,* they sent one of the slaves on some errand. Advancing a little farther, they sent the other slave also to call back [the former]. My unfortunate fate would have it [that I remained silent] as if some one had put a seal on my lips, and they did what they wished, and having occupied my attention in talk, they continued to lead me on; this dog, however, remained with me. When we had advanced a considerable distance, I saw neither fountains nor gardens, but a plain covered with thorns. There I had a call for making water, and sat me down to perform it. I saw behind me a flash like that of a sword; and, on looking back, my second brother struck me such a sword-cut, that my skull was cleft in twain.[320] Before I could call out, O savage! why dost thou murder me; my eldest brother gave me [a blow] on the shoulder. Both wounds were severe, and I staggered and fell; then these two pitiless ones mutilated me at their ease, and left me weltering in my blood. This dog, on seeing my condition, flew at them, and they wounded him likewise. After this, they gave themselves some slight wounds, and ran back to the encampment with naked feet and heads, and gave out, that 'some robbers have murdered our brother on that plain, and we ourselves also in a close encounter with them, have been wounded. Move off quickly, or else they

[316] The *farsakh,* or *farsang,* or *parsang,* is a measure of distance in Persia, and contains at the present day about 3¾ English miles. Herodotus reckoned the *[Greek: pasasaggaes]*; in his time at 30 Grecian stadia.

[317] *Salsabil* is the name of a fountain of Paradise, according to *Muhammadan* belief.

[318] The student is of course aware that in most languages a question is frequently equivalent to a negative, as in this sentence. A sapient critic, to whom I have more than once alluded, was pleased to honour me with the following profound remark on the reading given in the original, viz.—"There is a slip here in Forbes's edition, as well as the Calcutta one. The word *nahin,* 'not,' is omitted, which destroys the whole sense!!!"

[319] The *kaliyan* (or as the moderns say, *kaliyun*) is the Persian *hukka.*

[320] This is, as the vulgate hath it, "coming it a little too strong;" but be it remembered that Oriental story-tellers do not mar the interest of their narrative by a slavish adherence to probability.

will immediately fall on the caravan, and utterly plunder us all.' When the people of the *kafila* heard the name of robbers, they immediately became alarmed, and marched off and made their escape.

"My wife had [already] heard of the [former] conduct and precious qualities of these [brothers of mine,] and of all the treachery they had practised towards me; hearing now from these liars the events [that had occurred], she instantly stabbed herself to death with her dagger, and restored her soul to her Maker." O *darweshes!*[321] when the dog-worshipping *khwaja* had thus far told us of the adventures and misfortunes, I wept involuntarily on hearing them. The merchant having perceived [my grief,] said, "Lord of the world! if it were not a want of respect, I would strip myself naked, and show the whole of my body." Even on this, to [prove] the truth [of what he had related,] he tore his dress off his shoulders, and showed to us [his person]. In truth, there was not the space of four fingers on it free from wounds; and he took off his turban before me from his head, and there was such a great dint in his skull, that a whole pomegranate might be put into it. All the officers of state who were present shut their eyes, they had not the power of beholding [the shocking sight].

The *khwaja* then continued his narrative, saying, "O blessed majesty! when these brothers, as they thought, had finished their work and went away; on the one side, I lay wounded, and on the other side, this dog lay wounded near me. I lost so much blood from my body, that I had not the least strength or sensation left, and I cannot conceive how life remained. The spot where I lay was on the boundary of the kingdom of *Sarandip*, and a very populous city was situated near the place; in that city there was a great pagoda, and the king of that country had a daughter extremely well-favoured and beautiful.

"Many kings and princes were desperately in love with her. There, the custom of [wearing] the veil was unknown; for which reason the princess used to roam about, hunting all day with her companions. Near [the spot where I lay] was a royal garden; she had on that day got leave from her father, and had come to that same garden. Walking about by way of recreation, she chanced to pass over that plain; some female attendants also accompanied her on horseback. They came to the spot where I lay, hearing my groans, they stopped near me. Seeing me in this condition, they rode off to the princess, and said, that 'a miserable man and a dog are lying weltering in their blood.' On hearing this from them, the princess herself came near me, and, afflicted [at the sight,] she said, 'See if any life still remains.' Two or three of the attendants dismounted and having examined me, replied, 'He still breathes.' The princess instantly ordered them to lay me carefully on a carpet and carry me to the garden.

"When they brought me there, [the princess] having sent for the royal surgeon, gave him many injunctions respecting the cure both of myself and of my dog, and gave him hopes of a reward and a gratuity. The surgeon having thoroughly wiped my whole body, cleaned it from dust and blood, and having washed the wounds with spirits, he stitched them and put on plasters; and he ordered the extract of

[321] Here the king *Azad Bakht* speaks in his own person, and addresses himself to the four *darweshes.*

the musk-willow[322] to be dropped down my throat in lieu of water. The princess herself used to sit at the head [of my bed], and see that I was attended to; and two or four times during the day and night she made me swallow, from her own hands, some broth or *sharbat*. At last, when I came to myself, I heard the princess say with sorrow, 'What bloody tyrant hath used thee so cruelly? did he not fear even the great idol?'[323] After ten days, with the efficacy of the spirit of *bed-mushk*, and *sharbats*, and electuaries, I opened my eyes; and saw as if the whole court of *Indra* were standing around me, and the princess at the head of my bed. I heaved a sigh and wished to move myself, but had not sufficient strength. The princess said with kindness, 'O Persian, be of good cheer, and do not grieve; though some cruel oppressor hath used thee thus; yet the great idol has made me favourable towards thee, and thou wilt now recover.'

"I swear by that God who is one, and without a partner, that on beholding her I again became senseless; the princess also perceived it, and sprinkled me with rose water out of a phial held by her own fair hand. In twenty days my wounds filled up and granulated; the princess used to come [regularly] at night when all were asleep, and she then supplied me with food and drink. In short, after forty days, I performed the ablution [of perfect recovery];[324] the princess was extremely rejoiced, and rewarded the surgeon largely, and clothed me richly. By the grace of God, and the care and attentions of the princess, I became quite stout and healthy, and my constitution became sound; the dog also grew fat. She made me drink wine every day, listened to my conversation, and was pleased. I used also to amuse her by relating some agreeable stories and brief narratives.

"One day she asked to me, 'pray relate thy adventures, and tell me who you are, and how this accident has happened to you,' I related to her my whole history from beginning to end. On hearing this, she wept and said, 'I will now behave to thee in such a manner that thou wilt forget all thy [past] misfortunes,' I replied, 'God preserve you; you have bestowed on me a second existence, and I am now wholly yours; for God's sake, be pleased ever to regard me in this favourable manner.' In short, she used to sit all night with me alone; sometimes the nurse likewise stayed with her and heard my stories, and related [others herself.] When the princess used to go away and I remained alone, I used to perform my ablutions, and concealing myself in a corner, I used to say my prayers.

"Once it so happened, that the princess had gone to her father, and I was repeating my prayers in perfect security, after having performed my ablutions, when suddenly the princess, conversing with her nurse, entered, saying, 'Let us see what the Persian is now doing; whether he be asleep or awake!' But seeing that I was not in my place, she was greatly surprised, and exclaimed, 'Hey day! where is he gone? I hope he has not formed an attachment with some one else.' She began to examine every hole and corner in search of me, and at last came to where I was saying my prayers. She had never seen any one perform his prayers;[325] she stood

[322] With regard to the essence of *bed-mushk* vide note 120, page 23.
[323] The image of the Divine power in that country of Pagans.
[324] Vide note 90, page 18, respecting the *chilla*, or "period of forty."
[325] That is to say, she had never seen a *Muhammadan* at his prayers.

in silence, and looked on. When I had finished my prayers, and lifted up my arms to bless God, and prostrated myself, she laughed loudly, and said, 'What! is this man become mad? what various postures does he assume?'

"On hearing the sound of her laughter, I became alarmed. The princess advanced, and asked me, 'O Persian, what wast thou doing?' I could make no reply, on which the nurse said, 'May I take [the responsibility of] thy evils, and become thy sacrifice, it appears to me that this man is a *Musalman*, and the enemy of *Lat* and *Manat*;[326] he worships an unseen God. The princess immediately on hearing this struck her hands together, and said in great wrath, 'I did not know he was a Turk,[327] and an unbeliever in our gods, for which reason he had fallen under the wrath of our idol. I have erroneously saved him and kept him in my house,' Saying this she went away. On hearing [her words] I became disturbed, [and alarmed to know] how she would now behave to me. Through fear, sleep was driven from me, and until morning I continued to weep, and to bathe my face with tears.

"I passed three days and nights, weeping in this fear and hope. I never shut an eye [during this time.] The third night, the princess came to my apartment flushed with the intoxication of wine, and the nurse along with her. She was full of anger; and with a bow and arrows in her hand, she sat down outside of the room, on the border of the *chaman*;[328] she asked the nurse for a cup of wine, and after drinking it off, she said, 'O nurse! is that Persian who is involved in our great idol's wrath, dead, or does he yet live?' The nurse answered, 'May I bear your evils! some life still remains,' The princess said, 'He has now fallen in my estimation; but tell him to come out.' The nurse called me; I ran forth and perceived that the princess's face glowed through anger, and had become quite red. My soul remained not in my body; I saluted her, and having joined both my hands together, stood before her [in silent respect.] Giving me a look of anger, she said to the nurse, 'If I kill this enemy of our faith with an arrow, will the great idol pardon my guilt or not? I have already committed a great crime by having kept him in my house, and by supplying [his wants.]'

"The nurse answered, 'What is the princess's guilt? you did not in the least know him to be an enemy when you kept him [in your house;] you took compassion upon him, and you will receive good for the good you have done; and this man will receive from the great idol the reward of the evil which he has done.' On hearing these words, the princess said, 'Nurse, tell him to sit down.' The nurse made me a sign to sit down; I accordingly sat down. The princess drank another cup of wine, and said to the nurse, 'Give this wretch also a cup, then he will take his killing with more ease.' The nurse presented me a cup of wine; I drank it without hesitation, and made my *salam* [to the princess;] she never looked at me directly, but continued all along to give me furtive side glances. When I became elevated [with the effects of the wine,] I began to repeat some pieces of poetry; among others, I recited the following couplet:

[326] *Lat* and *Manat* were the two great idols of *Hindu* worship in former times.

[327] In the languages of southern India, *Turk* is the general appellation for a *Musalman*.

[328] The *chaman* is a small garden or *parterre*, which is laid out before the sitting room in the interior of the women's apartments; it means in general, *parterres* of flowers.

'I am in thy power, and if alive yet, what then?
Under the dagger, if one breathes awhile, what then?'

On hearing this verse, she smiled, and turning towards the nurse, she said, 'What art thou sleepy?' The nurse, guessing her motive, replied, 'Yes, sleep overcomes me.' She then took her leave, and went away.[329] After a short pause, the princess asked me for a cup of wine; I quickly filled it, and presented it to her; she took it gracefully from my hand and drank it off; I then fell at her feet; she passed her hand kindly over me, and said, 'O ignorant man! what hast thou seen bad in our great idol that thou hast betaken thyself to the worship of an unseen God?' I answered, 'Pray, be just, and reflect a little, whether that God [and He only,] is worthy of adoration, who, out of a drop of water, hath created a lovely creature like thee, and hath given such beauty and perfection, that in one instant thou canst drive into distraction the hearts of thousands of men. What a [contemptible] thing is an idol that any one should worship it? The stone-cutters have shaped a block of stone into a figure, and have spread it as a net to entangle fools. Those whom the devil beguiles, confound the Creator with the created; and they prostrate themselves before that which their own hands have formed. We are *Musalmans*, and we worship him who hath created us. For those [misguided idolaters], He hath created hell; for us [true believers], He hath destined paradise; if you will place your faith in God, you will experience the delights [of heaven], and distinguish truth from error, and you will find that your [present] devotion is false.'

"At length, on hearing these pious admonitions, the heart of that stony-hearted one became softened, and through the favour and mercy of God she began to weep, and said, 'Well, teach me thy faith,' I taught her the *kalima*, which she repeated with sincerity of heart, and having expressed penitence, and prayed for pardon, she became a [true] *Musalman*. I then threw myself at her feet [and thanked her]. Until the morning she continued reciting the *kalima*, and praying for pardon. Again she said, 'Well, I have embraced your faith, but my parents are idolators; what remedy is there for them?' I replied, 'what is that to thee? as any one acts, so will he be treated.' She said, 'They have betrothed me to my uncle's son, and he is an idolator; if I should be married to him tomorrow, which God forbid, he, an idolator, would cohabit with me, and I should bear issue, which would be a dreadful misfortune. We ought immediately to think of some remedy for this, so that I may be freed from such a calamity,' I replied, 'what you say is indeed reasonable; do whatever you think proper.' She said, 'I will remain here no longer, but go forth somewhere else.' I asked, 'by what means can you escape, and where will you go?' She answered, 'In the first place, do you leave me here, and go and abide with the *Musalmans* in the *sarai*, so that every one may hear of it, and not suspect you. You will there continue on the look out for [the departure of] vessels, and if any vessel sails for Persia, let me know; for which reason I will send the nurse to you frequently, and when you send me word [that all is ready,] I will come to you, and having embarked in the vessel, I will effect my escape and obtain my release from the hands of these ill-fated heathens,' I replied, 'I will devote myself as a sacrifice for your life and safety, but what will you do with the nurse?' She answered, 'Her

[329] The original uses a much stronger expression.

case can be easily settled; I will give her a cup of strong poison.[330] The plan was fixed upon, and when the day appeared, I went to the *sarai*, and hired a private apartment and went and resided therein. During this absence, I only lived in the hopes of meeting again. Two months[331] [after this event,] when the merchants of *Rum*, of Syria, and of *Isfahan* were assembled together, they formed the project of returning by water, and began to embark their merchandise on vessels. From residing together I had formed acquaintances with most of them, and they said to me, 'Well, sir, will you not also come [along with us]; how long will you stay in this country of infidels?' I answered, 'what have I wherewith I can return to my country? I have as my property this only, a female slave, a chest, and a dog; if you could give me a little room to stay in and fix its price, I shall then be at ease in my mind, and embark likewise.'

"The merchants allotted me a cabin,.and I paid the money for the hire of it. Having set my heart at ease, I went to the nurse's house under some pretext, and said, 'O mother, I am come to take leave of thee, and am now returning to my country; if I could through your kindness see the princess for a moment, it would be a great satisfaction to me.' At last, the nurse complied [with my request]. I said, 'I will return at night, and wait in such a place;' she replied, 'Very well,' Having settled [this point], I returned to the *sarai*, and carried my chest and bedding on board the vessel and delivered them in charge to the master, and added, 'I will bring my female slave on board to-morrow morning.' The master said, 'Come speedily, as we shall weigh anchor to-morrow early,' I answered, 'Very well.' When the night came, I went to the place I had fixed upon with the nurse, and waited. After a watch of the night had passed, the gate of the seraglio opened, and the princess came out dressed in soiled and dirty clothes, with a casket of jewels in her hand; she delivered the casket to me, and went along with me. As soon as it was morning, we reached the seaside, and embarking on a skiff we went on board the vessel; this faithful dog also went with me. When it was broad daylight, we weighed anchor and set sail. We were sailing along in perfect security, when the report of a cannon was heard from one of the ports. All [on board] were surprised and alarmed; the ship was anchored, and a consultation was held among us [to know] if the governor of the port intended some foul play, and what could be the cause of the firing of cannon.

"It happened, that all the merchants had some handsome female slaves [on board], and for fear lest the governor of the port might seize them, they locked them up in chests. I did so likewise, and having shut up my princess in my chest, I

[330] Literally, the poison of the *halahal*, as expression used to denote poison of the strongest kind. The *halahal* is a fabulous poison, said to have been produced from the ocean on the churning of it by the gods and *daityas*. Our critic says, on this word, that it means "deadly!!!" will he favour us with some authority on that point, better than his own?

[331] On the phrase, *do mahine men*, our critic comes out in great force. He says, "Mir Amman here sins against grammar; it should be, *do mahinon men!!!*" The critic is not aware, that when a noun follows a numeral it never requires the inflection plural en, except when it is to be rendered more definite? In reality, Mir Amman would be wrong if he had employed the reading recommended by the sapient critic; *do mahine men* means "in two months;" *do mahinon men* "in *the* two months" (previously determined upon).

locked it. In the meanwhile, the governor and his suite appeared on board a swift sailing vessel, and constantly nearing us, he came and boarded our ship. Perhaps the cause of his coming to us was this: that when the news of the nurse's death and the princess's disappearance became known to the king, in consequence of his being ashamed to mention the [princess's] name, he sent orders to the governor of the port, saying, 'I have heard that the Persian merchants have very handsome slaves with them, and as I wish to buy some for the princess, you will stop them, and send all the slaves that may be in the vessel to the royal presence. On seeing them, I will pay the full value for such as may be approved of, and the remainder shall be returned.'

"According to the king's orders, the governor of the port came himself on board our vessel for this purpose. Near my cabin was [the berth of] another person; he also had a handsome female slave locked up in his chest. The governor sat down on that chest, and began to collect all the female slaves [that could be found]; I praised God, and said, 'Well, no mention has been made of the princess.' In short, the governor's people put into their own vessel all the female slaves that were to be found; and the governor, laughing, asked the owner of the chest on which he was sitting, 'Thou hadst also a female slave?' The blockhead was frightened, and answered, 'I swear by your Honour's feet, I alone have not acted in this manner; all of us from fear of you have concealed our [handsome] female slaves in our chests.' The governor, on hearing this confession, began to search all the chests. He opened my chest also, and having taken out the princess, he carried her away with the rest. I fell into a strange state of despair, and said to myself, 'such a [dreadful] circumstance has occurred that thy life is gone for nothing; and now we must see how he will treat the princess.'

"In my anxiety for her, I forgot all fear for my own life; the whole day and night I spent in prayers to God [for her safety]. When the next early morn arrived, they brought back all the female slaves in their own vessel. The merchants were well pleased, and each took back his own. All returned, but the princess alone was not among them. I asked, 'What is the reason that my slave is not come back [with the rest]?' They answered, 'We do not know; perhaps the king may have chosen her.' All the merchants began to console and comfort me, and said, 'Well, what has happened is past; do not afflict yourself; we will all subscribe and make up her price, and give it to you.' My senses were utterly confounded; I said, 'I will not now go to Persia.' Then I addressed myself saying to the boatmen, 'O friends, take me with you, and land me on the shore.' They agreed, and I left the vessel and stepped into the boat; this dog likewise came along with me.

"When I reached the port, I kept to myself only the casket of jewels which the princess had brought with her; all my other property I gave to the governor's servants. I wandered everywhere in the way of search, that perhaps I might get some intelligence of the princess; but I could find no trace of her, nor could I get the smallest hint respecting that affair. One night I entered the king's seraglio by a trick, and searched for her, but got no intelligence. For nearly the space of a month I sifted every lane and house in the city; and through sorrow I reduced myself almost to death's door, and began to wander about like a lunatic. At last, I fancied that 'my princess must, in all probability, be in the governor's house, and nowhere else.' I went round and inspected the governor's house, to the intent that should I discover any passage I might enter it.

"I perceived a sewer high enough to allow a man to go in and out, but there was an iron grating at its mouth; I formed the resolution to enter [the house] by the way of this sewer; I took off my clothes, and descended into that filthy channel. After a thousand toils, I broke the grating, and entered the *chor-mahall*[332] through the sewer. Then, having put on the dress of a woman, I began to search and examine all around me. From one of the apartments a sound reached my ear, as if some one was praying fervently. Advancing towards the place, I saw it was the princess, who was weeping bitterly and was prostrating herself before her Maker, and praying to him thus, 'For the sake of thy prophet and his pure offspring,[333] deliver me from this country of infidels; and restore me once more in safety to the person who taught me the faith of *Islam*.' On seeing her, I ran and threw myself at her feet; the princess clasped me to her bosom, and upon us both a state of insensibility fell. When our senses were restored, I asked her what had happened to her; she answered, 'When the governor of the port carried all the female slaves on shore, I was offering up this prayer to God that my secret might not any how be known, and that I might not be recognised, and that your life might not be endangered. He is so great a concealer [of our shame], that no one knew I was the princess. The governor was examining every one with a view to purchase [some for himself]; when it came to my turn, he chose me, sent me secretly to his house; the rest he forwarded to the king.

"'When my father did not see me among those [slaves], he sent them all back. The whole of this artifice was had recourse to on my account. He now gives out, that the princess is very ill, and if I do not soon appear, then in a few days the news of my death will fly through the whole country; then the king's shame will not be [divulged]. But I am now greatly distressed, as the governor has other designs upon me, and always urges me to cohabit with him; I do not agree [to his desires]. Inasmuch as he [really] loves me, he has as yet waited for my acquiescence, and therefore he remains silent and quiet. But I dread [to think] how long matters can go on in this way; for which reason I have determined within myself, that when he attempts anything further, I will put myself to death. But now that I have met thee, another thought has arisen in my mind; if God is willing, except this mode, I see no other for escape.'

"I replied, 'Let me hear it; what sort of scheme is it?' She said, 'If you assist and exert yourself, it can be accomplished.' I said, 'I am ready to obey your commands; if you order me, I will leap into the burning flames, and if I could find a ladder, I would for your sake ascend to the sky; [in short], I will perform whatever you command.' The princess said, 'Go, then, to the temple of the great idol; and in the place where [the people take off[334] their shoes, there lies a piece of black canvas.

---

[332] The *chor-mahall* is a private seraglio.

[333] The twelve *Imams*.—Vide note 10, page 4.

[334] The threshold of a pagoda or mosque. The oriental people uncover their feet, as we do our heads, on entering a place of worship.

The custom of this country is, that whoever becomes poor and destitute, he having wrapt himself up in that piece of canvas, sits down in that spot. The people of this country who go there to worship, give him something, each according to his means.

"'In three or four days, when he collects some money, the head priests give him a *khil'at* on the part of the great idol, and dismiss him; having thus become rich, he goes away, and no one knows who he was. Go thou also, and sit under that canvas, and hide well thy hands and face, and speak to no one. After three days, when the priests and idolaters shall have given thee a *khil'at*, and [wish greatly to] dismiss thee; do not thou on any account get up from thence. When they entreat thee greatly, then tell them, "I do not want money nor am I avaricious of riches. I am an injured person, and am come to complain; if the mother of the *Brahmans* does me justice, it is well; otherwise the great idol will do me justice; and this same great idol will attend to my complaint against my oppressor." As long as the mother of the *Brahmans* does not come herself to thee, let any one entreat thee ever so much, consent thou not. At last, being compelled to it, she will come to thee herself; she is very old, for she is two hundred and forty years of age, and six and thirty sons, that have been born of her, are the chief priests of the temple; and she is highly respected by the great idol. For this reason she possesses such vast power that all the little and great of this country deem her command [a matter of] felicity; whatever she orders, that they perform with all their heart and soul. Lay hold of the skirt of her garment, and say to her, "O mother, if you do not exact justice from the oppressor to this injured traveller, I will dash my head on the ground before the great idol; he will at last pity me, and intercede for me with you."

"'When, after this, she asks thee all the particulars of thy complaint, tell her, "I am an inhabitant of Persia; I am come here from a great distance, both to perform a pilgrimage to the great idol, and in consequence of having heard of your justice. For some days I lived here in peace; my wife also came with me; she is young, her form and figure are excellent, and her features perfect. I do not know how the governor of the port saw her, but he forcibly took her away from me, and shut her up in his house. With us *Musalmans* it is a rule, that if a stranger sees one of our wives, or takes her away, it is right that the stranger be put to death by whatever means it may be accomplished, and the wife be taken back; and otherwise, we must abandon food and drink; for whilst the stranger lives, that wife is forbidden to the husband. Now, having no other resource, I am come hither; let us see what justice you do to me."' When the princess had fully instructed me in all these circumstances, I took my leave, and came out by the same sewer, and once more replaced the iron grating.

"As soon as the morning came, I went to the temple, and, having covered myself with the black canvas, I sat down. In three days' time so many pieces of gold, and silver, and articles of apparel were heaped up near me, that it appeared a regular store. On the fourth day, the priests, performing their devotion, and singing and playing, came to me with a *khil'at*, and wished to dismiss me. I would not agree to it, and called on the great idol for protection, and said, 'I am not come to beg, but to get justice from the great idol and the mother of the *Brahmans*; and until I get justice I shall not stir from hence.' On hearing this [determination], they went to the presence of the old woman, and related what I had said; after which a *Brahman* came to me and said, 'Come, the mother calls you.' I instantly wrapped myself up in the black canvas from head to foot, and went to the threshold [of her apartment]. I saw that the great idol was placed on a jewelled throne in which were set rubies, diamonds, pearls and coral; and a rich covering was spread on a golden chair, on which was seated, with great pomp and dignity, an old woman dressed in black, with cushions and pillows [around her], and near her stood two boys, ten or twelve years old, one on her right and one on her left. She called me before her; I advanced towards her with profound respect, and kissed the foot of the throne, and then took hold of the skirt [of her garments]. She asked me my story; I related it exactly as the princess had instructed mo to do.

"On hearing it, she said, 'Do *Musalmans* keep their wives concealed?' I replied, 'Yes, may it fare well with your children; it is an ancient custom of ours.' She said, 'Thine is a good religion; I will instantly give orders that the governor of the port, together with your wife, shall appear here, and I shall punish that ass in such a manner that he will not act so another time, and all shall prick up their ears and tremble.' She asked her attendants, 'Who is the governor of the port? How dares he take away by force the wife of another man?' They answered, 'He is such a one.' On hearing his name, she told the two boys who were standing near her, 'Take this man along with you instantly, and go to the king, and say, "That the mother declares, that this is the command of the great idol, that whereas the governor of the port commits excessive violence on the people; for instance, he has carried off [by force] this poor man's wife, and his guilt is proved to be great; therefore let an inventory be quickly taken of the delinquent's effects and property, and let them be delivered to this Turk, whom I esteem, otherwise you will be destroyed to-night, and you will fall under our wrath.' The two boys rose up, came out of the place, and mounted their horses; all the priests, blowing their shells, and singing hymns, went in their retinue.

"In short, the great and little of that country having conceived the dust of the spot where the feet of those boys trod as holy, used to take it up and put it to their eyes. In this manner, they went to the palace of the king. He heard of it, and came forth with naked feet for the purpose of their reception, and having conducted them with great respect, he placed them on the throne near himself, and asked them, 'What has given me the honour of your visit to-day?' The two young *Brahmans* repeated on the part what they had heard from the mother, and threatened him with the great idol's anger.

"On hearing it the king said, 'Very well,' and issued an order to his attendants, saying, 'Let some officers of justice go, and let them immediately bring the governor of the port, along with that woman into our presence, then shall I, having investigated his crime, inflict upon him deserved punishment.' On hearing [this order], I was greatly alarmed in my own heart, [and said to myself], 'This affair indeed is not quite so well; for if they bring the princess with the governor of the port, the matter will be discovered; what then will be my situation?' Being extremely fear-stricken in my mind, I looked up to God, but my countenance was overcast with anxiety, and my body began to tremble. The boys seeing my colour change, perhaps observed that this order was not agreeable to my wish; they instantly rose with vexation and anger, and said harshly to the king, 'O wretch, art thou become mad, that thou steppest aside from the great idol's obedience, and conceivest what we said to be untrue, that thou wishest to send for them both and verify [the circumstance]? Now, take care, thou hast fallen under the great idol's wrath; we have delivered our orders, now do thou look [to it], or the great idol will look [to thee].'

"On hearing these words, the king was so greatly alarmed, that, joining both his hands together, he stood [before the boys] and trembled from head to foot. Having made humble supplication, he endeavoured to appease them; but they would not sit down, and they remained standing. In the meantime, all the nobles who were present, began with one voice to speak ill of the governor, saying, 'He is indeed such a wicked man, and so tyrannical, and commits such offences, that we cannot relate the same before the royal presence. Whatever the mother of the *Brahmans* has sent word of, is all true; inasmuch as it is the great idol's decision; how can it be false?' When the king heard the very same story from all, he was much ashamed and regretful of what he had said. He instantly gave me a rich *khil'at;* and having written an order with his own hand, and sealed[335] with his sign manual, he consigned it to me; he also wrote a note to the mother of the *Brahmans*, and having laid trays of gold and jewels before the boys as presents, he dismissed them. I returned to the temple highly pleased, and went to the old woman.

"The contents of the king's letter which had arrived were as follows. After the usual compliments and tenders of service and devotion, [the king] had written, 'That according to the orders of your highness, the situation of governor of the fort has been conferred upon this *Musalman*, and a *khil'at*[336] has been bestowed on him. He is now at liberty to put the former governor to death; and all his effects and money now belong to this *Musalman*; he may do with him what he pleases. I hope my fault will be forgiven.' The mother of the *Brahmans* was pleased with the letter, and said, 'Let the music strike up in the *naubat-khana* of the *pagoda*.' Then she sent with me five hundred well-armed soldiers, who were good marksmen[337] with the musket, to go with me, and gave them orders to go to the port, seize its governor, and deliver him up to this *Musalman*, in order that he may put him to death with what torture he pleases. Also let them take care that, except this honoured [*Musal-*

[335] Asiatics do not sign their names, but put their seals to letters, bonds, paper, &c.; on the seal is engraven their names, titles, &c.; which absurd practice has frequently given rise to much roguery, and even bloodshed, as it is so easy, by bribes, to get a seal-cutter to forge almost any seal, a notorious instance of which appeared some twenty years ago in the case of the *Raja* of *Sattara*. Though the *Muhammadan* laws punish with severe penalties such transgressions, yet seal-cutters are not more invulnerable to the powers of gold than other men. Kings, princes, *nawwabs* &c., have a private mark, as well as a public seal, to official papers; and a private seal and mark for private or confidential papers.

[336] A *khil'at* or honorary dress is generally bestowed on a person when he is appointed to a new situation.

[337] Literally, "who could hit a *kauri* suspended by a hair." The *kauri* is a small round shell used to denote the minutest denomination of money. In Bengal it is about the hundredth part of a *paisa*.

man], no one be permitted to enter the [governor's] seraglio, and let them deliver over his money and effects [untouched to the new governor]. When he sends them back with his own accord, let them get a letter of approbation from him, and return to me.' She then gave me a complete dress from the wardrobe of the great idol, and having caused me to mount, she dismissed me.

"When I reached the port, one of my men proceeded before me, and informed the governor [of my arrival]. He was sitting like one in great perplexity, when I arrived my heart was already filled with rage; on seeing the harbour-master, I drew my sword, and struck him such a blow on the neck, that his head flew off like a stalk of Indian corn. Then having ordered the agents, the treasurers, the superintendants and other officials to be seized, I took full possession of the records; and then I entered the seraglio. There I met the princess; we embraced each other most tenderly, and wept, and praised the goodness of God; we wiped each other's tears; I then came out and sat on the *masnad*, and gave *khil'ats* to the officers [of the port], and re-established them in their respective situations; to the servants and slaves I gave promotion. To those people who had come as an escort from the temple, I gave presents and gratuities, and having bestowed dresses on their officers, I dismissed them. Then having taken with me jewels of great value, and pieces of fine cloth, and shawls, and brocaded stuffs and goods, and rarities of every region, and a large sum of money as a *nazar*[338] for the king, and for the nobles, according to their respective ranks, and for the priests and priestesses, to be divided among them, after one week I went to the idol-temple and laid the presents before the old woman.

"She gave me another *khil'at* of dignity, and a title. I then went to the audience of the king, and presented my *pesh-kash*. I addressed his majesty [on the best means] to remove the evil consequences of whatever acts of tyranny and injustice the [former] governor of the port had committed. For this reason, the king, the nobles, and the merchants were all well pleased with me, and the king showered many favours on me, and having given me a *khil'at* and a horse, he bestowed on me a title and a *ja-gir*,[339] with other dignities and honours. When I came out from the royal presence, I gave the servants and attendants so much, that they all began to pray [for my welfare]. In short, I became very happy in my condition; and I passed my days in that country in extreme ease and felicity, after marrying the princess; and I offered up thanks to God [for the happiness I enjoyed]. The inhabitants were quite happy through the equity of my administration; and once a month I used to go to the temple and the king's levee; his majesty, from time to time, conferred on me additional promotion.

"At last, he enrolled me as one of his privy counsellors, and did nothing without my advice; my life began to pass in extreme delight; but God only knows that

[338] The *nazar* or *pesh-kash* is a sum of money, &c., which, all oriental officials pay to the prince of the country, or to his favourites, &c., when appointed to their situations. Some people say that such things are done nearer home, with this difference, that among us it is a private transaction; whereas, in the East, it is an open one.

[339] *Ja-girs* are donations of lands, or, rather, of the revenues arising from a certain portion of land; strictly speaking, such a grant is a reward for military service, though it is sometimes bestowed without that condition.

I often thought on these two brothers [and was anxious to know] where they were and how they were. After the space of two years, a *kafila* of merchants arrived at the port from the country of *Zerbad,* and they were all bound for Persia; they wished to return to their own country by sea. It was the rule at that port, that whenever a *karavan* arrived there, the chiefs of the *karavan* used to present to me as a *nazar* some rare presents and curiosities of different countries. On the day following, I used to go to [the chief's] place of residence, and to levy ten per cent. on the value of his goods by way of duty; after which, I gave him permission to depart. In the same manner, those merchants from *Zerbad* likewise came to wait on me, and brought with them presents beyond value; the second day I went to their tents. There I perceived two men dressed in tattered old clothes, who bore packages and bundles on their heads, right into my presence. After I had examined [the packages], they carried them back; they laboured hard, and attended constantly.

"I looked at them with great attention, and perceived they were, indeed, my two brothers. At that time, shame and pride would not allow me to see them in such servitude. When I returned home, I desired my servants to bring those two men to me; when they brought them, I had clothes made up for them, and kept them near me. But these incorrigible villains again laid a plan to murder me. One day at midnight,[340] finding all off their guard, they came like thieves to the head of my bed. I had maintained a guard at my door from apprehensions for my life, and this faithful dog was asleep at the side of my bed; but the moment they drew their swords from the scabbard, the dog first barked, then flew at them; the noise he made awaked all; I, also alarmed, started up. The guards seized them, and I knew them to be themselves all over. Every one began to execrate them, [and said] 'notwithstanding all this kindness, how infamously they have behaved!'

"O king, peace be upon you, I also became at last alarmed [for my life]. There is a common saying, 'That the first and second fault may be pardoned, but the third punished.'[341] I determined then, in my own heart, to confine them; but if I had put them in the prison, who would have taken care of them? They might have perished from want of food and drink, or they might have contrived more mischief. For this reason, I have confined them in a cage, that they may be always under my own eye, then my mind will be at rest; lest being absent from my sight, they may hatch further wickedness. The honour and esteem which I evince towards this dog, are on account of his loyalty and fidelity. O, great God, a man without gratitude is worse than a faithful brute! These were the past events of my life, which I have related to your majesty, now, either order me to be put to death, or grant me my life; to the king command belongs."

On hearing this narrative,[342] I praised that man of honour, and said, your kindness has been uninterrupted, and there has been no limits to these fellows' shameless and villainous conduct; so true is it, "That if you bury a dog's tail for twelve years, it will still remain crooked as ever."[343] After this, I asked the *khwaja*

[340] As the *Musalmans* reckon their day from sun-set, this is no *bull*.

[341] Literally, "the third fault is that of the mother."

[342] The king here resumes his address to the four darweshes.

[343] A proverb synonymous to ours, of "What is bred in the bone, will never come out of the flesh."

the history of those twelve rubies which were in the dog's collar? He replied, "May the age of your majesty be a hundred and twenty years! After I had been three or four years governor of that port, I was sitting one day on the top of my house, which was high, for the purpose of viewing and enjoying the sea and plain beneath. I was looking in all directions, when suddenly, I perceived two human figures, who were coming along from one side of the wood, where there was no high road. Having seized a telescope, I looked at them, and saw they were of a strange appearance: I speedily sent some mace-bearers to call them [to my presence.]

"When they came, I perceived they were a man and a woman. I sent the woman into the seraglio to the princess, and called the man before me; I saw he was a youth of twenty or twenty-two years of age, whose beard and mustaches had commenced [growing;] but the colour of his face had become black as that of the *tawa*.[344] The hair of his head, and the nails of his fingers owing to the heat of the sun were greatly grown, and he looked like a man of the woods. He held on his shoulder a boy of about three or four years old, and two sleeves of a garment, filled [with something], were suspended like a collar round his neck; he cut a strange appearance, and was oddly dressed, I was greatly surprised, and asked him, 'O, friend, who art thou, and of what country art thou the inhabitant, and in what a strange condition do I see thee?' The young man began to weep bitterly, and taking off the two filled sleeves from around his neck, he laid them before me, and cried out, 'Hunger, hunger! for God's sake give me something to eat; I have subsisted for a long while on roots and herbs, and there is not a particle of strength remaining in me.' I instantly ordered him some bread, meat, and wine; he began to devour them.

"In the meantime, the eunuch brought from my haram several other bags which he found on [the stranger's wife.] I ordered them all to be opened, and saw that they contained precious jewels of every kind, each of which was equal in value to the amount of the king's revenue; each one was more valuable than another in weight, shape and brilliancy; and the whole apartment was illuminated with variegated colours, from the reflection of their different coloured rays. When the young man had eaten something, and drank a cup of wine, his senses returned; I then asked him, 'where did you get these stones?' He answered, 'My native country is *Azurbaijan*;[345] Having separated from my home and parents in my infancy, I have undergone many hardships; I was for a long while buried alive, and have often escaped from the claws of the angel of death.' I said, 'pray, young man, give me the details that I may fully comprehend [your story].' Then he began to relate his adventures as follows:—'My father was a merchant, and he used to travel constantly to *Hindustan*, China, *Khata, Rum,* and Europe. When I was ten years of age, my father set out for *Hindustan*, and wished to take me with him. Although my

[344] The *tawa* is a circular plate of malleable or cast iron, used for baking cakes or bannocks. It is slightly convex, like a watch-glass, on the upper side, where the bread is laid on; the under or concave side being, of course perfectly black. In Scotland, and in the northern counties of England, this domestic implement is called "the girdle," and is still in common use in places remote from towns.

[345] Till recently a province of Persia; the northern part of ancient Media. It is now, alas! fallen into the deadly grasp of the unholy Muscovite.

mother and various aunts remarked that I was yet a child, and not old enough to travel; my father did not mind them, and said, "I am now old; if he is not instructed under my own eye, I will carry the regret with me to my grave; he is the son of a man, and if he does not learn now, when will he learn?"

"'Saying this, he took me with him, in spite of their entreaties, and we set out. The journey was performed in health and safety, and when we arrived in *Hindustan*, we sold some of our goods there, and taking some rarities with us from thence, we set out for the country of *Zerbad*. This journey was likewise performed in safety; there also we sold and bought goods, and embarked on board a ship, to return the quicker to our country. One day, about a month after, we were overtaken by a storm and hurricane, and the rain began to fall in torrents; the whole earth and sky became dark as a mass of smoke, and the rudder broke; the pilot and master began to beat their heads; for ten days the winds and waves carried us where they pleased; the eleventh day the ship having struck against a rock, went to pieces. I did not know what became of my father, our servants and our goods.

"'I found myself on a plank, which floated for three days and nights beyond any control [of mine]. On the fourth day it reached the shore. I had just life enough remaining. I got off the plank, crawled along on my knees. I some how or other reached the dry land. I saw some fields at a distance, and many people were assembled there; but they were all black, and as naked as the day they were born; they said something to me; but I did not understand their language in the least. It was a field of the *chana*[346] pulse; the men, having lighted a large fire were parching the ears [of *chana*] and eating them; and some houses also appeared [near the spot]. Perhaps this was their usual food, and that they lived in those houses; they made signs to me also that I should eat. I plucked up some of the *graum*, roasted it, and began to toss it into my mouth; and having drank a little water, I laid down to sleep in a corner of the field.

"'After some time, when I awoke, a man, from among them came to me, and began to show me [by signs] the road; I plucked up some more of the *graum*, and followed the road [he pointed out]. A great level plain appeared before me, vast as the plain of the day of judgment.[347] I proceeded, eating the *graum* as I went; after four days, I perceived a fort; when I went near it, then I saw it was a very high fort, all built of stone, and each side of which was two *kos* in length, and the door was cut out of a single stone, and had a large lock attached; but I could see no trace of any human being. I proceeded on from thence and saw a hillock, the earth of which was in colour black as *surma*;[348] when I passed over the hillock, I saw a large city, surrounded with a rampart with bastions at regular intervals; and a river of great width flowed on one side of the city. Proceeding on, I reached a gate, and

[346] A kind of pea common in India; it is the ordinary food of horses, oxen, camels, &c., likewise of the native. By Europeans it is generally called *grum* or "*graum*."

[347] The *Muhammadans* believe that on the day of judgment all who have died will assemble on a vast plain, to hear their sentences from the mouth of God; so the reader may naturally conceive the size of the plain.

[348] The *surma* is a black powder made of antimony, which the Asiatic women use on their eyelids, to give a superior lustre to their black or hazel eyes; when applied with taste, it certainly has that effect. It is likewise used for sore eyes, but I cannot say with what success.

invoking God, I entered it. I saw a person who was dressed in the garment of the people of Europe, and seated on a chair; the moment he saw I was a foreign traveller, and heard me invoke God, he desired me to advance. I went up to him, and made him a *salam*; he returned my salutation with great kindness, and laid on the table instantly some bread and butter, and a roast fowl and wine, and said, "Eat thy belly full." I ate a little, and drank [some of the wine], and fell sound asleep. When the night came, I opened my eyes, and washed my hands and face; he gave me again something to eat, and said, "O son, relate thy story." I told him all that had happened to me. He then said, "Why art thou come here?" I became vexed, and replied, "Perhaps thou art mad; after hardships of long duration, I have at last seen the appearance of [human] dwellings. God has conducted me so far, and thou askest me why I am come here." He answered, "Go and rest thyself now; I will tomorrow tell thee what I have to say."

"'When the morning came he said to me, "There are in this room a spade, a sieve, and a leather bag; bring them out." I said to myself, God knows what labour he will make me undergo because he has made me eat of his bread; having no help for it, I took up those articles and brought them to him. He then ordered me to go to the black hillock [I had passed] and dig a hole a yard deep, and "whatever you find in it pass it through this sieve; whatever cannot pass through, put it in the leather bag, and bring it to me." I took all those implements and went there, and having dug as much [as I was ordered], I passed it through the sieve, and put what remained into the bag, [as directed]; I then saw they were all precious stones of different colours, and my eyes were dazzled with their brilliancy. In this manner I filled the bag up to the mouth, and carried it to that person; on seeing it, he said, "Whatever is in the bag take it for thyself, and go away from hence; for thy stay in this city will not do thee good." I gave for answer, "Your worship has, on your part, done me a great favour by giving me these stones and pebbles; but of what use are they to me? When I become hungry, I shall not be able to eat them nor to fill my belly; and if you give me more of them, what use will they be to me?? That person smiled, and said, "I pity thee, for thou, like me, art an inhabitant of the kingdom of Persia; for this reason I advise thee [against remaining here], otherwise it rests with thee. If thou art determined, at all hazards, to enter this city, then take my ring with thee; when thou reachest the centre of the market place, thou wilt find sitting there a man with a white beard—his face and general appearance are very like mine—he is my eldest brother—give him this ring—he will then take care of thee; act conformably to what he says, otherwise thou wilt lose thy life for nothing; my authority only extends as far as this; I have no entrance into the city."

"'I took the ring from him, and, saluting him, took my leave. I entered the city, and saw it was a very elegant place; the streets and market-places were clean and the men and women without concealment were buying and selling among themselves, and were all well dressed. I continued advancing on, and viewing sights. When I reached the four cross roads of the market place, such a crowd there was, that if you threw a brass plate, it would have skimmed over the heads of the people. The multitude were so close to each other, that one could with difficulty make his way through. When the concourse became less, I, pushing and jostling, advanced forward. I saw at last the person [described], seated on a chair, and a *chummak*[349] set with precious stones lay before him. I approached him, made him my *salam*, and gave him the ring; he looked at me with a look of anger, and said, "Why hast thou come here, and plunged thyself in calamity? Did not my foolish brother forbid thee?"

"'I replied, "he did forbid me, but I did not mind him." I then related to him all my adventures from beginning to end. That person got up, and taking me with him, he went towards his own house; his residence appeared like the abode of a king, and he had many servants and attendants. When he had retired to his private apartment and sat down, he said with mildness, "O son! what folly hast thou committed, that on thine own feet thou hast walked to thy grave? What unfortunate blockhead ever comes to this enchanted city?" I answered, I have already fully related to you my history; now indeed fate has brought me here; but do me the kindness to enlighten me on the customs and ways of this place, then shall I know for what reasons you and your brother have dissuaded me from staying here." The good man answered, "The king and all the nobles of this city have been excommunicated; strange are their manners and religion! In an idol temple here there is an idol, from whose belly the devil tells the name, sect, and faith of every individual; so, whatever poor traveller arrives here, the king has information of it; and he conveys the stranger to the pagoda, and makes him prostrate himself before the idol. If he prostrates himself, it is well; otherwise, they cause the poor wretch to be immersed in the river; and if he attempts to escape from the river, his private parts[350] become elongated to such a degree that he has to drag them along the ground. Such enchantment [has God] ordained in this city. I feel pity for thee on account of thy youth; but for thy sake I am going to execute a scheme I have formed that thou mayest be able to live at least a few days, and be saved from this calamity."

"'I asked, "What is the nature of the project [you have formed]? impart it to me." He replied, "I mean to have thee married; and to get thee the *wazir's* daughter for thy wife." I gave for answer, "How can the *wazir* give his daughter to a wretch so poor and destitute as myself? Will it be when I embrace his faith? This is what I never can do." He replied, "The custom of this city is, that whoever prostrates himself before the idol, if he be a beggar and demand the king's daughter, the king must deliver her up to him in order to gratify his wish, and that they may not grieve him. Now I am in the king's confidence, and he esteems me, for which reason all the nobles and officers of state of this place respect me. In the course of every week, they go twice to the pagoda on a pilgrimage, and there they perform their worship; so they will all assemble there to-morrow, and I will carry thee with me." Saying this, he gave me something to eat and drink, and sent me away to sleep. When the morning came, he took me with him to the pagoda; when we

[349] *Chummak* is the Turkish name for a kind of *baton* set with precious stones, and used by some of the officers of the palace as an insignia of state, like our rods, wands, &c.

[350] This ludicrous idea is to be found in the veracious "Voiage and Travaile" of Sir John Maundevile, Kt. Speaking of the "Yles abouten Ynde," he says, "men fynden there an Ile that is clept Crues," where "for the grete distresse of the hete, mennes ballokkes hangen down to their knees, for the grete dissolucioun of the body."

arrived there, I saw that people were going to and fro, and performing their devotions.

"'The king and nobles in front of the idol, near the priests, with heads uncovered, were respectfully seated; also unmarried girls and handsome boys, like *Hur* and *Ghilman*[351] were drawn up in lines on the four sides. The good old man spoke to me and said, "Now do whatever I say." I agreed, and said, "Whatever you command, that I will perform." He said, "First, kiss the king's hands and feet, then, lay hold of the *wazir's* dress." I did so. The king asked, "Who is this, and what has he to say?" The man replied, "This young man is my relation, and he is come from far to have the honour to kiss your majesty's feet, and with this expectation, that the *wazir* will exalt him by [admitting him] into his service, if the order of the great idol and your majesty's approbation be [to that effect]." The king said, "If he will embrace our faith and sect, and adopt our customs, then it will be auspicious [for him]." Immediately, [the drums of] the *nakkar-khana*[352] of the pagoda struck up; and I was invested with a rich *khil'at;* they then put a black rope round my neck, and dragged me before the seat of the idol, and having made me prostrate myself before it, they lifted me up.

"'A voice issued from the idol, saying, "O respected youth, thou hast done well to enter into my service; rely on my mercy and favour." On hearing these words, all the people prostrated themselves, and began to roll on the ground, and exclaimed, "Long may you prosper! why should it not be!" When the evening came, the king and the *wazir* mounted, and went to the *wazir's* house, and they made over to me the *wazir's* daughter according to their rites and ceremonies; they gave a great dowry and presents with her, and expressed themselves highly obliged, saying, that according to the commands of the great idol, they had given her to me. They settled us both in one house; when I saw that beauty, then [I perceived that] in truth her beauty was equal to that of a fairy, perfect from top to toe. All the beauties we have heard of, as peculiar to *Padmini*[353] females, were centred in her. I cohabited with her without ceremony, and experienced great delight. In the morning, after having bathed, I waited on the king; he bestowed on me the *khil'at* of marriage, and ordered that I should always attend his levee; at last, after some days, I became one of his majesty's counsellors.

"'The king used to be much pleased with my society, and often gave me presents and rich *khil'ats,* although I was rich in worldly treasures, for my wife possessed so much gold property and precious stones, that they exceeded all bounds and limits. Two years passed in extreme delight and ease. It happened that [my wife] the *wazir's* daughter, became pregnant; when the seventh and eighth months had passed, and she entered her full time, the pains came on; the nurse and mid-

[351] The *Hur* are celestial females, and the *Ghilman* beautiful youths, who are to attend upon all good Mahometans in Paradise.

[352] The *nakkar-khana* is the place at the portico of a temple or palace where drums are beaten at stated intervals. It is somewhat akin to the "belfry," of a Romish church, the childish and everlasting noise of which is supposed to constitute an important part of Christianity.

[353] *Padmini,* the highest and most excellent of the four classes of women among the *Hindus.*

wife came, and a dead child was brought forth; its poison infected the mother, and she also died. I became frantic with grief, and exclaimed, what a dreadful calamity has burst upon me! I was seated at the head of the bed, and weeping; all at once the noise of lamentations spread through the whole house, and women began to pour in [upon me] from all sides. Each as she entered, struck one or two blows with her hands on my head, and stood before my face, and began to weep. So many women were assembled [round me], that I was perfectly hidden among them, and nearly expiring.

"'In the mean time, some one from behind seized me by the collar, and dragged me along; I looked up, and saw it was the same man of Persia who had married me [to the *wazir's* daughter]. He exclaimed, "O blockhead! for what art thou weeping?" I replied, "O cruel! what a question thou askest! I have lost my empire, and the repose of my house is utterly gone, and thou demandest why I weep!" He said, with a smile, "Now weep on account of thy own death; I told thee at first, that perhaps thine evil fate had led thee here [to perish]; so it has turned out; now, except death, thou hast no release." At last, the people seized me, and led me to the pagoda; I saw that the king, the nobles, and thirty-six tribes of his subjects were assembled there; the wealth and property of my wife were all collected there; whatever article any one's heart desired, he took; and put down its price in cash.

"'In short, all her property was converted into specie; with this specie precious stones were purchased, and locked up in a small box; they then filled a chest with bread, sweetmeats, roast meat, dried and green fruits, and other eatables; and they put the corpse of my wife into another chest, and slung both the chests across a camel; they mounted me on it, and put the box of precious stones in my lap. All the *Brahmans* went before me singing hymns and blowing their shells, and a crowd for the purpose of wishing me joy came on behind. In this manner I was conducted out of the city, through the same gate by which I entered the first day. The moment when the same keeper of the gate saw me, he began to weep, and said, "O unfortunate, death-seized [wretch]! thou wouldst not listen to me, but by entering this city thou hast lost thy life for nothing! It is not my fault; I did dissuade thee." He said this to me; but I was so confounded, that I could not use my tongue to reply to him; nor were my senses in their right place, to foresee what would become of me at last.

"'They conducted me at last to the same fort, the door of which I had seen shut the first day [I entered this country]. The lock was opened with the assistance of many people united, and they carried in the corpse and the chest of food. A priest came up to me, and began to console me, saying, "Man is born one day, and one day dies; such is the [mode of] transmigration in this world; now these, thy wife, thy son, thy wealth, and forty days' food are placed here; take them, and remain here until the great idol is favourable to thee." In my wrath I wished to curse the idol, the inhabitants of that place, and their manners and customs, and to inflict blows and buffets on that priest. That same man of Persia in his own tongue, forbade me, and said, "Take care, do not on any account utter a word; if you should say anything whatever, they will burn you immediately. Well, whatever was in your destiny, that has taken place: rely now on the mercy of God; perhaps He will deliver you alive from this place."

"'In short, all of them, having left me by myself, went out of that fortress, and shut the door. At that moment I wept bitterly at my solitary and helpless state, and began to kick the corpse of that woman, saying, "O cursed corpse, if thou wast to perish in child-birth, why didst thou marry and become pregnant?" After thoroughly beating her, I again sat silent. In the meantime, the day advanced, and the sun became very hot; my brains began to boil, and I was dying by reason of the stench. On whatever side I looked, I saw the bones of the dead, and boxes of precious stones in heaps. I then, having gathered some old chests together, placed them over each other, so that there might be a shed against the heat of the day, and the dews of the night. I began to search for water, and on one side I saw something like a cascade, which was cut out of stone in the wall of the inclosure, and had a mouth like a pot. In short, my life was [sustained] for some time on the food [they had left with me], and the water [I had found.]

"'At last, the victuals were exhausted, and I became alarmed and complained to God. He is so beneficent that the door of the inclosure opened and another corpse was brought in; an old man accompanied it. When, having left him also, they went away, it came into my head to kill the old man, and take possession of his chest of provisions. So, having taken up the leg of an old chest, I went up to him; he was, poor wretch, sorely perplexed, seated with his head resting on his knees. I came behind him, and struck him such a blow, that his skull was fractured and his brains came out, and he instantly resigned his soul to God. I seized his stock of provisions, I began to live on it. For a long while this was my way, that whatever living beings came in with the dead, I used to kill the former, and having taken their provisions, I fared plentifully.

"'After some time, a young girl once came with a corpse; she was very handsome, and I had not the hard heart to kill her [as had hitherto been my practice]. She espied me, and swooned away through fear. I took up her stock of provisions, and carried it to where I lived; but I did not eat it alone; when I was hungry, I used to carry her some victuals, and we ate together. When the young girl perceived that I did not molest her, her timidity lessened daily and she became more familiar, and used to come to my shed. One day I asked her her story, and who she was; she replied, "I am the daughter of the king's *wakili mutlak*,[354] and had been betrothed to my uncle's son. On the day of the marriage night he was attacked with a colic, and was in such agonies from the pain, that he expired in an instant;[355] they brought me here with his corpse and have left me." She then asked to hear my story; I also related the whole to her, and said, "God hath sent thee here for my sake." She smiled and remained silent.

"'In this way mutual affection increased between us in a short time; I taught her the principles of the *Musalman* faith, and made her repeat our *kalima*. I then performed the marriage ceremony, and cohabited with her; she also became pregnant and brought forth a son. Nearly three years passed in this manner. When she

[354] The prime minister, or first officers of state, under the *Mughal* emperors.

[355] Literally, "instant of an instant." With regard to this idiomatic use of the genitive case, vide "Grammar," page 96, paragraph *b*.

weaned the child, I said to my wife, "How long shall we remain here, and how shall we get out from hence?" She replied, "If God takes us out, then we shall get out; otherwise we shall some day die here." I wept bitterly at what she said, and at our confinement, and continuing to weep, I fell asleep. I saw a person in my dream, who said to me, "There is an outlet through the drain; go thou forth." I started up with joy, and said to my wife, "Collect and bring with you all the old nails and bolts which belonged to the rotten chests, that I may [with their help] widen [the mouth of the drain]." In short, I having applied a large nail to the mouth of that drain, used to strike it with a stone until I became quite tired; however, after a year's labour, I widened the opening so much that a man could get through it.

"'I then put the very finest of the precious stones into the sleeves of the habits of the dead, and taking them with us, we three got out through the opening [I had made]. I offered up thanks to God [for our deliverance], and placed the boy on my shoulders. It is a month since we quitted the high road from fear, and have travelled through bye-paths of the woods and mountains; when hunger attacked us, we fed on grass and leaves. I have not strength left to say a word more; these are my adventures which you have just heard,' O mighty king,[356] I took pity on his condition, and having sent him to the bath, I had him well dressed, and made him my deputy. In my own house I had had several children by the princess, but they died one after another, when young; one son lived to five years of age, and then died; from grief for him my wife died also. I was greatly afflicted, and that country became disagreeable to me after her loss; my heart became quite sad, and I determined to return to Persia. I solicited the king's leave to depart, and got the situation of the governor of the port transferred to the young man [whose story I have just related]. In the meantime the king died also; I took this faithful dog and all my jewels and money with me, and came to *Naishapur,* in order that no one should know the story of my brothers. I have become well-known as the dog-worshipper; and owing to this evil fame, I to this day pay double taxes into the exchequer of the king of Persia.

"It so happened that this young merchant went to *Naishapur,* and owing to him I have had the honour to kiss your majesty's feet." I asked[357] the *khwaja* Is not this [young merchant] your son? He answered, "Mighty sire, he is not my son; he is one of your majesty's own subjects; but he is now my master or heir, or whatever you choose to call him." On hearing this, I asked the young merchant, "what merchant's son art thou, and where do thy parents reside?" The youth kissed the ground, and beseeching pardon for his life, replied, "This slave is the daughter of your majesty's *wazir;* my father came under the royal anger on account of this very *khwaja's* rubies, and your majesty's orders were, that if in one year my father's words should not be verified, he should be put to death. On hearing [the royal mandate], I assumed this disguise and went to *Naishapur;* God has conducted the *khwaja,* together with the dog and rubies, before your majesty, and you have heard all the circumstances; I now am hopeful that my aged father may be released."

On hearing these circumstances from the *wazirzadi,* the *khwaja* gave a groan,

[356] Here the *khwaja* resumes his own story to *Azad Bakht.*
[357] The king, *Azad Bakht,* speaks in his own person.

and helplessly fell down. When rose water was sprinkled over his face, he recovered his senses, and exclaimed, "O, dire mishap! that I should have come from such a distance, with such toil and sorrows, in the hope that, having adopted the young merchant for my son, I should make over to him by a deed of gift, all my wealth and property, that my name might not perish, and every one should call him *khwaja-zada;*[358] but now my imaginations have proved vain, and the affair has turned out quite the contrary. He, by becoming a woman, has ruined the old man. I fell into female snares, and now the saying may be applied to me, 'Thou remainedst at home, and didst not go to pilgrimage; yet thy head was shaved, and thou art scoffed by all.'"[359]

To shorten my story, I took pity on agitation, and groans and lamentations, and called him near me, and whispered in his ear some glad tidings, and added, "do not grieve; I will marry thee to her, and, if God pleaseth, thou shalt have children from her, and she shall [now] be thy master." On hearing these welcome words, he became altogether comforted. I then ordered them to conduct the *wazir-zadi* to the seraglio, and to take the *wazir* out of prison, bathe him in the bath, dress him in the *khil'at* of restoration to favour,[360] and bring him quickly before me. When the *wazir* arrived, I went to the end of the *farsh*[361] to receive him, and conceiving him my superior, I embraced him, and bestowed on him anew the writing case of the *wazirship*.[362] I conferred also titles *jagirs* on the *khwaja*, and fixing on a happy hour, I married him to the *wazir's* daughter.

In a few years, he had two sons and a daughter born to him. In short, the eldest son is now *Malikut-Tujjar*, and the youngest, the chief manager of my household. O *Darweshes*, I have related these adventures to you for this reason, that last night, I heard the adventures of two of your number; now you two who remain, fancy to yourselves that I am still where I was last night, and think me your servant, and my house your *takiya;*[363] relate your adventures without fear and stay some days with me. When the *Darweshes* perceived that the king was very kind to them, they said, "Well, as your majesty condescends to form amity with *Darweshes*, we both will also relate our adventures: be pleased to hear them."

---

[358] The son of a *khwaja* or merchant of the highest grade.

[359] When *Musalmans* go on pilgrimage to *Mecca*, they shave their heads on their arrival there; the ridicule is, to have incurred the shaving without the merit of the pilgrimage.

[360] Called the *khil'at sarafrazi*, i.e. of exaltation.

[361] The *farsh* is the carpet or cloth which is spread in the room, where company is received, or the king's audience is held; for the king to advance to the end of the *farsh* to receive the *wazir*, is a mark of respect, which Asiatic princes seldom pay, even to their equals.

[362] The insignia of the *wazir's* office in India and Persia, is the *kalumdan*.

[363] The abode of a *fakir* is called a *takiya*.

ADVENTURES OF THE THIRD DARWESH.

The third *Darwesh,* having sat down at his ease,[364] began thus to relate the events of his travels.

"O friends, the story of this pilgrim hear;
That's to say, hear the tale of what has happened to me;
How the king of love hath behaved to me,
I am going to relate it in full detail, O, hear."

This humble being is the prince of Persia; my father was king of that country, and had no children except myself. In the season of my youth, I used to play with my companions at *chaupar*[365] cards, chess, and backgammon; or mounting my horse, I used to enjoy the pleasures of the chase. It happened one day, that I ordered my hunting party, and taking all my friends and companions with me, we sallied forth over the plains. Letting loose the hawks [of various sorts] on ducks and partridges, we followed [them] to a great distance. A very beautiful piece of land appeared in sight; as far as the view extended, for miles around, what with the verdure and the red flowers, the plain seemed like a ruby. Beholding this delightful scene, we dropped the bridles of our horses and moved on at a slow pace [admiring the charming prospect]. Suddenly, we saw a black deer on the plain, covered with brocade, and a collar set with precious stones, and a bell inlaid with gold attached to its neck; fearless it grazed, and moved about the plain, where man never entered, and where bird had never flapped a wing. Hearing the sound of our horses' hoofs, it started, and lifting up its head, looked at us, and moved slowly away.

On perceiving it, such became my eagerness that I said to my companions, remain where you are, I will catch it alive, take care you do not advance a step, and do not follow me. I was mounted on such a swift horse, that I had often gallopped him after deer, and confounding their bounds, had seized them one after another with my hand. I pushed after it; on seeing me, it began to bound, and swiftly fled away; my horse also kept pace with the wind, but could not overtake the very dust it raised. The horse streamed with sweat, and my tongue also began to crack from thirst; but there was no alternative. The evening was approaching, and I did not know how far I had come, or where I was. Having no other chance [of getting the animal], I employed stratagem towards it, and having taken out an arrow from the

[364] The phrase *kot bundh baithna* signifies to squat down as a person does when easing nature, the two hands being clasped together round the legs a little below the knees.

[365] *Chaupar* is a very ancient Indian game of the nature of backgammon, played by four people, each having four men or pieces. A full description of it is given in the Ayeeni Akbary, London, 1800, vol. 1st, page 253.

quiver, I adjusted my bow, drew the arrow to its full length, aimed it at its thigh, and pronouncing the name of God, I let it fly. The very first arrow entered its leg, and, limping away, it went towards the foot of the mountain. I dismounted from my horse, and followed it on foot; it took to the mountain, and I at the same time gave it chase. After many ascents and descents, a dome appeared; when I got near it, I perceived a garden and a fountain; but the deer disappeared from my sight. I was greatly fatigued, and began to wash my hands and feet [in the fountain].

All at once the noise of weeping struck my ears, as issuing from the dome, and as if some one was exclaiming, "O, child, may the arrow of my grief stick in the heart of him who hath struck thee; may he derive no fruit from his youth, and may God make him a mourner like me." On hearing these words, I went to the dome, and saw a respectable old man, with a white beard, and well dressed, seated on a *masnad*, and the deer lying before him; he was drawing the arrow from its thigh, and uttering imprecations [on the shooter]. I made him my *salam*, and joining my hands together, I said, "Respectable sir, I have unknowingly committed this fault; I did not know it [was your deer]; for God's sake pardon me." He answered, "You have hurt a dumb animal; if you have committed this cruel act through ignorance, God will forgive you." I sat down near him, and assisted him in extracting the arrow; we pulled it out with great difficulty; and having put some balsam to the wound, we let [the deer] go. We then washed our hands, and the old man gave me some food to eat, which was then ready; after satisfying my hunger and thirst, I stretched myself out on a four-footed bedstead.

After having fed well, I slept soundly through fatigue. In that sleep, the noise of weeping and lamentation struck my ears; rubbing my eyes, when I looked round, then neither the old man nor any one else was in that apartment. I lay alone on the bed, and the room was quite empty. I began to look with alarm in all directions, and perceived a *parda* in a corner which was down; going to it, I lifted it up, and saw that a throne was placed there, on which was seated an angelic woman of about fourteen years of age; her face was like the moon, and her ringlets on both sides [of her head] hung loose; she had a smiling countenance; and she was dressed like a European, and with a most charming air; she was seated [on the throne] and looking forward. The venerable old man lay prostrate before her, with his head on her feet, and he was weeping bitterly, and he seemed to have lost his senses. On seeing the old man's condition, and the woman's beauty and perfection, I was quite lost, and having become lifeless, I fell down like a corpse; the old man seeing my senseless state, brought a bottle of rose water, and began to sprinkle it over my face; when I recovered, I got up, and went up to the angelic woman and saluted her; she did not in the least return my salute, nor did she open her lips. I said, "O lovely angel, in what religion is it right to be so proud, and not to return a salute.

"'Although to speak little is becoming, yet not so much so;
If the lover is dying, even then she would not open her lips.'

For the sake of Him who hath created thee, pray give me an answer; I am come here by chance, and the pleasing of a guest is a requisite duty." I talked much to her, but it was of no use; she heard me, and sat silent like a statue. I then advanced, and laid my hand on her feet; when I touched them, they felt quite hard; at last, I perceived that this beautiful object was formed of stone, and that *Azur*[366] had formed this statue. I then said to the idol-worshipping old man, "I struck an arrow in thy deer's leg, but thou hast with the dart of love pierced my heart through and through; your curse has taken place; now tell me the full particulars of these [strange circumstances]; why hast thou made this talisman, and why, having left [human] habitations, dost thou dwell in woods and mountains? Tell me all that has happened to thee."

When I pressed him greatly, he said, "This affair has indeed ruined me; dost thou also wish to perish by hearing it?" I exclaimed, "Hold, thou hast already made too many evasions; answer to the purpose, or else I will kill thee." Seeing me very urgent, he said, "O youth, may God the Almighty keep every person safe from the scorching flame of love; see what calamities this love hath produced; for love, the woman burns herself with her husband, and sacrifices her life;[367] and all know the story of *Farhad* and *Majnun*; what wilt thou gain by hearing my story? Wilt thou leave thy home, fortune and country, and wander for nothing?" I gave for answer, "Cease, keep thy friendship to thyself; conceive me now thy enemy, and if life is dear to thee, tell me plainly [thy story]." Perceiving there was no alternative, his eyes filled with tears, and he began to say, "The following is this miserable wretch's story:—This humble servant's name is *Ni'man Saiyah*. I was a great merchant; arrived to these years, I have traversed all parts of the world for the purpose of trade, and have been admitted to the presence of all kings.

"Once the fancy came into my mind that I had wandered over the regions of the four corners [of the world], but never went to the Island of the Franks,[368] and never saw its king, citizens and soldiers—I knew nothing of its manners and customs—so that I ought to go there also for once. I took the advice of my acquaintances and friends, and resolved [on the voyage]; I took with me some rarities and presents from various places, such as were fit for that country, and collecting a *kafila* of merchants, we embarked on board a ship and set sail. Having favourable winds, we reached the island in a few months and put up in the city. I saw a magnificent city, to which no city could be compared for beauty. In all the *bazars* and streets the roads were paved and watered; such was the cleanliness that a bit of straw could not be seen; why then make mention of dirt? The buildings were of every variety, and at night the streets were lighted, at intervals, by two rows of lamps; without the city were delightful gardens, in which rare flowers and shrubs and fruits were seen [in rich profusion], such as no where else could be [seen] except in Paradise. In short, whatever I may say in praise of this [magnificent city]

[366] *Azur*, the father of Abraham, was a famous statuary and idol-worshipper, according to the ideas of *Muhammadans*.

[367] Alluding to the *Hindu* custom of the wife's burning herself with the corpse of her husband; in these cases, perhaps, fear of the priesthood, &c., is a stronger motive than love for the defunct.

[368] By the Island of the Franks, it is most probable that the author means Britain. The description of the capital is more adapted to London sixty years ago than to any other European city. This, *Mir Amman* might have learned from some of the resident Europeans, while he filled up the rest from his own luxuriant imagination.

would not exceed [the truth].

"The arrival of our merchants was much talked of. A confidential eunuch[369] mounted on horseback, and attended by many servants, came to our *kafila,* and asked the merchants, "Who is your chief?" They all pointed to me; the eunuch came to my place; I rose up to receive him with respect, and we saluted each other; I seated him on the *masnad,* and offered him the pillow; after which I asked him to tell me what was the occasion which afforded me the honour of his visit; he replied, 'The princess has heard that some merchants are arrived, and have brought much merchandise, for which reason she has desired me to bring them to her presence; so come, and take along with you whatever merchandise may be fit for the courts of kings, and gain the happiness of kissing her threshold.'

"I gave for answer, 'To-day, indeed, I am greatly fatigued; to-morrow I will attend her with my life and property; whatever I have by me, I will present as a *nazar* [to the princess], and whatever pleases her, the same is her majesty's property.' Having made this promise, I gave him rosewater and *betel,* and dismissed him. I called all the merchants near me, and whatever rarities each had, we collected together, and those of my own I took also, and went in the morning to the door of the royal seraglio. The door-keeper sent word of my arrival, and orders came to bring me to the presence; the same eunuch came out, and taking my hand in his, he led me along, whilst we talked in friendly converse. Having passed the apartments of the female attendants of the princess, he conducted me into a noble apartment. O friend, you will not believe it, but so beautiful was the scene, that you might say the fairies had been let loose there with their wings shorn. On whatever side I looked, there my sight became transfixed, and my limbs were torn away [from under me]; I supported myself with difficulty, and reached the royal presence. The moment I cast my eyes upon the princess, I was ready to faint, and my hands and feet trembled.

"I contrived, with some difficulty, to make my salutation. Beautiful women were standing in rows to the right and left, with their arms folded. I laid before the princess the various kinds of jewels, fine clothes, and other rich rarities that I had brought with me; from these she selected some, (inasmuch as they were all worthy of choice). She was greatly pleased, and delivered them to her head-servant, and he said to me, that their prices should be paid the next day, according to the invoice. I made my obeisance, and was pleased within myself that under this pretext I should have to come again the next day. When I took my leave and came out, I was speaking and uttering words like those of a maniac. In this state I came to the *serai,* but my senses were not right; all my friends began to ask what was the matter with me; I replied, that from going and returning so far, the heat had affected my brain.

"In short, I passed that night in tossing and tumbling [about in my bed]. In the morning, I went again and presented myself [to wait on the princess], and entered the seraglio along with the confidential servant, and saw the same scene I had seen the day before. The princess received me kindly, and sent every one

[369] The "eunuch" is of course out of place in a Christian city; at least he does not hold the same rank as in the East.

[present] away, each to his own occupation. When there became a dispersion of them, she retired to a private apartment, and called me to her. When I entered, she desired me to sit down; I made her my obeisance, and sat down. She said, 'As you have come here, and have brought these goods with you, how much profit do you expect on them?' I replied, 'I had an ardent desire to see your highness, which God hath granted, and now I have got all I wished; I have acquired the prosperity of both worlds. Whatever prices are marked in the invoice, half is the prime cost, and half profit.' She replied, 'No, whatever price you have marked down shall be paid; moreover, you shall receive presents besides, on condition that you will do one thing, which I am about to order you.'

"I replied, 'This slave's life and property are at your service, and I shall think as the happiness of my destinies if they can be of any use to your highness; I will perform [what you desire] with my life and soul.' On hearing these words, she called for a *kalam-dan*, wrote a note, put it into a small purse made of pearls, wrapped the purse in a fine muslin handkerchief, and gave it to me; she gave me likewise a ring which she took from off her finger, as a mark [by which I might make myself known]; she then said to me, 'On the opposite side [of the city] is a large garden, its name is *Dil-kusha*, or "Delight of the Heart." Go you there. A person named *Kaikhusru* is the superintendent [of the garden]; deliver into his hands the ring, and bless him for me, and ask a reply to this note, but return quick, as if you ate your dinner there and drank your wine here;[370] you will see what a reward I shall give you for this service.' I took my leave, and went along inquiring my way. When I had gone about two *kos*, I saw the garden. When I reached it, an armed man seized me, and led me into the garden gate. I saw there a young man with the looks of a lion; he was seated on a stool of gold, with an air of state and dignity, having on an armour [forged] by *Da,ud*,[371] with breast plates, and a steel helmet. Five hundred young men, holding each in his hands a shield and sword, and equipped with bows and arrows, were drawn up in a line, and ready [to execute his orders].

"I made him my *salam*, and he called me to him; I delivered him the ring, and, paying him many compliments, I showed him the handkerchief, and mentioned also the circumstance of having brought him a note. The moment he heard me, he bit his finger with his teeth, and slapping his head, he said, 'Perhaps your evil destiny hath brought you here. Well, enter the garden; an iron cage hangs on a cypress tree, in which a young man is confined; give him this note, receive his answer, and return quickly.' I immediately entered the garden; what a garden it was! you might say that I had entered alive into Paradise. Every individual parterre bloomed with variegated flowers; the fountains were playing, and the birds were warbling [on the trees]. I went straight on, and saw the cage suspended from the tree, in which I perceived a very handsome young man. I bent my head with respect, and saluted him, and gave him the sealed and enveloped note through the bars of the cage. That young man opened the note and read it, and inquired of me about the princess with great affection.

[370] In the original it is water; the meaning is obvious enough.

[371] Most probably the name of some famous armourer.

"We had not yet done speaking, when an army of negroes appeared, and fell on me on all sides, and began to attack me without delay with their swords and spears; what could one single unarmed man do? In a moment they covered me with wounds; I had no sensation or recollection of myself. When I recovered my senses, I found myself on a bed, which two soldiers were carrying along [on their shoulders]; they were speaking to each other; one said, 'Let us throw the corpse of this dead man on the plain; the dogs and crows will soon eat it up.' The other replied, 'If the king should make investigation, and learn this circumstance, he will bury us alive, and grind our children to paste; what! are our lives become a burthen to us, that we should act so rashly?'

"On hearing this conversation, I said to the two [ruffians] Gog and Magog, 'for God's sake take some pity on me, I have still a spark of life left; when I die, do with me what you please; the dead are in the hands of the living;[372] but tell me what has happened to me; why have I been wounded, and who are you? pray explain thus much to me.' They then having taken pity on me, said, 'The young man who is confined in the cage is the nephew of the king of this country; and his father was previously on the throne. At the time of his death he gave this injunction to his brother: 'My son, who is heir to my throne, is as yet young and inexperienced; do you continue to guide the affairs of state with zeal and prudence; when he is of age, marry your daughter to him, and make him master of the whole empire and treasury.'

"After saying this his majesty died, and the younger brother became king; he did not attend to the [late king's] last injunctions; on the contrary, he gave it out that [his nephew was] mad and insane, and put him into a cage, and has placed such strict guards on the four sides of the garden that no bird can there flap its wing; and many a time he has administered to [his nephew] the poison called *hala-hal*;[373] but his life is stronger and the poison has had no effect. Now the princess and this prince are lover and mistress; she is distracted at home, and he in the cage; she sent him a love-letter by your hands; the spies instantly conveyed intelligence [of this circumstance] to the king; a body of Abyssinians were ordered out and treated you thus. The king has consulted his *wazir* on the means of putting to death this imprisoned prince, and that ungrateful wretch has persuaded the princess to kill the innocent prince with her own hands in the king's presence.'

"I said, 'Let us go, that I may see this scene even in my dying moments.' They at last agreed [to my request], and the two soldiers and myself, though wounded, went to the scene and stood in silence in a retired corner. We saw the king seated on his throne; the princess held in her hand a naked sword; the prince was taken out of the iron cage, and made to stand before [the king]; the princess, becoming an executioner, advanced with the naked sword to kill her lover. When she drew near the prince, she threw away the sword and embraced him. Then that lover said to her, 'I am willing to die thus; here, indeed, I desire thee,—there, also, I shall wish for thee.'[374] The princess said, 'I have come, under this pretext to behold

[372] A Persian proverb.

[373] That is poison of the strongest kind.—Vide note on this word in page 108.

[374] Meaning in this world and the next.

thee.' The king, on seeing this scene, became greatly enraged, and reproached the *wazir*, and said, 'Hast thou brought me here to see this sight?' The [princess's] confidential servant separated the princess from the prince, and conducted her to the seraglio. The *wazir* took up the sword, and flew with rage at the prince to end with one blow his unfortunate existence. As he lifted up his arm to strike, an arrow from an unknown hand pierced his forehead, so that [his head] was cleft in twain, and he fell down.

"The king, seeing this mysterious event, retired into his palace; and they put the young prince again into the cage, and carried him to the garden; I likewise came out from where I was. On the road, a man called me and conducted me to the princess; seeing me severely wounded, she sent for a surgeon, and enjoined him very strictly, 'cure this young man quickly, and perform the ablution of recovery. Your welfare depends on it; as much care and attention as you bestow on him, so many presents and favours you will receive from me.' In short, the surgeon used his skill and assiduity according to the princess's injunctions, and at the end of forty days, having caused me to be bathed and washed, he presented me to the princess. She asked me, 'Is there now anything else left to be done.' I replied, that through her humanity I was quite recovered. The princess then gave me a rich *khil'at* and a large sum of money, as she had promised; yea, she even gave me as much more, and then dismissed me.

"I took all my friends and servants with me, and set out from that country [to return home]. When I reached this spot, I desired all of them to return to their native country, and I erected on this hill this building, and got a statue made of the princess. I took up my residence here, and having rewarded my servants and slaves according to their respective merits, I dismissed them, saying, whilst I live, I leave it to you to provide me with food; beyond this act, you are your own masters. They supply me with subsistence from gratitude, and I, with heart at ease, worship this statue; whilst I live, this will be my sole [care and] employment; these are my adventures which you have just heard." O, *Darweshes*! on hearing his story, I, having thrown the *kafni* over my shoulders, and having put on the habit of a pilgrim, set out with extreme desire to see the country of the Franks. After long wandering over mountains and through woods, I began to resemble *Majnun Farhad*.

At last, my strong desire carried me to the same [European] city [where the old statue-worshipper had been]; I wandered through its streets and lanes like a lunatic, and I often remained near the seraglio of the princess; but I could get no opportunity to have an introduction to her. I was greatly vexed that I should not obtain the object for which I had undergone such misery and toil, and come so far. On day, I was standing in the *bazar* when all at once the people began to run away, and the shopkeepers having shut up their shops, also fled. What crowds there were [a moment before], and how desert the place became [all of a sudden]! I soon perceived a young man rushing forward from a side street; he was like *Rustam* in appearance, and roared like a lion; he flourished a naked sword in each hand; he was in armour, with a pair of pistols in his girdle, and kept muttering something to himself like an inebriated maniac; two slaves followed him, clothed in woollen, and bearing on their heads a bier covered with velvet of *Kashan*.

On seeing this sight, I determined to proceed with it; those I met dissuaded me from it, but I would not hear them. Pushing forward, the young man went towards a grand mansion; I also went along with him. He looked back, and perceiving me, he wished to give me a blow and cut me in two; I swore to him that this was the very thing I wished, saying, "I forgive you my blood; relieve me by some means or other from the misery of life, for I am grievously afflicted; I have knowingly and voluntarily put myself in your way; do not delay [my execution]." Setting me determined to die, God infused compassion into his heart, and his anger cooled, and he asked me with much kindness and gentleness, "Who art thou and why art thou tired of life?"

I replied, "Sit down awhile that I may tell you; my story is very long and tedious. I am caught in the claws of love, for which reason I am desperate." On hearing this, he unfastened his waist band, and having washed his hands and face, he took some food and gave me some likewise. When he finished his meal, he said, "Say what has befallen thee?" I related all the adventures of the old man and the princess, and the cause of my going there, [i. e. to Europe]. On hearing them he wept at first, and then said, "What numbers of homes this unfortunate [princess] has ruined! Well, thy cure is in my hands; it is probable that through the means of this guilty being thou wilt attain thy wishes; do not give way to anxiety; be confident." He then ordered the barber to shave me, and to apply to me the bath;[375] his slave brought me a suit of clothes and dressed me: then the young man said to me, "This bier which thou seest is that of the late young prince, who was confined in the iron cage; another *wazir* murdered him at last through treachery; he indeed has obtained release though he has been wrongfully slain. I am his foster brother; I put that *wazir* to death with a blow of my sword, and made the attempt to kill the king; but he entreated mercy, and swore that he was innocent; I having spurned him as a coward, allowed him to escape. Since then, my occupation has been this, to carry the bier, in this manner, through the city, on the first Thursday of every moon, and to mourn for the [murdered prince]."

On hearing these circumstances, from his mouth, I attained some consolation, saying, "If he should wish it, then my desires will be accomplished; God has favoured me greatly, since he has made such a mad man well inclined towards me; so true is it, that if God is favourable, all goes well." When the evening came, and the sun set, the young man took up the bier, and instead of one of the slaves, he put it on my head and took me along with him. He said, "I am going to the princess, and will plead for thee as much as I am able; do not thou open thy lips, but remain silent and listen." I replied, "Whatever you advise, I will strictly do; God preserve you, for you feel pity on my case." That young man proceeded towards the royal garden, and when we entered it, I perceived a marble platform of eight sides, in an open space of the garden, on which was spread an awning of silver tissue with pearl fringe, and erected on poles set with diamonds; a rich brocade *masnad*, with pillows, was spread under the awning. The bier was placed there, and we were both ordered to go and sit under a tree [which he pointed out].

In a short time, the lights of flambeaux appeared, and the princess herself

[375] Barbers in Asia not only shave but wash persons in the private and public baths.

arrived, accompanied by some female attendants before and behind her; melancholy and anger were visible in her looks; she mounted the platform and sat down [on the *masnad*]. The foster-brother stood before her with folded arms, then sat down at a respectable distance on a corner of the *farsh*. The prayer for the dead was read; then the foster-brother said something; I having applied my ear, was listening with attention. At last, he said, "O princess of the world, peace be upon you! The prince of the kingdom of Persia, hearing, in your absence, of your beauty and excellence, has abandoned his throne, and becoming a pilgrim like *Ibrahim Adham*;[376] he is arrived here, after overcoming many difficulties and undergoing great fatigue. The pilgrim hath quitted *Balkh*[377] for thee; he hath wandered for some time through this city in distress and misery; at last, forming the resolution to die, he joined me; I attempted to alarm him with my sword; he presented his neck, and conjured me to strike without delay, adding, that was his wish. In short, he is firmly in love with you; I have proved him well, and have found him perfect in every way. For this reason I have mentioned him to you; if you take pity on his case and be kind to him, as he is a stranger, it would not be doing too much [on the part] of one who fears God and loves justice."

On hearing this speech, the princess said, "Where is he? if he is really a prince, then it does not signify, let him come before us." The foster-brother got up and came [to where I was] and took me with him. I, on seeing the princess, became exceedingly overjoyed, but my reason and my senses departed. I became dumb; I had not power to speak. The princess shortly after returned [to her palace], and the foster-brother came to his own residence. When we reached his house, he said, "I have related all the circumstances [you mentioned] to the princess from beginning to end, and have likewise interceded for you; now do you go there every night without fail and indulge in pleasure and joy." I fell at his feet; [he lifted me up and] clasped me to his bosom. All the day, I continued counting the hours until the evening came, that I might go and see the princess. When the night arrived, I took leave of that young man, and went to the princess's lower garden; I sat down on the marble platform, reclining on my pillow.

A hour after, the princess came slowly, attended by one female servant only, and sat down on the *masnad;* it was through my happy destinies that I lived to see this day! I kissed her feet; she lifted up my head, and embraced me, and said, "Conceive this opportunity as fortunate; mind my advice; take me from hence, and go to some other country." I replied, "Come along." After having thus spoken, we both got out of the garden, but we were so confused, through wonder and joy, that we could not use our hands and feet, and we lost our road; we went along, in another direction, but found not a place of rest. The princess got angry, and said, "I am now tired, where is your house? hasten to get there; otherwise what do you mean to do? My feet are blistered; I shall [be obliged to] sit down somewhere on the road."

I replied, "My slave's house is near; we have now reached it; be easy in your mind, and march on." I indeed told a falsehood, but I was at a loss where to take

[376] A prince of *Khurasan,* who quitted a throne in order to lead a life of piety.

[377] A celebrated city of *Khurasan,* famous in former times for its riches.

her. A locked door appeared on the road; I quickly broke the lock, and we entered the place; it was a fine house, laid out with carpets, and flasks full of wine were arranged in the recesses, and bread and roast meat were ready in the kitchen. We were greatly fatigued, and drank each of us, a glass of Portugal wine with our meat, and passed the whole night together in mutual bliss. In this scene of felicity when the morning dawned, an uproar was raised in the town that the princess had disappeared. Proclamations were issued in every district and street; and bawds and messengers were despatched with orders, that wherever she was to be found, she might be seized [and brought to the king]; and guards of royal slaves were posted at all the gates of the city. Those guards received orders not to let an ant pass without the royal permission; and that whoever would bring any intelligence of the princess should receive a *khil'at* and a thousand pieces of gold as a present. The bawds roamed through the whole city and entered every house.

I, who was ill fated, did not shut the door. An old hag, the aunt of Satan (may God make her face black), with a string of beads in her hand, and covered with a mantle, finding the door open, entered without fear, and standing before the princess, lifted up her hands and blessed her, saying, "I pray to God that he may long preserve you a married woman, and that thy husband's turban may be permanent! I am a poor beggar woman, and I have a daughter who is in her full time and perishing in the pains of child-birth; I have not the means to get a little oil which I may burn in our lamp; food and drink, indeed, are out of the question. If she should die, how shall I bury her? and if she is brought to bed, what shall I give the midwife and nurse, or how procure remedies for the lying-in woman? it is now two days since she has lain hungry and thirsty. O, noble lady! give her, out of your bounty, a morsel of bread that she may eat the same along with a drink of water."

The princess took pity on her, and called her near her, and gave her four loaves, some roast meat, and a ring from her little finger, saying, "having sold this, make jewels [for your daughter] and live comfortably; and come occasionally to see me, the house is yours." The old hag having completely gained the object she came in search of, poured heartfelt blessings on the princess, saluted her and trotted off. She threw away the loaves and meat at the door, but kept the ring snug, saying to herself, "the clue to trace the princess is now in my possession." As God wished to preserve us from this calamity, just then the master of the house arrived; he was a brave soldier, mounted on an Arab horse, with a spear in his hand, and a deer hanging by the side of his saddle. Finding the door of his house open, the lock broken, and the old hag coming out of it, he was enraged, and seized her by the hair and dragged her to the house. He tied both her feet with a rope, and hung her on the branch of a true with her head down and her feet uppermost; so that in a short time the old devil died in agonies. The moment I saw the soldier's looks, I was overcome with such fear that I turned quite pale, and my heart began to tremble with dread. That brave man seeing us both alarmed, gave us assurances of safety, and added, "You have acted very imprudently; you have done the deed and left the door open."

The princess, smiling, said, "The prince said it was the house of his slave, and brought me here under a deception." The soldier observed, "The prince said truly, for all the people are the slaves and servants of princes; all are reared and fed from their favour and protection. This slave is yours without purchase; but to conceal secrets is consonant to good sense. O, prince, you and the princess's coming to this humble roof, and honouring me with your presence, will be a source of happiness to me in both worlds; and you have thus dignified your slave. I am ready to sacrifice my life for you; in no way will I withhold either it or my property [from your service]; you may repose here in confidence; there is now no danger. If this vile bawd had gone away in safety, she would have brought calamity [upon you]; remain here now as long as you please, and let this servant know whatever you require; he will procure it. What is the king! angels themselves shall have no tidings of your being here." The brave fellow spoke such words of comfort, and gave such confidence, that we became more easy in our mind. Then I spoke, "Well said, you are a brave fellow; when I am able, I will show you the return for this kindness; what is your name?" He answered, "This slave's name is *Bihzad Khan*. In short, for the space of six months, he performed from his heart and soul all the duty required, and we passed our time very comfortably.

One day, my country and my parents recurred to my recollection, which made me pensive and melancholy. Seeing my thoughtful looks, *Bihzad Khan* joined his hands together, and stood before me,[378] and began to say, "If on the part of this slave any failure has occurred in performing his duty, then let the same be stated." I said, "For God's sake, why mention this? you have behaved to us in such a manner, that we have lived in this city as comfortably as any one does in his mother's womb; for I had committed such an act that every individual straw had become my enemy. Who was such a friend to us, that we could have tarried here a moment? May God preserve you in happiness! You are a brave man." *Bihzad Khan* then said, "If you are tired of this place, I will conduct you in safety wherever you wish to go." I then said, "If I could reach my own country, I should see my parents; I am in this state; Lord knows what may have been their condition. I have attained the object for which I quitted my country; and it is proper I should now return [to my relations]; they have no tidings of me, whether I am dead or alive; [God knows] what sorrow they may feel in their hearts." That brave man replied, "It is very proper,—let us go." Saying this, he brought a Turkish horse for me, which could travel a hundred *kos* a-day, and a swift quiet mare of unclipped wings[379] for the princess, and made us both mount; then putting on his cuirass and arming himself completely, he mounted on his horse and said, "I will go before, do you follow me with full confidence."

When we came to the city gate, he gave a loud cry, and with his mace broke the bolt, and frightened the guards; he vociferated to them, "Ye rascals, go and tell your master that *Bihzad Khan* is carrying off the princess *Mihrnigar*, and the prince *Kamgar*, who is his son-in-law; if he has any spark of manhood, then let him come out and rescue her; do not you be saying that I carried her off in silence and by stealth, otherwise let him stay in the fort and enjoy his repose." This news soon reached the king; he ordered the *wazir* and general to seize the three rebel-

[378] The attitude of respect, common in the East, when a servant has a request to make of his master; or a very inferior person of one who is greatly his superior.

[379] Meaning, "of surpassing speed."

lious ones, and bring them tied neck and heels to the royal presence, and cut off their heads and lay them before the throne. After a short time, a numerous body of troops appeared, and the heavens and earth were darkened by a whirlwind of dust. *Bihzad Khan* placed the princess and me on the abutment of an arch of the bridge which, like the bridge of *Jaunpur*, consisted of twelve arches, and he himself turned about, and pushed his horse towards the troops; he rushed in among them like a growling lion; the whole body was dispersed like a flock of sheep,[380] and he penetrated to the two chiefs and cut off both their heads. When the chiefs were killed, the troops dispersed, as the saying is, that "All depends on the head; when it is gone, all is lost." The king came immediately to their assistance, with a body of armed troops; *Bihzad Khan* completely defeated them also.

The king fled; so true it is that "God alone gives victory;" but *Bihzad Khan* behaved so bravely, that perhaps even *Rustam* himself could not have equalled his valour. When he saw that the field of battle was cleared, and that no one remained to pursue him, and that there was nothing to apprehend, he came confidentially to the place where we were, and taking the princess and me along with him, he pushed forward. The duration of the journey is rendered short; we reached the boundaries of my country in a short time. I despatched a letter to the king, (who was my father), mentioning my safe arrival; he was quite rejoiced on reading it, and thanked God [for His goodness]. As the withered plant revives by water, so the joyful tidings renovated his drooping spirits; he took all his *amirs* with him, and advanced for the purpose of receiving me as far as the banks of a large river, and an order for boats [to cross us over] was issued to the superintendent of rivers. I saw the royal train from the opposite bank; from eagerness to kiss my father's feet, I plunged my horse into the river, and swimming over, I rode up to the king; he clasped me with eager fondness to his [paternal] bosom.

At this moment, another unforeseen calamity overwhelmed us. The horse on which I was mounted was perhaps the colt of the mare on which the princess rode, or they had been perhaps always together, for seeing my horse plunge into the river, the mare became restive, followed my horse, and likewise plunged into the river with the princess, and began to swim. The princess being alarmed, pulled the bridle; the mare was tender mouthed and turned over; the princess struggled, and sank with the mare, so that not a trace of either was ever seen again. On seeing this circumstance, *Bihzad Khan* dashed into the river on horseback to afford assistance to the princess; he got into a whirlpool and could not extricate himself; all his efforts with his hands and feet were vain, and he also sank. The king seeing these sad circumstances, sent for nets and had them thrown into the river, and ordered the boatmen and divers [to look for the bodies]; they swept the whole river, but could find nothing.[381] O *Darweshes!* this dreadful occurrence affected me so much that I became mad and frantic; I became a pilgrim, and wandered about, ever repeating these words,—"Such has been the fate of these three; that you have seen, now view the other side." If the princess had vanished or died anywhere, I should

[380] In the original, the word is *kai,* or the green scum that floats on stagnant water. "*Bihzad Khan,* dispersed the enemy as *kai* is dispersed when a stone is thrown into the water," is nearly the original simile.

[381] Literally, "merely continued bringing up the soil from the bottom."

then have some kind of consolation for my heart, for I would have gone in search of her, or have borne the loss with patience; but when she perished before my eyes [in this dreadful manner], I could not support [the shock]. At last, I determined to perish with her in the stream, that I might perhaps meet my beloved one in death.

I according plunged into that same river one night in order to drown myself, and went up to the neck in the water; I was on the point of stepping forward and diving down, when the same veiled horseman who saved you two,[382] came up and seized my arm; he consoled me, and said to me, "Be comforted; the princess and *Bihzad Khan* are alive; why do you uselessly throw away your life? such events do occur in the world. Do not despair of the help of God; if you live, you will some day or other meet the two persons [for whom you are going to sacrifice your life]. Proceed now to the empire of *Rum*; two other unfortunate *Darweshes* are gone there already; when you meet them, you will attain your wishes." O *Darweshes!* I am come here to you, according to the advice of my heavenly Mentor; I firmly hope that each of us will gain the desires of his heart. These have been this pilgrim's adventures, which he hath related to you fully and entirely.

[382] The first and second *Darweshes*.

ADVENTURES OF THE FOURTH DARWESH.

The fourth *Darwesh* began with tears the relation of his adventures in the following manner:—

"The sad tale of my misfortunes now hear,
Pay some attention, and my whole story hear;
From what causes I distressed have come thus far,
I will relate it all,—do you the reason hear."

O, guides [to the path] of God,[383] bestow a little attention. This pilgrim, who is reduced to this wretched state, is the son of the king of China; I was brought up with tenderness and delicacy, and well educated. I was utterly unacquainted with the good and evil of this world, and imagined [my life] would ever pass in the same manner. In the midst of this extreme thoughtlessness this sad event took place; the king, who was the father of this orphan, departed [this life]. In his last moments, he sent for his younger brother, who was my uncle, and said to him, "I now leave my kingdom and wealth behind me, and am going to depart; but do you perform my last wishes, and act the part of an elder. Until the prince, who is the heir to my throne, has become of age, and has sense to govern his kingdom; do you act as regent, and do not permit the army and the husbandmen to be injured or oppressed. When the prince has arrived at the years of maturity, give him advice, and deliver over to him the government; and having married him to your daughter, *Roshan Akhtar,* retire yourself from the throne. By this conduct, the sovereignty will remain in my family, and no harm will accrue to it."

After this speech, [the king] himself expired; my uncle became ruler, and began to regulate the affairs of government. He ordered me to remain in the seraglio, and that I should not come out of it until I reached [the years of] manhood. Until my fourteenth year I was brought up among the princesses and female attendants, and used to play and frisk about. Having heard of [my intended] marriage with my uncle's daughter, I was quite happy, and on this hope I became thoughtless, and said to myself, that I shall now in a short time ascend the throne and be married; "the world is established on hope."[384] I used often to go and sit with *Mubarak,* a negro slave, who had been brought up in my late father's service, and in whom much confidence was [placed], as he was sensible and faithful. He also had a great regard for me, and seeing me advancing to the years of manhood, he was much pleased, and used to say, "God be praised, O prince, you are now a young man, and, God willing, your uncle, the shadow of Omnipotence, will shortly fulfil the injunctions [of your late father], and give you his daughter, and your

[383] One of the many epithets applied to *Darweshes* in the East.

[384] A Persian proverb.

father's throne."

One day, it happened that a common female slave gave me, without cause, such a slap, that the marks of her five fingers remained on my cheek. I went, weeping, to *Mubarak;* he clasped me to his bosom, and wiped away my tears with his sleeve, and said, "Come, I will conduct you to-day to the king; he will perhaps be kind to you on seeing yon, and, conceiving you qualified [in years], he may give up to you your rights." He led me immediately to my uncle's presence; my uncle showed me great affection before the court, and asked me, "why are you so sad, and wherefore are you come here to-day?" *Mubarak* replied, "He is come here to say something [to your majesty]." On hearing this, he said of himself, "I will shortly marry the young prince." *Mubarak* answered, "It will be a most joyful event." The king immediately sent for the astrologers and diviners into his presence, and with feigned interest asked them, "In this year what month, what day, and what hour is auspicious, that I may order the preparations for the prince's marriage?" They perceiving what were [the king's real wishes], made their calculations, and said, "Mighty sire, the whole of this year is unpropitious; no day in any of the lunar months appears happy; if this whole year pass in safety, then the next is most propitious for a happy marriage."

The king looked towards *Mubarak,* and said, "Reconduct the prince to the seraglio, if God willing, after this year is over, I will deliver up my trust to him; let him make himself perfectly easy, and attend to his studies," *Mubarak* made his *salam,* and taking me along with him, reconducted me to the seraglio. Two or three days after this, I went to *Mubarak;* on seeing me, he began to weep; I was surprised, and asked him, saying, "My father, is all well? what is the cause of your weeping?" Then, that well wisher, (who loved me with heart and soul), said, "I conducted you the other day to that tyrant; if I had known it, I would not have carried you there," I was alarmed, and asked him, "What harm has occurred from my going? pray tell me truly," He then said, "All the nobles, ministers, and officers of state, small and great, of your father's time, were greatly rejoiced on seeing you, and began to offer up thanks to God, saying, 'Now, our prince is of age, and fit to reign. Now, in a short time, the right will devolve upon the rightful [heir]; then he will do justice to our merits, and appreciate the length of our services.' This news reached the ears of that faithless wretch,[385] and entered his breast like a serpent. He sent for me in private, and said, 'O *Mubarak,* act now in such a manner, that by some stratagem or other the prince may be destroyed; and remove the dread of his [existence] from my heart, that I may feel secure.' Since then I am quite confounded, for your uncle is become the enemy of your life." When I heard this dreadful news from *Mubarak,* I was dead without being murdered, and fell at his feet from fear of my life, and said, "For God's sake, I relinquish my throne; by any means, let my life be saved." That faithful slave lifted up my head, clasped me to his breast, and said, "There is no danger, a thought has struck me; if it turns out well, then there is nothing to fear; whilst we have life, we have everything. "It is probable that, by this scheme [of mine] your life will be preserved, and you will attain your wishes."

Giving me these hopes, he took me with him, and went to the apartment

[385] The regent; the fourth *Darwesh's* uncle.

where the deceased king, my father, used to sit and sleep; and gave me every confidence. There a stool was placed; he told me to lay hold of one of its legs, and taking hold of the other himself, we removed the stool, and he lifted up the carpet that was beneath it, and began to dig the floor. A window appeared suddenly, to which were attached a chain and lock. He called me near him; I apprehended within myself that he wished to butcher me, and bury me in the place he had dug. Death appeared [in all its horrors] before my eyes; but having no other alternative, I advanced slowly and in silence towards him, repeating within myself my prayers to God. I then saw a building with four rooms inside of that window, and in every room ten large vases of gold were suspended by chains; on the mouth of each vase was placed a brick of gold, on which was set the figure of a monkey inlaid with precious stones. I counted thirty-nine vases of this kind in the four rooms, and saw one vase filled with pieces of gold, on the mouth of which there was neither the brick, nor the figure of the monkey, and I also saw a vat filled to the brim with precious stones. I asked *Mubarak,* "O my father, what talisman is this? whose place is this, and for what use are those figures?" He replied, "The following is the story of those figures of monkeys which you see:—Your father from his youth formed a friendship and kept up an intercourse with *Maliki Sadik,* who is the king of the *jinns.*

"Accordingly, once every year, [his late majesty] used to visit *Maliki Sadik* and stay near a month with him, having carried thither with him many kinds of essences,[386] and the rarities of this country, [as a present]. When he took his leave, *Maliki Sadik* used to give him the figure of a monkey made of emerald, and our king used to bring it and place it in these lower rooms; no one but myself knew the circumstance. Once I observed to your father, O mighty king, you carry with you thousands of rupees'-worth of rarities, and you bring back from thence the figure of a lifeless monkey in stone; what is the advantage of this [exchange] in the end? In answer to my question, he smiling, said, 'Beware, and do not, in any way divulge this secret; the information [you receive] is on this condition. Each one of these lifeless monkeys which thou seest has a thousand powerful demons[387] at his command, ready to obey his orders; but until I have the number of forty monkeys complete, so long are all these of no use, and will be of no service to me.' So one monkey was wanting [to complete the efficient number] in that very year, when the king died.

"All this toil then has been of no avail, nor has the advantage of it been displayed. O prince, I recollected this circumstance on seeing your forlorn situation, and determined within myself to conduct you by some means or other to *Maliki Sadik,* and mention to him your uncle's tyranny. It is most likely that he, recollecting your father's friendship for him, may give you the one monkey which is wanting [to complete the number]; then, with their aid, you may get your empire, and reign peaceably over China and *Machin,*[388] and your life, at least, will be secured

[386] According to the fabulous system of *jinns, divs, paris, &c.,* in Asia, it is supposed that the *jinns* and *paris* live on essences, &c. The *divs* are malignant spirits or beings, and live on less delicate food.

[387] *Divs* or demons; the malignant race of *jinns.*

[388] *Chin* and *Machin,* is the general name of China among the Persians.

by this proceeding, if nothing else can be done; I see no other way to escape from the hands of this tyrant, except the plan I propose." On hearing all these consoling circumstances from *Mubarak*, I said to him, "O friend, you are now the disposer of my life; do whatever is best with regard to me." Giving me every confidence, he went to the *bazar* to buy some *'itr* and *bukhur*,[389] and whatever he deemed fit to be carried [as a present for *Maliki Sadik*].

The next day, he went to my impious uncle, who was a second *Abu-Jahal*,[390] and said, "Protector of the world, I have formed a plan in my heart for destroying the prince, and if you order me, I will relate it." That wretch was quite pleased, and said, "What is the plan?" Then *Mubarak* said, "By putting him to death [here], your majesty will be highly censured in every way; but I will take him out to the woods, finish him, bury him, and return; no one will be conversant [of the fact]." On hearing this plan of *Mubarak's*, the king said, "It is an excellent [plan]; I desire this, that he may not live in safety; I am greatly afraid of him in my heart, and if thou relievest me from this anxiety, then in return for that service thou shalt obtain much; take him where thou wilt, and make away with him, and bring me the welcome tidings."

Being in this manner at ease with regard to the king, *Mubarak* took me with him, and having also taken the presents, he set out from the city at midnight, and proceeded towards the north. For a whole month he went on without stopping; one night we were trudging along, when *Mubarak* observed, "God be praised, we are now arrived at the end of our journey." On hearing this exclamation, I said, "O friend, what dost thou say?" He replied, "O prince, do not you see the army of the *jinns*?" I answered, "I see nothing except you." *Mubarak* then took out a box containing *surma*, and with a needle applied to both my eyes the *surma* of *Sulaiman*. I instantly began to see the host of the *jinns* and the tents and encampments of their army; they were all handsome, and well dressed. Recognising *Mubarak*, they all embraced him, and spake to him facetiously.

Proceeding onwards, we at length reached the royal tents, and entered the court. I saw they were well lighted, and stools of various kinds were arranged in double rows, on which were seated men of learning, philosophers, *darweshes*, nobles, and the officers of state; servants of various grades with their arms across were in waiting, and in the centre was placed a throne set with precious stones, on which was seated with an air of dignity, the king, *Maliki Sadik*, with a crown of his head, and clothed in a tunic set with pearls. I approached him and made my salutation; he desired me with kindness to sit down, and then ordered dinner; after having finished [our repast], the *dastar-khwan* was removed, and he having looked towards *Mubarak*, asked my story. *Mubarak* replied, "This prince's uncle now reigns in the room of his father, and is become the enemy of his life, for which reason I have run off with him from thence, and have conducted him to your majesty; he is an orphan, and the throne is his due; but no one can do anything without a

[389] *Bukhur* is a kind of frankincense.

[390] *Abu-Jahal*, or "the father of obstinacy," or "of brutality," was the name of an Arab. He was uncle to the prophet *Muhammad*, and an inveterate opposer of the latter's new religion.

protector; with your majesty's assistance, this injured [youth] may get his rights; recollect the return due for his father's services, afford him your assistance, and give him the fortieth monkey, that the number may be completed, and the prince, having gained his rights [with their aid],[391] will pray for your majesty's long life and prosperity; he has no other visible resource except your majesty's protection."

On hearing all these circumstances, *Maliki Sadik,* after a pause, said, "In truth, the return for the deceased king's services, and his friendship for me, are great; and, considering that this helpless prince is overwhelmed with misfortunes, that he has quitted his lineal throne to save his life, and is come as far as this, and has taken shelter under the shadow of our protection, I shall in no way be wanting [to afford him my assistance] as far as I am able, nor will I pass him over; but I have an affair in hand; if he can do it and does not deceive me—if he executes it properly, and acquits himself fully in the trial, I then promise that I will be a greater friend to him than I was to the late king, his father, and that I will grant him whatever he asks." I joined my hands, and replied, "This servant will most cheerfully perform as far as he is able, whatever services your majesty may require; he will execute them with prudence and vigilance, and without deceit, and think it a happiness to him in both worlds." The king of the *jinns* observed, "You are as yet a mere boy, for which reason I warn you so repeatedly, that you may not deceive me, and plunge yourself in calamity." I answered, "God, through the good fortune of your majesty, will make it easy to me, and I will, as far as in me lies, exert myself to your satisfaction."

Maliki Sadik, on hearing [these assurances], called me near him, and taking out a paper from his pocket book, showed it to me, and said, "Search where you think proper for the person whose portrait this is; find her out and bring her to me; when you find out her name and place, go before her, and express great affection to her from me; if you perform this service, then whatever expectations you may have from me, I will exceed them in the performance; otherwise you will be treated as you deserve." When I looked on that paper, I perceived such a beautiful portrait in it, that a faintness came over me; I supported myself with difficulty through fear, and answered, "Very well, I take my leave; if God favours me, I shall execute what your majesty commands." Saying this, I took *Mubarak* with me, and bent my course towards the woods. I began to wander from city to city, from town to town, from village to village, and from country to country, and to inquire of every one [I met] the name and place [of the fair one whose portrait I had]; but no one said "Yes, I know her," or "I have heard of her from some one." I passed seven years in this wandering state, and suffered every misery and perplexity; at last, I reached a city which was populous, and contained many grand edifices; but every living creature there was repeating the great name,[392] and worshipping God.

I saw a blind beggar of *Hindustan* begging alms, but no one gave him a *kauri,* or a mouthful; I wondered at it, and pitied him; I took out a piece of gold from my pocket, and gave it to him; he took it, and said, "O donor! God prosper you; you

[391] The forty figures of monkeys would give the possessor a power over the *divs* and *jinns,* and having them at his command, he could easily overset the usurper, *alias* his uncle.

[392] The *Ismi A'zam,* or great name of God.—See note 254, p. 75.

are perhaps a traveller, and not an inhabitant of this city." I replied, "In truth, I have wandered distractedly for seven years; I cannot find the smallest trace of the object for which I set out, and have this day reached this city. The old man poured blessings on me, and went on; I followed him; a grand building appeared without the city; he entered it, and I also followed, and saw that here and there the building had fallen down, and was out of repair.

I said to myself, "This edifice is fit for princes; what an agreeable place it will be when in repair? and now, through desolation, what an appearance it has! but I cannot conceive why it is fallen into ruin, and why this blind man lives in it." The blind man was going on feeling his way with his stick, when I heard a voice, as if some one was saying, "O father, I hope all is well; why have you returned so early to-day?" The old man, on hearing this question, replied, "Daughter, God made a youthful traveller have pity on my condition; he gave me a piece of gold; it is many a-day since I have had a bellyful of good food. So I have purchased meat, spices, butter, oil, flour, and salt; and I have also procured such clothes for you as were necessary; cut them out, sew them and wear them; and cook the dinner, that we may partake of it, and then offer up our prayers for the generous man [who has been kind to us]; although I do not know the desires of his heart, yet God knows and sees all; and will grant the prayers of us destitute ones." When I heard the circumstance of his severe fasting, I wished much to give him twenty pieces of gold more; but looking towards the quarter from whence the sounds came, I saw a woman who resembled exactly the portrait I had. I drew it out and compared it, and perceived that there was not a hairbreadth of difference. A deep sigh escaped from my bosom, and I became senseless. *Mubarak* took me in his arms and sat down, and began to fan me; I recovered a little sensation, and was gazing at her, when *Mubarak* asked, "What is the matter with you?" I had not yet answered him, when the beautiful female said, "O young man, fear God, and do not look at a strange female;[393] shame and modesty are necessary to every one."

She spoke with such propriety that I became enchanted with her beauty and manners. *Mubarak* comforted me greatly, but he did not know the state of my heart; having no alternative, I called out and said, "O you creatures of God, and inhabitants of this place! I am a poor traveller; if you call me near you, and give me some place to put up in, it will be an important matter [for me]." The old man called me to him, and recognising my voice, he embraced me, and conducted me to where the lovely woman was seated; she went and hid herself in a corner. The old man asked me thus: "Tell thy story; why hast thou left thy home, and wandered about alone, and of whom are you in search?" I did not mention *Maliki Sadik's* name, nor did I say anything about him; but thus told [my supposed tale]. "This wretch is the prince of China and *Machin*; so that my father is still king; he purchased from a merchant this picture for four *lakhs* of rupees; from the moment when I beheld it, my peace of mind fled, and I put on the dress of a pilgrim; I have searched the whole world, and have now found the object here; the same is in your power."

[393] Alluding to the Asiatic custom of the women being concealed from the view of all, except their husbands or very near relations.

On hearing these words, the old man heaved a heavy sigh, and said, "O friend, my daughter is entangled in great misfortunes; no man can presume to marry her and enjoy her." I replied, "I am in hopes you will explain more fully." Then that strange man related thus his story;—"Hear, O prince! I am a chief and grandee of this unfortunate city; my forefathers were celebrated, and of a great family; God the Most High bestowed on me this daughter; when she became a woman, her beauty and gracefulness and elegance of manners were celebrated; and over the whole country it was said, that in such a person's house is a daughter, before whose beauty even angels and fairies are abashed; how can a human creature, therefore, be compared to her! The prince of this city heard these praises, and became enamoured of her by report without seeing her; he quitted food and drink, and became quite restless.

"At last, the king heard of this circumstance, and called me at night in private and mentioned to me how matters stood; he coaxed me so with fine speeches, that at last he got my consent to an alliance [by marriage] with him. I likewise [naturally] reflected that as a daughter was born to me, she must be married to some one or other; then what can be better, than to marry her to the prince? this the king also entreats. I accepted the proposal, and took my leave. From that day the preparations for the marriage were begun by both parties; and on an auspicious hour, all the *kazis* and *muftis*,[394] the learned men and the nobles were convened, and the marriage rites were performed; the bride was carried away with great *eclat*, and all the ceremonies were finished. At night, when the bridegroom wished to consummate the nuptial rites, such a noise and uproar arose in the palace, that the people without who mounted guard were surprised. They wished that having opened the door of the room, they might see what was the matter; but it was so fastened from the inside, that they could not open it. A moment after, the noise of lamentation became less; they then broke open the door from its hinges, and saw the bridegroom with his head severed from his [body], and [his limbs] still quivering; and the bride foamed at the mouth, and rolled senseless in the dust mingled with [her husband's] blood.

"On seeing this horrible sight, the senses of all present forsook them; that such grief should succeed such felicity! The dreadful intelligence was conveyed to the king; he flew [to the spot], beating his head; all the officers of state were soon assembled there, but no one's judgment was of any use in ascertaining the [cause of] this [mysterious] affair; at length the king, in his distracted state, ordered the ill-fated, luckless bride's head to be cut off likewise. The moment this order was issued from the king's lips, the same clamour arose; the king was alarmed, and from fear of his life, he ran off, and ordered the bride to be turned out of the palace. The female attendants conveyed this [unfortunate] girl to my house. The account of this strange event soon spread over the whole kingdom, and whoever heard it was amazed; and owing to the prince's murder, the king himself and all the inhabitants of the city became bitter enemies of my life.

"When the public mourning was over, and the fortieth day completed, the

[394] The *kazis* and *muftis* are the judges in Turkey, Arabia, Persia and *Hindustan*, of all civil and religious causes; they likewise marry, divorce, &c.

king asked counsel of the officers of state, saying, 'What is next to be done?' They all said, 'Nothing else can be done; but in order to console your majesty's mind, and inspire it with patience, to put the girl and her father to death, and confiscate their property.' When this punishment of me and mine was determined on, the magistrate received orders [to put it in execution]; he came and surrounded my house [with guards] on all sides and sounded a trumpet at the gate, and was about to enter in order to execute the king's orders. From some hidden quarter, such showers of stones and bricks were poured on them that the whole band could not stand against it, and covering their faces, they were dispersed hither and thither; and these dreadful sounds issued, which even the king himself heard in his palace; 'What misfortune impels thee! what demon possesses thee! if thou desirest thy welfare, molest not that fair one, or else the fate that thy son met with by marrying her, thou shalt experience the like doom by being her foe; if thou now molestest her, thou wilt rue its consequences.'

"The king fell into a fever through fear, and instantly ordered that 'No one should molest these evil-fated persons; to say nothing to them, to hear nothing from them, but to let them remain in their house, and that no one should injure or oppress them.' From that day, the magicians, conceiving this mysterious event to be witchcraft, have used all their exorcising arts and spells to destroy its effects; and all the inhabitants of this city read [prayers] from the glorious *Kur,an*, and pronounced the great name of God. It is a long while since this awful scene took place, but to this day the mysterious secret has not been developed, nor do I know anything about it; I once asked the girl what she had seen with her own eyes; she replied, I know nothing more than that when my husband wished to consummate our marriage, I saw the roof instantly open, and a throne set with precious stones descended through the aperture, on which was seated a handsome young man dressed in princely robes, and many persons in attendance upon him, came into that apartment; and were ready to put the prince to death. That young man came up to me and said, "Well, my love, where to will you now escape from me?" They had the appearance of men, but with feet like goats; my heart palpitated, and I fainted through fear; I do not know what afterwards happened.'

"From that period we have both thus lived in this ruined place; and from the fear of offending the king, all our friends have forsaken us; when I go out to beg, no one gives me a *kauri*; moreover, it is not allowed me even to stand before their shops; this unfortunate girl has not a rag to cover her nakedness, nor sufficient food to satisfy her hunger. From God I only pray for this, that our deaths should ensue, or that the earth may open out and swallow this ill-fated girl: death is better than such existence; God has perhaps sent thee here for our good; so that thou tookest pity on us, and gave us a piece of gold, which has enabled us to have good food and clothes for my daughter. God be praised, and blessed be thou; if she was not under the influence of some *jinn* or fairy, then I would give her for thy service like a slave, and think myself happy. This is my wretched story; do not think of her, but abandon all thoughts on that head."

After hearing this sad narrative, I entreated the old man to accept me as his son-in-law, and if evil be my future doom, then let it come; but the old man would on no account agree to my request. When the evening came, I took my leave of him, and went to the *sarai*. *Mubarak* said, "Well, prince, rejoice, God has favoured you, and your labours are not thrown away." I answered, "I have to-day used many fair speeches, but that infidel old man will not consent; God knows if he will give her to me or not." My mind was in such a state that I passed the night in great restlessness, and wished the morning was come that I might return [and see her]; I sometimes fancied, that if the father should be kind and agree to my wishes, *Mubarak* would carry her away for *Maliki Sadik*. I then said to myself, "Well, let us once get possession of her; I will then get over *Mubarak*, and enjoy her." Again my heart was filled with apprehensions, that even if *Mubarak* should likewise agree to my project, the *jinns* would serve me as they had served the prince; moreover the king of this city will never consent, that after the murder of his son, another should enjoy [his bride].

I passed the whole night without sleep, agitated by this project. When the day appeared, I issued forth, and went to the *chauk*, and purchased some pieces of fine cloth and lace, and fresh and dried fruits; and carried them to the old man. He was greatly pleased, and said, "That to every one nothing is dearer than life, but even if my life could be of any use to thee, I would not grieve to sacrifice it, and give thee now my daughter; but I fear that by doing so, I might endanger thy life, and the stain of this reproach would remain upon me to the day of judgment." I answered, "I am now in this city, helpless, it is true, and you are my father in every respect, temporal and spiritual, but [consider] what pains, fatigues and miseries I have undergone, and what buffetings I have for a long while suffered to attain the object of my wishes, before I arrived here. God has likewise made you kind towards me, since you consent to marry her to me, and only hesitate on account of my safety; be just for a moment, and reflect that to save our heads from the sword of love, and screen our lives from its danger, is not commendable in any religion; let what will happen, I have lost myself in every way; and to possess the object of my love, I consider as my existence. I do not care if I live or perish; moreover, despair will finish my days without the assistance of fate, and I will stand forth as your accuser on the day of judgment."

In short, in such altercations, in hesitations between refusal and acquiescence, a tedious month passed heavily over my head, accompanied with future hopes and fears; I used every day to devote my services to the old man, and every day, with flattering speeches, I entreated him [to grant my boon]. It came to pass, that the old man fell sick; I attended him during his illness; I used always to relate his case to the physician, and whatever medicine he ordered, I used to get them, and administer them to him; I used to dress with my own hand his rice and pulse and other light diet, and gave it to him to eat. One day he was [uncommonly] kind, and said, "O young man, thou art very obstinate; I have repeatedly told thee of all the evils which will ensue if thou persistest in thy object, and have often warned thee not to think of it. Whilst we have life, we have every thing, but thou art determined to jump into the abyss; well, I will to-day mention thee to my daughter; let us hear what she says." O holy *Darweshes*, on hearing these enchanting words, I swelled so with joy, that my clothes could scarce contain me; I fell at the old man's feet, and exclaimed, "You have now laid the foundation of my [future happiness and] existence." I then took my leave and returned to my abode, I passed the whole night in talking of this circumstance with *Mubarak*; where was sleep, and where was hunger! Early in the morning I again went and saluted the old man; he said, "Well, I give you my daughter—God bless you with her—I have put you both under his protection—whilst I have life, stay with me; when my eyes are closed, then do what you wish; you will then be master of your own actions."

A few days after [this conversation], the old man died; we mourned for him and buried him. After the *tija*,[395] *Mubarak* brought this beautiful daughter to the *serai* in a *doli*,[396] and said to me, "She belongs, [pure and untouched], to *Maliki Sadik*; beware you do not play false, and lose the fruits of your labour."

I replied, "O friend, what has *Maliki Sadik* to do here? my heart will not mind me, and how can I have patience? let what will happen, whether I live or perish, let me now enjoy her." *Mubarak*, having lost all patience, replied, with anger, "Do not act like a boy; now, in an instant, matters will change dreadfully; do you think *Maliki Sadik* far off, that you disregard his injunctions? He explained every circumstance to you on taking leave, and warned you of the consequences; if you act according to his directions, and convey her safe and sound to him, he has a royal mind, and may regard the toils you have undergone with a favourable eye, and give her to you; how different will the case be then! you will preserve his unbounded friendship, and gain the sincere affection [of your mistress]."

At last, [from the force of his] threats and admonitions, I remained silent; I bought two camels, and mounting on *kajawas*,[397] we set out for the country of *Maliki Sadik*. We pursued our journey, and at last reached a plain, where loud noises were heard. *Mubarak* exclaimed, "God be praised, our labours have turned out well, for lo! the army of *jinns* is here arrived." He met them at last, and asked them where they intended to go. They replied, "The king has sent us forward for the purpose of receiving you, and we are now under your orders; if you command us, we will convey you in a moment to the presence [of the king]." *Mubarak*, turning to me, said, "See how, after all our toils and dangers, God has favoured us before the face of the king; what is the need of haste now? if some misconduct should occur, which God forbid, then the fruits of our labours would be lost, and we should fall under the king's displeasure." They all answered, "You are the sole master in this; proceed as you please." Although we were comfortable in every way, yet we made it our business to march day and night.

When we approached [the place where the king was], I, seeing *Mubarak* asleep, fell at that beautiful woman's feet, and bewailing to her the restless state of my heart, and my helpless condition, owing to the threats of *Maliki Sadik*, and that from the day I had seen her picture, I had forsworn sleep and food and repose; and now that God had shewn to me this day, I still remained an utter stranger to her. She replied, "My heart is also inclined towards you, for what toils and dangers

[395] The *tija* is the same as the *siyum*.—See note 286, page 91.

[396] A kind of litter for the conveyance of women and the sick.

[397] A kind of litter for travelling in Persia and Arabia; two of them are slung across a camel or a mule; those for camels carry four persons.

have you undergone for my sake, and with what labour and difficulty have you brought me away; remember God, and do not forget me; let us see what may be revealed from behind the curtain of mystery." On saying this, she wept so loud that she was nearly suffocated. Such was my state, and such was hers! In the meantime, *Mubarak's* slumbers were broken, and seeing us both in tears, he was greatly affected, and said, "Be comforted; I have an ointment which I will rub over the body of this fair one; from the smell of it the heart of *Maliki Sadik* will be disgusted, and he will perhaps abandon her to you."

On hearing this plan of *Mubarak's*, my heart was greatly revived; and, embracing him fondly, I said, "O friend, you are now in the place of a father to me; owing to you my life was saved, now also act so that I may still live on, otherwise I must perish in this grief." He gave me every friendly assurance. When the day appeared, we heard the noise of the *jinns*, and saw that many personal attendants of *Maliki Sadik* were arrived, and had brought two rich *khil'ats* for us, and a covered litter with a network of pearls accompanied them. *Mubarak* rubbed the ointment over my beloved's body; and having caused her to be richly dressed, he conveyed her to *Maliki Sadik*. On beholding her, the king rewarded me greatly, and having honoured and dignified me, he made me sit down [near himself], and said, "I will behave to thee such as no one has as yet done to any one; the kingdom of thy father awaits thee, besides which thou art in the place of a son to me." He was talking to me in this gracious manner, when the beautiful woman appeared before him, and suddenly at the smell of that ointment, his brain became confused, and his mind distracted; he could not endure that smell; having got up, he went out and called *Mubarak* and me; he addressed himself to *Mubarak*, and said, "Well, sir, you have truly performed the injunctions [I gave].

"I had warned you, that if you deceived me, you would incur my displeasure; what smell is this? now see how I will treat you." He was very angry; *Mubarak*, from fear, opened his trowsers, and showed his condition,[398] and said, "Mighty king, when I undertook this business, according to your commands, I then cut off my privities, and put them in a box, sealed it, and delivered it over in charge to your treasurer, and putting some ointment of Solomon on the mutilated parts, I set out on the errand." On hearing this reply from *Mubarak*, the king of the *jinns* looked sternly at me, and said, "Then, this is thy doing;" and getting into a rage, he began to abuse me. I immediately perceived from his words that he would put me to death. When I felt convinced of this from his looks, despairing of life, I became desperate, and snatching the dagger from *Mubarak's* waist, I plunged it into the king's belly; on receiving the stab, he bent down and staggered; I wondered, for I thought he must assuredly have perished; I then perceived that the wound was not so effective as I imagined, and could not account for it; I was staring [with surprise] when he rolled on the ground, and assuming the appearance of a tennis ball, he flew up to the sky. He ascended so high, that at last he disappeared; a moment after, flashing like lightning, and vociferating some meaningless words in his rage, he descended, and gave me such a kick, that I swooned away, and fell flat on my back, and became as one lifeless. God knows how long I remained ere I came to

[398] Viz., his state of castration.

my senses; but when I opened my eyes I saw that I was lying in such a wilderness, where, except thorns and briars, nothing else was to be seen; at that moment my understanding was of no avail to fix on what I should do, or where I should go. In this state of despondence, I gave a sigh, and followed the first path that offered; if I met any one any where, I inquired after the name of *Maliki Sadik*; he, thinking me mad, answered that he had not even heard his name.

One day, having ascended a mountain, I likewise determined to throw myself [off its summit], and end my existence; just as I was ready to jump off, the same veiled horseman, the possessor of *Zu-l-fakar*,[399] appeared and said, "Why do you throw away your life; man is exposed to every pain and misery; your unhappy days are now over, and your propitious ones are coming; go quickly to *Rum*—three afflicted persons like thee are gone there before thee—meet them, and see the king of that country; the wishes of all five will be fulfilled in the same place." This is my story which I have just related; at last, from the happy tidings of our difficulty-solving guardian,[400] I am come into the presence of your worships, and have also been kindly received by the king, who is the shadow of Omnipotence; we ought all now to be comforted."

This conversation was passing between the king *Azad Bakht* and the four *Darweshes*, when a eunuch came running from the royal seraglio and with respectful salutation, wished his majesty joy, and added, "This moment a prince is born, before whose refulgent beauty the sun and moon are abashed." The king was surprised, and asked, "No one was pregnant[401] in appearance; who has brought forth a son?" The eunuch replied, "*Mahru*, the female slave, who for some time hath lain under your majesty's displeasure, and lived like an outcast in a corner [of the seraglio], and no one from fear ever went near her or asked after her state; on her the grace of God hath been such, that she hath borne a son like the moon."

The king was so rejoiced, that he nearly expired from excessive joy; the four *Darweshes* also blessed him, and said, "May thy house be ever happy, and may thy son prosper; and may he grow up under thy shadow." The king replied, "This is owing to your propitious arrival, for otherwise I had no idea of such an event; if you give me leave, I will go and see him." The *Darweshes* answered, "In the name of God, go." The king went to the seraglio, and took the young prince in his lap, and thanked God; his mind became easy; pressing the infant to his bosom, he brought it and laid it at the *Darweshes'* feet; they blessed it, and exorcised all evil spirits from approaching it. The king commanded the preparations of a festival to be made [on the happy occasion], and the royal music struck up, and the door of the treasury was opened; with princely donations he made the poor[402] rich; on all the officers of state he bestowed a two-fold increase of lands and higher titles, and to the army he gave five years' pay as a present; to the learned and holy he gave pensions and lands; and the wallets of the beggars were filled with pieces of gold and silver; and the *ryots*[403] were excused from paying any revenue for three

[399] *Zu-l-fakar*, the name of a famous sword that *'Ali* used to wear.

[400] The veiled horseman, *'Ali Mushkil-Kusha*.

[401] In the original there is a play on the words *haml* and *hamal*.

[402] Literally, "he made the man in want of a *kauri* the master of a *lakh* [of rupees].

[403] *Ryots* (a corruption of the word *ra'iyat*) are the husbandmen in India; the tillers

years, and that whatever they cultivated during this period, they should keep for themselves.

Throughout the whole city, in the houses of the high and the low, wherever one looked, there were merry dances; in their joy, every one, small and great, felt himself a prince. In the midst of these rejoicings, the sounds of lamentation and weeping issued suddenly from the seraglio; the female servants, of all descriptions, and the eunuchs, ran out, scattering dust upon their heads, and said to the king, "When we had washed and bathed the prince, and delivered him to the bosom of the nurse, a cloud descended from the sky and enveloped the nurse; a moment after, we saw the nurse prostrate and senseless, and the little prince gone; what a dreadful calamity has occurred!" The king was thunderstruck on hearing this wonderful occurrence; and the whole country mourned [for the sad event]; for two days no one dressed any victuals, but fed on their grief, and drank their own blood, for the prince's loss.

In short, they began to despair of their lives, living in this manner; on the third day the same cloud appeared, and a cradle studded with jewels, and with a covering of pearls, descended from it into the area of the seraglio; the cloud then disappeared, and the servants found the little prince in the cradle sucking his thumb; the royal mother immediately invoking blessings upon him, took him up in her arms, and pressed him fondly to her bosom; she saw that he was dressed in a jacket of fine muslin embroidered with pearls, and had a child's bib of brocade, and many ornaments set with jewels on his hands and feet, and a necklace with nine gems on his neck, and there was a child's rattle with golden balls placed by his side. Through joy all [the female attendants] were transported; and they began to offer up prayers, saying, "May all thy mother's wishes be gratified, and mayest thou attain a period of mature old age."

The king ordered a new grand palace to be built and furnished with carpets, and kept the four *Darweshes* in it; when he was disengaged from the affairs of state, he used to go there, sit with them, and to provide everything for them and wait on them; but on the first Thursday night of every month the same cloud descended, and took away the prince, and after keeping him two days, it used to bring him back, with such rich toys and rarities of every country, and of every description, in his cradle, that on beholding them, the minds of the spectators were confounded with astonishment. In this manner, the prince reached in safety his seventh year; on the birthday the king *Azad Bakht* said to the *Darweshes*, "O holy men, I cannot conceive who carries the prince away and brings him back; it is very wonderful; let us see what will be the end of it." The *Darweshes* said, "Do one thing; write a friendly note to this purport, and put it into the prince's cradle, viz.:—'Having seen your friendship and kindness [to my son], my heart wishes most anxiously to meet you, and if by way of amity you favour me with your tidings, my heart will be highly gratified, and my wonder will cease.'" The king, according to the

of the soil who rent small parcels of land from the government, through the medium of the *zamin-dar*, who is a servant of government and not the proprietor of the land, as some have erroneously supposed. The word means keeper of the land, and not the proprietor. In fact, he is like the Irish middleman, in every sense of the word.

Darweshes' advice, wrote a note to this purport on paper sprinkled with gold, and put it in the golden cradle.

The prince, according to custom, disappeared; and in the evening *Azad Bakht* was sitting with the *Darweshes* and conversing with them, when a folded paper fell near the king; he opened it and read it, and found that it was an answer to his note; these two lines were written in it: "Conceive me likewise anxious to see you; a throne goes for you; it is best that you should come now, that we may meet; all the preparations of enjoyment are ready; your majesty's place alone is empty." The king *Azad Bakht* took the *Darweshes* with him, and ascended the celestial throne; it was like the throne of Solomon, and mounted into the air; proceeding on, it descended in a place where grand edifices and sumptuous preparations appeared; but it could not be perceived if any one was there or not. In the meantime some one rubbed the eyes of all five with the *surma* of *Sulaiman*; two drops of tears fell from the eyes of each, and they saw an assembly of the fairies, who were waiting to receive them, dressed in rich habits of various colours, with vials of rose-water in their hands.

Azad Bakht advanced amidst two rows consisting of thousands of fairy-born creatures, standing in respectful order, and in the centre was placed an elevated throne inlaid with emeralds, on which was seated leaning on pillows, with an air of great dignity, *Malik Shah Bal,* the son of *Shah-rukh;* a beautiful little girl of the fairy race was seated before him, and was playing with the young prince *Bakhtiyar*. Chairs and seats were arranged in rows on both sides of the throne, on which the nobles of the fairy race were seated. *Malik Shah Bal* stood up on seeing the king *Azad Bakht* and descended from his throne and embraced him, and taking him by the hand, he seated him on the throne by the side of himself, and they began to converse together with much cordiality; the whole day passed in feasting and hilarity, and music and dancing. The second day, when the two kings met, *Shah Bal* asked *Azad Bakht* the reason for bringing the *Darweshes* with him.

Azad Bakht related fully their adventures as he had previously learned, and interceded for them, and asked [the king's] assistance, saying, "These have undergone many hardships, and suffered great misfortunes; and if now, through your favour, they attain their wishes, it will be an act of great merit, and I also will be grateful for it through life; by your kind assistance they will all reach the summit of their desires." *Malik Shah Bal,* after hearing [these adventures, replied, "Most willingly; I will not fail to obey your commands." Saying this, he looked sternly at the *divs* and fairies [who were present], and he wrote letters to the great *jinns,* who were chiefs in different places, and ordered them, that on receiving his commands, they must repair speedily to the presence, and if any one should delay in coming, he should be punished, and brought as captive; and that whoever possessed any persons of the human species, male or female, he must bring them along with him; that if [a *jinn*] having concealed any one, should detain the same, and it be known hereafter, the concealer and his wife and family shall be exterminated, and no vestige of them will remain.

Receiving these written orders, the *divs* were dispatched in all directions. A great warmth of friendship arose between the two kings, and they passed their time in amicable conversation, amidst which *Malik Shah Bal,* turning round to the *Darweshes,* said, "I had a great wish to have children, and had resolved, if God gave me a son or a daughter, to marry it to the offspring of some king of the human race. After this resolve, I learned that my wife was pregnant; at last, after counting with anxiety each day and hour, the full period arrived, and this girl was born. According to my determination, I ordered the *jinns* to search the four corners of the world, and that whatever king had a prince born to him, to bring the child quickly to me with care; agreeably to my orders, the *jinns* flew instantly to the four corners of the earth, and after some delay, brought this young prince to me.

"I thanked God, and took the child in my lap, and loved it dearer than my own daughter; I could not bring myself to separate him from my sight for a moment, but used to send him back for this reason, that if his parents did not see him, they would be greatly afflicted. For this reason I sent for him once every month, and after keeping him with me a few days, I sent him back. If it please God the Most High, now that we have met, I will marry them to each other; all are liable to death, then let us, whilst we are alive, see their marriage performed."

The king *Azad Bakht,* on hearing this proposal of *Shah Bal's,* and seeing his amiable qualities, was greatly pleased and said, "At first the prince's disappearance and re-appearance raised very strange aprehensions in my breast, but I am now, from your conversation, easy in my mind, and perfectly satisfied; this son is now yours; do with him whatever you please." In short, the intercourse between the two kings was like that of sugar and milk, and they fully enjoyed themselves. In the space of less than ten days, mighty kings of the race of the *jinns,* from the rose garden of *Iram,*[404] and from mountains and islands, (to call whom the fairies had been dispatched) all arrived at the court [of *Shah Bal*]. In the first place, *Maliki Sadik* was ordered to produce the human creature he had in his possession; he was much vexed at it, and sad, but having no remedy, he produced the rosy-cheeked fair one [the blind man's daughter]. Next, he demanded of the king of *'Umman*[405] the daughter of one of the *jinns* for whom the prince of *Nimroz,* the bull rider, went mad; he likewise made many excuses, but produced her at last. When the daughter of the king of the Franks and *Bihzad Khan* were demanded, all present denied having any knowledge of them, and swore by Solomon [to that effect].

At last, when the king of the sea of *Kulzum* was asked if he knew anything of them, he hung down his head, and remained silent. *Malik Shah Bal* had a deference for him, and entreated him to give them up, and gave him hopes of future favour and even threatened him. Then he also joined his hands together, and said, "Please your majesty, the particulars of that circumstance are as follows:—When the king [of Persia] came to the river *Kulzum* to meet his son, and the prince from eagerness plunged his horse into the flood, it chanced that I had gone out that day to roam about and to hunt. I passed by the place, and the cavalcade stopped to behold the

[404] A famous garden in Arabia Felix; it is also applied to the garden in Paradise, in which all good Mahometans, according to their belief, are to revel after death.

[405] *'Umman* is the name of the southern part of *Yaman* or Arabia Felix; the country which lies between the mouth of the Persian Gulf and the mouth of the Red Sea; the sea which washes this coast is called the sea of *'Umman* in Persia and Arabia, as the Red Sea is called the sea of *Kulzum.*

scene. When the princess's mare carried her also into the stream, my looks met hers, and I was enchanted, and gave instant orders to the fairy race to bring her to me, together with the mare. *Bihzad Khan* plunged in also after her on horseback; I admired his bravery and gallantry, and had him seized likewise; I took him with me, and returned home; so they are both safe, and with me."

Saying this, he sent for them both before *Malik Shah Bal*. Great search had been made for the daughter of the king of Syria, and strict inquiries were put to all present, but no one acknowledged having her, or knowing anything about her. *Malik Shah Bal* then asked if any king or chief was absent, and if all were arrived; the *jinns* answered, "Mighty sire, all are present except one named *Musalsal Jadu*, who has erected a fort on the mountain *Kaf* by the means of magic; he, from haughtiness, is not come, and we, your majesty's slaves, are not able to bring him by force; the place is strong, and he himself also is a great devil."

On hearing this, *Malik Shah Bal* was very angry, and an army of *jinns, 'afrits* and fairies were sent with orders, that if he came of his own accord, and brought the princess with him, well and good, but otherwise subdue him, and bring him tied by the neck and heels, and raze his fort to the ground, and drive the plough, drawn by an ass, over it. Immediately, on the orders being given, such numbers of troops flew to the place, that in a day or two the rebellious haughty chief was brought in irons to the presence. *Malik Shah Bal* repeatedly asked about the princess, but the haughty rebel gave no reply. The king at length got angry, and ordered him to be cut to pieces, and his skin stretched and filled with chaff;[406] a body of fairies were ordered to go to the mountain of *Kaf*, and search for the princess; they went and found her, and brought her to *Malik Shah Bal*. All these prisoners and the four *Darweshes*, seeing the strict orders and justice of the king *Shah Bal*, were greatly rejoiced, and admired him highly; the king *Azad Bakht* was also much pleased. *Malik Shah Bal* then ordered the men to the palace, and the women to the royal seraglio; the city was ordered to be illuminated, and the preparations for the marriages to be quickly completed; [all was instantly made ready], as if the order alone was wanted to be given.

One day, a happy hour being fixed upon, the prince *Bakhtiyar* was married to the princess *Roshan Akhtar*; and the young merchant of *Yaman*[407] was married to the princess of *Dimashk*; and the prince of Persia[408] was married to the princess of *Basra*; and the prince of *'Ajam*[409] was married to the princess of the Franks; *Bihzad Khan* was married to the daughter of the king of *Nimroz*; and the prince of *Nimroz* was married to the *jinn's* daughter; and the prince of China[410] was married to the daughter of the old blind man of *Hindustan*; she who had been in the possession of *Maliki Sadik*. Through the favour of *Malik Shah Bal*, every hopeless person gained

[406] A mode of punishment used in former times in Persia, India, and Arabia, against great enemies or atrocious delinquents. Such treatment the poor emperor Valerian experienced from the haughty *Shapur* or *Shabar* (the Sapores of the Greeks), king of Persia or Parthia.

[407] The first *darwesh*.

[408] The second *darwesh*.

[409] The third *darwesh*.

[410] The fourth *darwesh*.

his desires, and obtained his wishes; afterwards, they all enjoyed themselves for forty days, and passed their time, night and day, in pleasures and festivity.

At last, *Malik Shah Bal* gave to each prince rich and rare presents, and dismissed them to their different countries. All were pleased and satisfied, and set out and reached their homes in safety, and began their reigns; but *Bihzad Khan*, and the merchant's son of *Yaman*, of their own accord, remained with the king *Azad Bakht*, and in the end the young merchant of *Yaman* was made head steward to his majesty, and *Bihzad Khan* generalissimo of the army of the fortunate prince *Bakhtiyar*; whilst they lived, they enjoyed every felicity. O God! as these four *Darweshes* and the king *Azad Bakht* attained their wishes, in like manner grant to all hopeless beings the wishes of their hearts, through thy power and goodness, and by the medium of the five pure bodies,[411] the twelve *Imams*, and the fourteen innocents,[412] on all of whom be the blessing of God! Amen, O God of the universe.

When this book was finished, through the favour of God, I took it into my mind to give it such a name, that the date should be thereby found out.[413] When I made the calculation, I found that I had begun to compose this work in the end of the year of the *Hijra* 1215, and owing to want of leisure, it was not finished until the beginning of the year 1217; I was reflecting on this circumstance, when it occurred to me that the words *Bagh O Bahar* formed a proper title, as it answered to the date of the year when the work was finished; so I gave it this name. Whoever shall read it, he will stroll as it were through a garden; moreover, the garden is exposed to the blasts of winter, but this book is not; it will ever be in verdure.

When this *Bagh O Bahar* was finished, the year was 1217; do you now stroll through it night and day, as its name and date is *Bagh O Bahar*; the blasts of winter can do it no injury; for this *Bahar*[414] is ever green and fresh; it hath been nourished with the blood of my heart, and its (the heart's) pieces are its leaves and fruits;—all will forget me after death;—but this book will remain as a *souvenir*; whoever reads it, let him remember me. This is my agreement with the readers; if there is an error, excuse it; for amidst flowers lie concealed the thorns; man is liable to faults and errors, and he will fail, let him be ever so careful. I have no other wish except this, and it is my earnest prayer. O my Creator, that I may ever remain in remembrance of Thee, and thus pass my nights and days! That I may not be questioned with

---

[411] The five pure bodies are *Muhammad*, the prophet; *Fatima*, his daughter; *Ali*, her husband; and *Hazan* and *Husain*, their children.

[412] The fourteen innocents are the children of *Hazan* and *Husain*.

[413] By an arithmetical operation called in Persian *Abjad*; as Persian letters have arithmetical powers, the letters which compose the words *Bagh O Bahar* added up, produce the sum 1217. From the inscription on most *Muhammadan* tombs, and those on the gates of mosques, the dates of demise and erection can be ascertained. We had the same barbarous custom in Europe about the thirteenth and fourteenth centuries; see the Spectator (No. 60,) on this ridiculous subject, which was considered as a proof of great ingenuity.

[414] A pun on the word *Bahar*, which means spring, when flowers are in full bloom; but the French word *printemps* conveys more exactly the compound signification; for *Bahar* not only means spring, but an agreeable spring. The Persians are as fond of these *double entendres* as any other people; their poetry is strewed with them, and so is their prose. It is not, however, to be considered as a model of pure taste.

severity on the night of death, and the day of reckoning! O God, in both worlds shower thy favours on me, through the mediation of the great prophet!

SUPPLEMENTAL NOTE.

It must be allowed, that the author has displayed great adroitness in the "denouement" of his tale. In the course of a few pages all the principal characters, male and female, are suddenly produced, safe and unscathed, before the reader. To be sure, this is done by the aid of a little "diablerie," but then it is done very neatly,—much more so than in some of the clumsy fictions of the late Ettrick Shepherd, to say nothing of the edifying legends about the Romish saints which the good people of southern Europe are taught to swallow as gospel. Finally, be it remembered, that Oriental story-tellers have never subscribed to Horace's precept,—

"Nec deus interait, nisi digens vindice nodus
Inciderit"

On the contrary, their rule is, when, by a free use of the supernatural, you have got the whole of your characters into a regular *fix*, it is but fair that you should get them off by the same means.

THE END.

Lector House believes that a society develops through a two-fold approach of continuous learning and adaptation, which is derived from the study of classic literary works spread across the historic timeline of literature records. Therefore, we aim at reviving, repairing and redeveloping all those inaccessible or damaged but historically as well as culturally important literature across subjects so that the future generations may have an opportunity to study and learn from past works to embark upon a journey of creating a better future.

This book is a result of an effort made by Lector House towards making a contribution to the preservation and repair of original ancient works which might hold historical significance to the approach of continuous learning across subjects.

HAPPY READING & LEARNING!

LECTOR HOUSE LLP
E-MAIL: lectorpublishing@gmail.com

www.ingramcontent.com/pod-product-compliance
Lightning Source LLC
LaVergne TN
LVHW101914220826
846093LV00008B/247

* 9 7 8 9 3 9 0 2 1 5 3 9 3 *